Lesbian Sex

By The Author:

with Bonnie Lopez and Marcia Quackenbush, *Period,* a book about menstruation for pre-menstrual girls. Published by Volcano Press: S.F.

Lesbian Sex

JoAnn Loulan

Drawings by Barbara Johnson
Technical Drawings by Marcia Quackenbush

Spinsters Ink
San Francisco

10-9-8-7-6-

Spinsters Ink
803 De Haro Street
San Francisco, CA 94107

Cover Art and Interior Drawings: Barbara Johnson
Cover Design: Linda Szyniszewski, Elephant Graphics
Technical Drawings: Marcia Quackenbush
Design and Production: Sherry Thomas and Jean Swallow
Typesetting: Maxine Morris and Kim Corsaro, Coming Up! Graphics
Printed in the U.S.A.

Portions of the proceeds from this book will go to a foundation for the support of women artists.

ISBN: 0-933216-13-0
Library of Congress Catalog Card Number: 84-52008

Dedication

This book is dedicated to all the women who have been and will be forced to be silent for so long. Thank you for your gift of existing. Only because of you we have been able to speak our names.

Acknowledgements

There are many that I have to thank for the appearance of this book.

My lover and my son have put up with the preoccupation I have had for nine months for this new "baby." This has been evidenced by my son coming up with new phrases like "I'm working on the 'puter honey." My lover also must be credited with getting me through my fear of computers. It is only with this constant love and support that I could write this so quickly. She has yet to convince me, however, that as long as these micro chips are at it, these machines should never break down. (And for the price they should also speak a couple of languages and do the dishes once in a while.) She also gave me much constructive criticism which helped to increase the quality of this book.

My friends may want to look at the picture of me in this book to remember what I look like. They too have continued to call and support me no matter what I have given them in return. Thanks a lot to each and every one of you.

The women who specifically helped with the making of the book are many. It started with the many lesbians I have worked with over the years who have given me both the information I used and the reason to write this volume. These women requested the written word, not just my incessant ramblings at every public and private lesbian gathering in the last ten years. Dotty Calabrese was one of the women that helped to make these contacts with so many lesbians possible by her part in making the sexuality weekends a success.

Joani Blank must be credited with giving me the impetus to actually start. She said, "How about writing a book on lesbian couples and sex and I'll publish it." I said, "Are you nuts? I have a six-month-old child." She asked me again a year later and when I finally got to a proposal she told me she was preoccupied with other projects.

Sherry Thomas became the next woman publisher to come along and say, "Hey I'll publish whatever you want to say about sex." To a headstrong Leo this sounded great. I started writing and then in January she came to my house and said, "Well, can you be done in June?" I thought maybe she hadn't noticed that I had a two-year-old by that time, a full time job counseling, and a few years emotional sobriety that should have given me the ability to say no. But I said yes. Sherry not only played this role, but has all along been the greatest inspiration. She always gave me the lift when I needed it, spurring me on. When she took over her end of the job, she gave many wonderful suggestions, was thorough, professional and dedicated. Without her this book would still be a few discs sitting in a box beside my computer.

Coletta Reid has been the major editor of this book. She has, in fact, taken pages of text and dislodged the dangling participles, the run on and on and on sentences, the misplaced modifiers, the problems of tense and voice. Let's face it, I'm a talker, not a writer. Thank the goddesses Coletta is a writer. Her brilliance was especially evident when I got the fifty page "Barriers to Sex" chapter back from her and it was twenty pages long and nothing I had said was left out. She created miracles like this over and over. You would all be still reading this book years later if Coletta hadn't done her craft so well. She also gave me wonderful support and believed in the project always.

Marcia Quackenbush has collaborated on a number of projects with me. This one was no exception. She was in at the beginning, helping to organize it, shaping the homophobia chapter and working with me on various parts of the manuscript throughout the project. Her illustrations in the physiology chapter have also given much to the book. She continues to be a tremendous support as a loving friend.

Marny Hall was a great help in contributing the chapter on couple dynamics. Her years of work in this field has been a great inspiration to me. I appreciate all her support for the rest of the book. My alter-ego as her little sister for the years we have known each other is very glad she's a part of this project.

Jill Lessing's contribution of the "Sex and Disability" chapter is very important to the lesbian community. Her life as a therapist, long-time lesbian, co-mother, disabled woman, and friend has been a gift to me for many years. She and E.L. Keir also contributed a fantastic section to the "Barriers" chapter on the cultural oppression of fat women.

My cousin Sandie Fujita was a great editor and word processor for some of the chapters. She contributed intensely (which is her Aries nature) to whatever parts of the book she came across.

There are many others that helped in various ways like proofreading, editing, organizing: Jean, Meredith, Sukey, and more.

Finally, I want to acknowledge the women who will read this book. You are so brave to pick up a book with the title of *Lesbian Sex*. You are among a changing tide that will hopefully help to create room for all of us in all our diversities in this culture we live in.

Table of Contents

Part V: Be Your Own Camp Director

Appendices

Introduction

This is a book about lesbian sex, written by a lesbian counselor, for lesbians. Over the last seven years more than 2,000 lesbians have come to my sexuality workshops and to my therapy practice to talk about sexuality and sexual concerns. Many of you have urged me to write about what I've learned so that we can all share in creating a body of knowledge about lesbian sexuality. This book is a direct result of your sharing with me detailed, intimate and specific information about your sexual lives and problems. I wish to thank you—clients and workshop participants—for your openness and participation. Without you, this book wouldn't exist.

I have very strong views about sexuality and you will encounter most of them in this book. I believe that sexual practice, like other areas in our lives, can be changed with willingness and consciousness. Just like building muscles, learning self-defense or learning new skills, we can learn how to have more sexual pleasure. We can take responsibility for our sexual lives. We don't need to believe that how we like to have sex has been dropped on us from Venus. We don't have to accept our sex lives as they are, without rhyme or reason.

I am here to tell you that our powerlessness and passivity in regards to our sexuality is unnecessary. We have the means within ourselves to create the kind of sex lives that we want. I have seen lesbians change. I know it's possible, and I've written this book to share with you what I know about how to do it.

Accordingly, this book was written with a specific intent in mind: to help you achieve the kind of sex life you want. The real core of this book is the "homework" chapter which includes dozens of specific sexual exercises designed to help you. All of them have been tried by garden-variety lesbians similar to you and all of them have worked for somebody. Not every exercise may work for you, but there will be some that are just what you need.

Friends who've read through the rough draft tell me that reading the homework exercises is a real turn-on. I hope that they're a turn-on for you, too. I suggest that you browse through them first before reading the rest of the book. Then, as you read the book, you'll have some idea of what they're like and what I'm referring to when I say, *"Try exercise XY-3 in the homework chapter."*

At the beginning of the homework chapter you'll find all of the exercises listed. There is very clear, simple directions for each group of exercises. Make time each week to do this work. Decide ahead of time. Make a commitment to yourself that you are going to change what is making you uncomfortable about your sex life. We must stop passively waiting for Ms. Right, or the moon to shift, or our acne to go away, or the arms race to stop. We must do something now.

Along with the idea of being responsible for our own sex lives and being able to change them, goes the idea that we're not responsible for anyone else's sexual pleasure (regardless of what our partners might say). We do have a responsibility to be there and be present for the other during sex; we are part of our partners' having a good time, but we are not the reason she does or doesn't. Each of us gets to be our own camp director and explore and ask for what gives us pleasure.

In line with that, this book is written for individuals. It is not primarily aimed at couples. Even when I talk about couples I'm discussing the needs of the individual within the couple. Maybe some day I'll write about sexual dynamics within couples, (goddess knows, we need it) but that is a different book.

I have tried to write directly, clearly, and without a lot of technical language. I don't think that you should have to go to medical school or learn Latin to know about your body, how it works, and what feels good. When I've used technical terms, it's so you can use them when referring to or reading other books. I have also tried to be as explicit as possible, to say what we actually do and how we do it. I know that may make some of you uncomfortable, but I hope you'll be less uncomfortable by the end. I have used quotes throughout to emphasize points. These are from women that I have talked with over the last seven years. I have tried to include women of different ethnic backgrounds, women of all classes, women from different religious groups, and women from numerous geographic areas.

This is a practical book, and, as such, it focuses on problems and how to solve them. I don't think our sex lives are dominated by problems; in fact, I know they aren't. The energizing and pleasurable aspects of lesbian sex are a major reason most of us are lesbians. But this book is not aimed at extolling the virtures of lesbian sex; it's aimed at helping you have the sex life that you want.

Loving ourselves is a key ingredient in doing anything, but certainly when it comes to sex this is a major element. Our lack of tolerance and acceptance for our own sexuality is something which keeps us from learning and changing our bodily responses. Loving our lesbianism is implicit in this book. Though we may be filled with homophobia, there is also something about being lesbian that energizes each of us. Even when talking about specific issues, I feel it is important to know that I am talking from a frame of love.

I believe that sexuality is strongly connected to all aspects of our lives. That's why this is not a book that focuses narrowly on what we do in bed. This is not a book about sexual techniques, although scads of them are in here. It's about the issues in our lives and how they affect our sexuality. I have tried to be comprehensive, to see sex as integral to who we are and how we interact. That's why you'll find chapters on sex and sobriety, sex and motherhood and sex and disability.

I also believe in diversity and plurality. I feel that all of us can benefit from encouraging difference within our community. Learning from each other is one of the advantages of being in a community.

Included in the physiology chapter is a new model of the Female Sexual Response Cycle—the JoAnn Loulan model. I have synthesized this model from information gleaned from talking with lesbians like yourself, and I think it describes more accurately than any other how women respond during sex. I have called it "The Willingness Model" because it starts with the premise that women can begin to have sex because we are willing. We do not have to be experiencing great desire or physical excitement; we can initiate sex because we want to. What a revolutionary idea! Women don't have to be overcome by the heat of desire to want to have sex. Two other revolutionary ideas are part of this model. One is that women can experience shutdown at any point in the cycle. There is always the possibility of no longer being present with the experience. No phase of the cycle automatically brings on the next phase. Nothing is inevitable. The other idea is that pleasure can be experienced anywhere along the way regardless of the stage at which you stop. You don't have to experience orgasm or resolution to experience pleasure. Every sexual experience regardless of its duration and movement along the cycle can be pleasurable. What a wonderful gift to ourselves that we have recognized and made this fact explicit.

I am a mother; a lesbian; a white, upper middle-class Leo who was raised Catholic in the country in the Midwest. I am also the adult child of an alcoholic. I trained as a marriage and family counselor in California and have been counseling lesbians since 1977.

Along with Dotty Calabrese and Scotti Cassidy, I regularly offer Lesbian Sexuality Workshops at an ocean retreat in the Bay Area of California. These weekend workshops for twenty lesbians have been happening since 1978 and are always full and have a waiting list, even when we do six a year. "Sex Camp" as Ann Hollingsworth aptly named the workshop, is a place to talk about our sex lives, get support, and learn some simple ideas for healing ourselves. No one is expected to have sex with anyone; rather we are there to learn and perhaps to unlearn. We think that sex is a learned process and that we can all benefit from having more information about it. So sex camp is a place for communication with hope that communication will encourage us to explore and accept our own sexuality.

I hope that you like this book and that it leads you to better know what sexually pleases you. Pleasure is one purpose of sexual experience and I endorse your having choice about your routes to that goal.

This book is for each of us. A call to making our sex lives ours again. For so many years we have given our sex lives away to the closest person, family member or government. We don't have to do that anymore. Here it is in black and white. You can have what you want out of sex. This is not a dress rehearsal. This is your life, make it what you want.

I would really love to know what you think and how you feel about this book; please write me in care of the publisher. Good reading.

JoAnn Loulan

Lesbian Sex

I. This Is Your Life:

Where We Start

Barriers
To Our Sexuality

For centuries now sex has been defined by men. How sex should be done, with whom and how often has been determined by men's sexual needs. Women have never been consulted about what in sexuality makes sense to us. It is no accident that our voices have been unheard; it is the result of sexism. Only recently have women begun to find their own voice and state the truth about their own sexuality. Just as we have redefined pregnancy as natural and not an illness, we are in the midst of redefining for ourselves what sexual desire is, what the "normal" amount of sexual activity is, what our natural rhythms of sexuality are.

No group is in a better position than lesbians to discover what women's sexuality is all about. Two women together without the psychological and physiological needs and demands of men can provide a lot of information about female sexuality. As travelers on a new frontier, we have an opportunity to chronicle the events and pass the information down to other women.

But first we have to get through all the obstacles that make most women less than enthusiastic about sex. For women, sex in our society is colored by sexism, homophobia and sexual trauma. We are not able to come to sexual experience freely, openly, and without fear.

Objectification Of Our Bodies

The most pervasive result of sexism in our culture is the way women's bodies are objectified. Most of us are seen primarily as bodies all our lives. Women are used as objects in advertising—"See this body, buy this car, bike, cigar, toothpaste, liquor, etc." Our bodies are always available for men to judge, as they rate who we are by how our bodies meet their standards. Songs, books and movies all stress that we must look good and constantly change ourselves, so we can get a man or keep the one we've got.

We have become so alienated and separated from our bodies that we don't even know how they work. This often includes knowing little about our sexual responses, and we end up with two strangers in bed—our partner and ourselves.

> "I have never known any woman who was happy with her body. If she was, she was afraid of losing that body, so she was always dieting, exercising, criticizing herself. Men don't seem to do this ever."

> "Our bodies are almost separate from us. Always being evaluated by us as if it was a commodity."

Some of us finally get comfortable with our bodies, then they change. Our good feelings are so tenuous, that any change— pregnancy, gaining or losing weight, menopause, for example— throws us back into insecurity.

> "I finally was feeling good about being fat then I went back to my parents for a visit and now I feel terrible about myself again."

> "The first thing I do when I think of dating is whether anyone will be interested in my body. I've lost some of my pubic hair since I've gotten older, it makes me feel almost embarrassed. I just stay discouraged."

Insecure feelings about our bodies take a constant toll on our sex lives. Some women's sex lives may not be affected by objectification, but that seems to be rare.

> "Lesbians claim that because they don't want men, they are not affected by the garbage from the culture about women's bodies. Then how come they

4

are just as uptight about wrinkles, fat and facial hair
as the rest of the culture?''

In addition to the general ways that all of us as women have
learned to objectify our bodies, women in target groups have the
added burden of specific stereotypical assumptions about our
bodies. Fat women, women of color, and disabled women all
receive messages about our bodies or our sexuality that are
specifically aimed at our identities.

Those of us who have disabilities have long received messages
that we may be figures of curiosity but not of attractiveness. The
effects of this external devaluing and our internal responses to it
are discussed in detail in the chapter on sex and disability.

There exists in the world, including the lesbian community,
the mistaken idea that fat is a matter of choice. Because of this,
many people feel that the hostility directed against fat women is
justified, even asked for. Therefore, while self-hatred and body
hatred are common to all of us as women, fat women are in a
special position because the hostility and blame are generally extremely blatant as well as socially sanctioned.

When looking for ways to express our sexuality, those of us
who are fat run into many obstacles. Many lesbians would not even
consider a fat partner. And, because they feel justified in their prejudice, they are often openly insulting. Others might take advantage of fat women's vulnerability for one-sided encounters. Still
others make love with fat women but express their fat hatred in subtle ways, such as not really looking at your body, or deep into your
eyes, or focusing only on your face. Perhaps they will avoid touching
the areas that are fat on your body such as your belly or thighs and
will concentrate only on the "acceptable" areas such as the breasts.
This kind of ignoring is very painful.

When we do find a partner who can accept fat, more difficulties still can arise. After years of internalized messages, it may
be difficult for some fat women to feel relaxed, to express needs
and to feel free to let go.

Ways to help move through this for all of us are, first of all,
to become educated on fat liberation politics. If you are thin, take
responsibility to bring the subject up yourself and find out what
sensitivities your fat lover may have. You can use that as a basis
for then exploring each other's bodies slowly and sensitively and

with a spirit of adventure, learning, and playfulness. Work to adopt a form of touching that will express complete acceptance and liking for your lover's body. If you are fat, working towards self-love and loving acceptance of your own body will help create a rewarding sex life, enhance communication, and aid you in projecting yourself out into the world as the beautiful woman you are.

Those of us who are women of color know that we have long been targets for sexual stereotyping. Specific ethnic groups are assigned sexual characteristics (very passive, earthy, sexually hot) and many lesbians perpetuate these stereotypes in their expectations. Because of internalized racism, we may even find issues of stereotyping coming up when our partner is also a woman of color.

> "I'm sick of asking white women out and feeling that they just heard me say I wanted to have sex with them. I'm black and know the stereotypes are out there, but I keep expecting lesbians to see me for who I am."

> "Being a Japanese, out lesbian is unique enough in some places, but I'm also very aggressive sexually. I think white, black and brown women expect me to just fade into the woodwork or something."

> "I don't really know other Latina lesbians. I live in the midwest and there aren't many around. All I know is that when it comes to sex, my Catholic upbringing is what shows the most. I am shy and almost embarrassed. My lover, Shelley, is white and I keep thinking I'm letting her down when I hear other lesbians say to her that it must be fun to go home with a brown woman instead of another uptight white woman."

The same process of assigning sexual stereotypes is also true for different classes. Whether you are working or upper class, your sexual life is judged and stereotyped by middle class assumptions. These assumptions change—sometimes the upper class is seen as cold and aloof, sometimes as sexually indiscriminant and having sex without accepting responsibility. Working class women are sometimes seen as sexually promiscuous or otherwise as un-sophisticated and uptight. None of these assumptions are always true. The middle class fluctuates between any of these positions, as do women from any class.

> "I'm all the things that are supposed to make you uptight sexually. I'm upper class, Catholic, and midwestern. Well, I had a great time at an all-girl's boarding school because nobody ever thought we'd be sexual."

> "I was really surprised to find that not only did my middle class lover expect that I would not know how to save money because I was raised poor, but she also thought I would want to have sex all the time. She was sick of dating women who were up-tight about sex and associated it with the fact that they were middle class. Well, she got another one that was uptight about sex."

To heal ourselves from the objectification of our own bodies by this culture, we need to start with our own truth about our bodies. Talk with your friends about what you really feel about your body. Few of us have the kind of bodies glorified by white, middle class male culture. If we are women of color the white standard makes us doubt whether our hair color or texture is beautiful and whether our skin is acceptable. The body shapes of different races are ignored by the clothing industry. Everything is made to fit white, thin, fourteen-year-old boys; there is no room for hips, breasts and thighs. If we have big thighs, fat arms, no waist, wide shoulders, or a round large butt, there isn't a piece of clothing in most department stores that will fit.

Each of us has to learn to love her own body shape without benefit of the support of the culture. Talk with your friends about what you really feel about your body. Don't just talk about your weight and height, but also how you feel about the smell of your genitals. Let other women know why you do not relate to your breasts or explain how you really hate your period and wish you did not have a uterus.

Take off all your clothes and look at yourself in a mirror for fifteen minutes a day. At the end of a week look at yourself for one hour. Yes, one hour. You would probably rather spend an hour doing nearly anything else. Look at your body for an hour. Have conversations with different parts of your body. Tell your bottom what you really think. See if your bottom has a reply. Do this for every part. See if you like particular parts and not others. Why?

Do exercises S-1, 3, 4, 5, 6 in the homework chapter. Pay attention to all the ways you separate yourself from your body, and to the ways that you do not pay attention to the needs and desires of your body. Make friends with your body as if it were a new person. Take it on a date, do what it wants. Allow yourself to pay attention to the depth of your hatred. Then allow yourself to concentrate on why your body is such a good friend. Let yourself really feel the joys of your skin, your bone structure, your flesh. Allow the part of you that loves your body to be present and verbal.

Sexism

Our training as girls to be passive, and non-initiating affects our ability to be sexual. The all pervasive assumption that men are responsible for women's sexuality is sexist. As teenagers, boys are expected to ask us out on dates, ask us to go steady, ask us to have sex. As men, they are supposed to be in charge of when we get married and when and how we have sex. Men are even assumed to be in control of our orgasms—when we have them, how we have them and how often we have them. It's not surprising we don't feel powerful about our sexual selves under these circumstances.

> "I had no training in how to be sexual. My mother always said my husband would know. What if you never grow up to have a husband?"

> "Since I was taught all my life to not have sexual thoughts, it is all I can do to force myself to stay turned on to some woman long enough to have sex."

As lesbians we are greatly affected by our training to be passive. We often do not even have the simple skills of being able to ask another out on a date. We frequently struggle with what is appropriate behavior for a woman who loves women. Even after having been a lesbian for years, we may not know the kind of specific sexual information we need in order to have a fulfilling sex life. We feel foolish asking questions or revealing our ignorance after having had numerous women partners. We still have a hard time getting information on how to initiate sex, create new ways of being sexual and actually execute sexual techniques.

> "Okay, you tell me. How do you tell a woman you have had one dance with that you would like to go to bed with her? It's supposedly wrong to have sex without any time spent together. Well, as far as I'm concerned, I think each of us is attracted to someone right off the bat. Rarely it may take a while to get turned on. Once that comes, however, why waste any time? I just can't find the words."

> "Florence and I have been together for four years. We just don't know how to enhance our sex lives and feel like there is no where to go to find out the information."

> "When I was sexual with men, I always left my sex life up to them. Now that I am with women, I have to choose for myself. I never learned how to do that."

The single most important aspect in learning how to have rewarding sex is acceptance—accepting ourselves just the way we are, the way we, as women, like to have sex. That may mean very different things to different women. It can mean wanting to have sex once a month, or once a year, or never. It can mean feeling that snuggling and making out are as rewarding as having finger-vagina sex. It can mean that oral sex is the ultimate pleasure. It can mean opting for companionship rather than the perfect sex life. A woman-oriented sex standard may mean having sex be regulated by your menstrual cycle (even after a hysterectomy or during menopause this cycle can be active). Willingness may be the most important part of your sexual response, not desire or orgasm. Frankly, we do not even know what a woman-oriented standard would be like. We have been following a male standard for so long we are not clear about our own needs. *Exercises SL-1 though 4; C-2, G-1, G-5, and S-1 through 6 in the homework chapter can help you practice self-acceptance.*

Homophobia

Sexism lays the groundwork for homophobia. As women, we are assumed to be asexual if we're not involved with men. Women are not seen as having an independent, aggressive sexuality of their own.

Ironically though, once we are seen as lesbians, we're viewed as purely sexual beings. Our genital contact with other women sets us apart and defines us. Sometimes we accept that label ourselves and question our own lesbianism if we are celibate, infrequently sexual or primarily companionate in our relationships.

It is important for us to talk out loud about our own homophobia. As the culture is permeated by homophobia, it's impossible for us not to have absorbed some of it. It's not a fact to feel guilty about or deny, but rather to acknowledge and explore. Homophobia can hurt us less if we are open about harboring it. The following chapter discusses in more details the ways that homophobia directly affects our sexuality. *Exercises H-1 through 3 in the homework chapter can help you reconcile your feelings.*

Rape Trauma

The sexual trauma experienced by women in our culture is another result of sexism. It is a short step from objectification to men using violence to sexually overpower women. Forty percent of women have experienced sexual assault by the age of eighteen (Russell). Both rape and incest have profound and long-lasting effects on our ability to experience sex whole-heartedly.

The sexual experience of a woman who has been raped is often negatively affected for the rest of her life. Considering that in the U.S. a woman is raped every six minutes (Brownmiller), the serious impact of rape on the lives of women cannot be overestimated. Lesbians are raped no less than other women. Although the lesbian community has been in the forefront of establishing rape hotlines and rape crisis centers, educating the police, the medical professions and the public, individually we are still as vulnerable to the pain of rape as other women.

Our private sex lives can be just as affected. We may still have flashbacks, feel powerless, fall into depression, and demand of ourselves that we be finished with our pain after a specific time.

"I just know everyone is sick of hearing about my rape. I hate myself for bringing it up again and again, but nothing else seems so significant to me."

"I'm still so depressed about being raped a year ago that I don't want to work."

"I'm afraid. I won't go out after dark. I generally have stopped living my life. I wonder will this ever end?"

"I have flashbacks to when I was raped almost every time I have sex. Especially with oral sex. I just try to ignore my mind and focus on the experience I'm involved with at the moment."

"After I was raped, I wasn't able to have sex for two years. Once I started again, I had a terrible time. Finally five years later I feel like being sexual sometimes."

After you have experienced the profound violation of self that is involved in rape, it is important to talk about it as much as you can. Talk about it to as many people as will listen. Keep talking about it. If you do not want to talk about it or are sure your friends are tired of listening, look at why you want to be silent. Are you ashamed? Are you angry? Have you asked your friends directly if your talking about your rape is tiring to them? Promise yourself that you will ask one friend a week to listen to you talk about your rape experience. Keep talking. Even as violent and obvious an incident as rape can be denied and "forgotten," leaving permanent scars and effects. Work on not letting this happen to you.

Find a counselor in your town and go to her. She will have ways to help you with your healing. She will be there just to listen to you. She can concentrate on your pain and on your healing rather than on her own. Tell her every detail no matter how minute or seemingly unimportant.

Our culture says that women are responsible for their own assaults. Even if intellectually you reject that piece of male rationalization, you've probably internalized it somewhere. Dig it out. Explore out loud every way you feel responsible. Let other women be there for you and remind you that no man has the right to rape you regardless of the circumstances.

"I never thought I would be ashamed if I was raped. Once it happened to me, I felt like I was so stupid to walk in the dark in this big city by myself."

"My lover wants to make love with me even though I was raped last month. I can't believe she would ever want to touch my genitals again."

Organizing or joining a group for rape survivors can be a tremendously empowering step. Healing yourself from the psychological and physical damage of rape needs to be your priority. *Exercises A-1 through 7 in the homework chapter can help.* Take as much time and energy as you need. You are Number One for you.

Incest Survivors

The sexual consequences of incest are generally even more deeply ingrained in our physical and psychic structures than those of rape. If our first sexual experience occurred with a trusted older family member or friend, sexual experience and violation are originally linked for us. The incest survivor has no model for a trustworthy and safe family. She has no experience of being able to rely on or be protected by those who purport to love her. She has no training in setting sexual limits or boundaries, in making assertive demands or in refusing sexual advances. Intimacy has been bound up with betrayal and abandonment.

The first difficult issue for the incest survivor is the secrecy that shrouds incestuous experiences encouraging the survivor to "forget" them and to doubt her own intuitions. She is left with vague, uncomfortable feelings about her father, grandfather, mother, uncle, sister or brother. Often our first job is to re-learn to trust our own intuition regardless of corroboration by anyone in our family. Trust that if you feel that you were abused, you were.

"I could never believe that something so terrible as my father molesting me could have happened in my family. But I keep having these memories that my father french kissed me when I was a little girl. I was always afraid of him. I never wanted him to be near me, especially if we were alone."

"I have these vague feelings that one time my brother came into my room in the middle of the night and touched me under the covers. I don't remember when that was, but I know it wasn't the only time. I don't know how I know, I just know."

Dealing with the ambivalence we feel about people we love who also violated, betrayed and abandoned us remains a major issue throughout our lives.

"Do I love them or hate them? They provided me with everything I needed, gave me a home and a family, but did not really care for me."

"I love my grandfather so much, why would he put his finger in my vagina?"

"Sometimes I wish I had simply been raped on the street. It's weird to say I wished that. But having to see my father for the rest of my life after he raped me in high school is almost too much to bear."

"I just want to forget that I was a victim of incest. When I go to a holiday dinner, I keep saying 'how could that woman do what she did to me?' I think I'm lying."

Incest creates serious sexual complications in the lives of survivors. Often sex becomes separated from emotional attachment. Sometimes the survivor has learned to "numb out", leave her body or otherwise detach during sexual experience. Often sex has become something too frightening or threatening to engage in.

"There is no way I have ever been willing to have sex with someone that I really care about. My father touching me the way he did, I just can't imagine sex could be loving and caring."

13

"My grandfather forced me to have sex with him; now the only people in my life that I have trusted have been friends. Lovers fall into a category that is always being tested. Will someone who is attracted to my body be someone I can really love?"

If you are an incest survivor, slow, gradual healing over time will probably be necessary. This time may be weeks, months or even years after acknowledging an incest experience. During the time of healing, your sex life may be seriously disrupted. You may not want to have sex at all. Tell your partner ahead of time, when you are not in a sexual situation, that you are a survivor of incest. Let her know where you stand about sex. Let her know if you have not had sex for a long time, or if you have had sex infrequently. Tell her that if you are going to have sex, you must stop as soon as you feel un-comfortable. Engage in sex, and then stop every time you have an uncomfortable flashback or sensation. Do this every ten seconds if necessary. *Do exercises A-1 through 7 with yourself. If you have a partner you are willing to trust, try exercises AP-1 through 5.* They can help you with your general fear of loss of control.

If you are in a committed relationship, your partner may not be able to stand by you through your healing. You need to honor your feelings, and your partner needs to honor hers. Healing from incest is a difficult process to go through, even for the partner of a survivor. When a woman is a partner of an incest survivor, it may be difficult to participate in a process of which someone else is seem-ingly "in charge." *If you are a partner of someone who has sur-vived sexual abuse, do exercises PA-1 through 3.*

Do not be discouraged; each of you must take care of yourself. Working on someone else's time schedule may give you each a lot of resentment and anger. The survivor and her partner(s) need to tell the truth above all. The survivor has been through some period of her life when everyone was lying . That must end, even at the expense of a relationship. Not telling the truth will eventually separate you anyway. Start today telling the truth. Waiting until next week will not make talking openly any easier. Time passing only makes truth-telling more difficult.

Forming or joining a support group of incest survivors can be invaluable; talking with other women with similar experiences is very healing. What you are going through, many other women are going through too. You are not alone; at least one in every five women has survived incest (Russell, 1983). We are all learning to heal ourselves, in whatever ways we can. Accepting yourself and your own ways of healing is imperative to that process.

Healing

Healing from the sexism, homophobia and sexual trauma perpetrated in our society is necessary for every woman regardless of her individual experiences. Each day spend some time alone with yourself. Take this time to thank yourself for putting up with the world around you. Let yourself know (say it out loud, write it down) that you love yourself. If you do not honestly feel that way, find one thing in the last week that made you have warm feelings for yourself. Recount that time, revel in it, do not just pass it off as something that happened by accident. Focus on what about you is unique. During this time alone, forgive yourself for all the parts of you or your actions that is not perfect. Forgive yourself for being human. Practice this ritual every day for a month. At the end, you will have another perspective to call upon when you are berating yourself. Learning to accept ourselves comes only after consistent effort. Work at stopping your negativity about yourself and allowing youself to talk about your positive aspects. As we each accept ourselves and our sexuality, we will break through our sexual blocks and create a body of knowledge about what women's sexuality is truly all about.

Homophobia

As with all irrational fears, homophobia affects those who are feared as well as those who fear. As I have said in the previous chapter, homophobia affects lesbians' lives in many ways. In most states it is illegal for consenting adults to engage in homosexual acts in private. Gay people are not legally protected from discrimination on the job or in housing as are other minorities. Because gay people have not yet won the fight for fair employment, we have to worry about whether it's safe for us to come out on the job. Similarly, young lesbians and gay men have to decide whether or not to come out at school.

To avoid awkwardness or dishonesty, many of us just refrain from talking openly about our personal lives. Our co-workers and co-students see us as shy, withdrawn, reserved, snobbish—when actually we are trying to protect ourselves from *their homophobia!*

When people have personal problems, it's natural for most to turn to family for support. Some families of gay people are loving and helpful, others are hostile and angry, and most fall somewhere in between. For lesbians, even families that try to be supportive may express homophobia in unconscious ways.

"Well, you know it's fine with me if you're gay, dear, but for God's sake don't tell your father."

"I'm sure this is *just* a phase."

"Oh, you're bringing your lover to your sister's wedding? Well, fine. Uh . . . what does she look like?"

> "I know your friend is really important to you,
> but I still don't understand why you can't spend the
> holidays here with us."

> "We'd love to have you visit anytime, but I must
> say in all honesty that your new friends are not
> welcome here."

> "I knew when you sent all your skirts home that
> you were a lesbian, just keep it to yourself."

We've all had similar experiences with straight friends, room-mates, neighbors, or even grocery clerks.

Race, class, religious and cultural experiences impact how we may come out to our families. There are many of us who cannot ever come out to our families. Whatever our background, this kind of hiding takes its toll on our sex lives.

> "As a black woman, I was raised in a small com-
> munity within a city. Whenever you did something
> everyone else knew about it. So my mother is very
> concerned about what the neighbors think. I don't feel
> I could ever tell her about my lifestyle."

> "My family is pretty typical for Asians in Hawaii.
> The men were the only ones who counted and a les-
> bian was seen as a true aberration. My family would
> never accept me in that way, so I just don't tell them."

> "Not only was my family Jewish, but my father
> was a survivor of the holocaust. To imagine that I
> wasn't going to marry a Jewish man and have children
> that would carry on the family, the traditions—well
> my family would rather think I was dead. So they ask
> all the time when I'm getting married, and I just ig-
> nore them. I'm sure my sex life suffers, because I do
> feel I'm betraying them."

> "Being Catholic, there is no room for lesbianism
> in my family. I want to tell them about my love for
> women, but it would be too hard for them."

Many lesbians spend most of their time with other lesbians just to avoid awkward situations. But we come up against homophobia there too. What about that lover you had who didn't want to be seen in public with you because you were "too butch"? Or the woman you were involved with for three years who did not call herself a lesbian because she didn't want to restrict her identity with meaningless labels?

Dealing with other people's issues about homosexuality is stressful. It affects the way we see others and the way we see ourselves. Internalized homophobia can lead to damaged or low self-esteem, which in turn results in lowered expectations, depression, anxiety, and inability to fully carry out our responsibilities. Homophobia gets ingrained so deeply that even lesbians who are at ease with their sexuality encounter homophobia within themselves. Taking on the oppressive attitudes of those around us makes us feel bad about who we are: lesbians.

> "Sometimes when I have my young son around a group of lesbians I hope he doesn't go and tell his friends what he hears. When I pay attention to that fear of mine it makes me so sad that I have hatred of being a lesbian."

> "Even though I do public speaking about being a lesbian, I'm really nervous when Esther and I are around my family. I'm always afraid she'll try to hold my hand and make my family uncomfortable. Then I hate myself for feeling that way."

We all have homophobia. We cannot grow and develop in this culture without experiencing within ourselves the fear the culture has of homosexuality. *Homework exercises H-1 to H-3 may help you explore your own homophobia.* The first step towards overcoming our internalized homophobia is to face it honestly.

Many gay parents do not talk with their children about the fact that they are gay. By "protecting" them from knowing who we are, we act as though there is something horrible about us. Children of gay parents *do* know who their parents are being sexual with, whether their parents tell them or not. I recently talked with a seven year old who told me, "When Isabel first moved in with us, I thought she was just there to help my mom with the rent. Then I saw how close they were. I felt so dumb!"

If our internalized homophobia is very strong, we may begin isolating ourselves from gay *and* straight people. We may feel intense sadness about being gay because we do not fit in, because we are not accepted. We turn this sadness inward and it becomes depression. We make judgments against ourselves, instead of turning outward in anger at the culture that disowns us.

Some people say, "But these are just ways to protect ourselves. If I come out as a lesbian at work, I'll be out of a job. That's not internalized homophobia, that's survival." The reality of cultural homophobia and the resultant discrimination cannot and should not be denied. But we can't let ourselves be forced by this reality into buying what the majority culture tells us: that we should hide our sexuality, that we are bad or less important in some way because of it. Believing this feeds our own internalized homophobia.

How Homophobia Affects Lesbian Sexuality

Initiating dates is difficult for lesbians because most of us never learned how to ask someone out. We were supposed to wait for the boys to ask us! This skill that most men began to develop gradually at about age thirteen is expected to bloom suddenly in a lesbian who comes out at eighteen or twenty-nine or forty-two. Two women attempting to get together face this process with little experience and a lot of awkwardness. Internalized homophobia profoundly affects even this aspect of our lives.

> "I used to think that the only reason I was afraid to ask a woman out would be because I was a woman of color and she wasn't. Now I think that maybe it has more to do with being afraid she'll be offended cause I'm thinking she's gay. See I'm nervous asking out a sister too."

> "Even though I came out as a teenager, no one taught me how to ask someone for a date. There just was no one to get advice from in 1943."

Families are remarkably powerful, and we carry family messages about all kinds of things into our adult lives. It is common for women to have no memories of lesbianism being mentioned in their families. It was a word, and a concept, that some of us never heard. It's typical for children to believe that things they have no words for are either bad or wrong. It is a struggle to fight a message as pervasive as this. One woman I worked with told me, "Every time I feel attracted to another woman, all I hear is my mother's voice saying that lesbians are disgusting."

The community around us affects us as well. I am reminded of one of my clients who was single and interested in dating. At that time, our county was facing a referendum on homosexual rights; as the election drew near, the newspapers were filled with vicious assertions about homosexuals. My client said, "I think about approaching a woman and asking her out to dinner, and then I see us at some restaurant with crowds of angry people smashing the windows, trying to get to us and chasing us through the streets. I feel so shaken after this vision that I say to myself, 'forget it.' And I don't ask her out."

Clearly there are a lot of obstacles we must overcome just to feel we can ask someone out. The next problem we face is who to ask. Our choices are very limited. Usually we rely on our circle of friends to introduce us to other lesbians. Most of us would not ask a woman out if we did not already know she was gay.

Men do not wonder whether a woman is straight before asking her out. They assume she is heterosexual. A man may have some doubts about whether a woman will say "yes", but he certainly isn't going to worry about offending her by admitting his attraction to her. We lesbians look for clues about a woman's sexual orientation and drop hints to observe her response. Even if an opportunity arises to express our attraction, we often choose to remain silent rather than risk insulting her or other (straight) people present. We feel, in fact, that we do not have the right to exhibit affection, attraction or sexuality except in private or in all-gay groups.

Most people in our western culture have a hard time discussing sexuality. We are embarrassed, we feel like novices, and sometimes we are actually ashamed of what we do sexually. Lesbians, in addition, often have no words for the things we do, while the words we *do* have may carry negative connotations. It is difficult to overcome these challenges and begin to talk about our sexuality. But as we talk about sex to one another, we will learn that we are all having the same kinds of struggles...and we will find solutions together.

The cultural message we hear is that sex between two women is immoral, dirty, disgusting. Lesbian sex is profoundly affected by this message. For example, many women find it unpleasant to touch another woman's genitals. They do not like the feel or the smell, or they are uncomfortable putting their fingers into someone's vagina. Oral sex may be difficult for such women because of the unfamiliar smell and taste of genitals, and the sense that there is something "unsanitary" about it all. Even being sensual and loving in a non-genital physical way (hugging, kissing, caressing) can be very hard for some of us. Our task now is to learn a new message about sex: we do not need to feel shame about who we are and how we choose to get our sexual fulfillment.

> "When I am having sex with a woman I often flash to the negative messages I hear all the time. I wonder how people can think we are sick, yet I do sometimes question whether I should be having oral sex with a woman."

Public negativity about our sexuality directly affects our sex lives. Sometimes we feel self-disgust while being sexual. Some of us have never actually been sexual with another woman because we've internalized the idea that it's sick.

When women experience cultural and internalized homophobia, attractions may be very strong but the ability to respond sexually to such attractions may be limited. A client of mine expressed this problem very well:

> "I knew I was attracted to girls when I was very young, but I read passages in the Bible that 'proved' homosexuality was wrong. Now, when I start to lick my lover's genitals, I sometimes have a flashback to stories in the Bible, and I have visions of lesbians going to hell."

This client found herself avoiding sex just to keep from experiencing this pain.

In lesbian relationships, there are two women struggling to overcome negative messages about sex; two people with deeply ingrained homophobia, and the resulting wish to avoid the sexual acts that bring forth anxiety about lesbianism. Frequently these feelings are unconscious. The end result is that sex is neither as frequent nor as fulfilling as each would wish. I often hear:

> "Well, when I'm ready for sex, she's too tired, and when she's ready, I have to go to a meeting. We are just hardly every ready at the same time."

If this situation happens frequently, the couple needs to ask whether they are using excuses to keep from dealing with anxiety around sex.

Even a woman like Billie Jean King (may the story rest in peace) had to act as if her lesbianism was a mistake. If a woman of such prominence and established position in the sports world cannot acknowledge her lesbianism, who can? The daily act of having to live a double life—one that you show in public, one that you act in private—negatively influences our sexual expression. It is difficult to be sexual with someone you have denied all week at work. Switching gears from being "friends" outside your home to passionate lovers inside has a devastating effect on our ability to be sexually free.

One way that lesbians have internalized homophobia is to participate in our own form of "performance anxiety". We often try to prove we love being lesbians by feeling we have to be fantastic lovers, or by being sexual perfectionists. Some of us may even become "hypersexual".

> "I always felt I had to be the world's greatest lover. I was always adding new activity to my repertoire. When I discovered that my overwhelming concerns were my own homophobia I was amazed."

> "When I'm having sex, I feel as though I am on stage. Every act is being graded. I have never had a lover say that. I think I believe the world is out to get me because I am a lesbian."

Some members of the lesbian community foster homophobia by trying to establish "politically correct" ways in which lesbians may express their sexuality. We live in a culture that arrogantly decides where a person lives, what kind of work she can do, and how many rights she has all based on her race, class, sex and sexual preference. Carrying on in the fashion of the culture around us, we arbitrarily dictate at various points in time that lesbians: can only be "butch" or "femme"; must be feminist and cannot have any gender roles whatsoever; cannot or must engage in sado-masochism; must have orgasm for a sexual experience; cannot have sex with men; must be non-monogamous; must be monogamous; cannot date and be sexual with lots of women; must be in love to be sexual; cannot be sexual with friends; should be sexual with friends. We do not support other lesbians whose views differ from our own, and we justify this lack of support by politicizing sex.

The majority culture engages in more than enough legislating around sexual behavior, and we lesbians do not need to also dictate what is or is not acceptable lesbian sex. Sex should dwell within the privacy of our own lives. If we do not like a particular sexual act, we do not have to engage in it. Sex between two consenting women means that what they do and how they do it is between them. Our beds are not large enough to hold our families, politicians, society *and* the lesbian community.

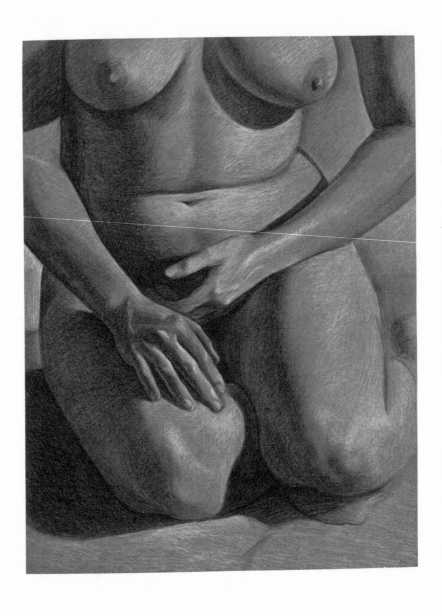

II. You Don't Have To Know Latin To Know Your Body:

What We Do & How Our Bodies Work

Physiology

In this society we are not encouraged to look at our genitals. It is unlikely that our mothers or our junior high sex classes gave us mirrors and flashlights and encouraged us to look "down there." If you haven't looked at your own genitals or if it's been a while, now is the time to do it. Choose a time when you can have total privacy and an unlimited span of time. You may want to masturbate too so you can see how your genitals change during arousal, excitement, orgasm, or resolution. *Doing exercises G-1 through G-9 and S-1 through S-8 from the homework chapter may help.*

Each woman's genitals are as individual as her nose. Contrary to the standard drawings in books, we are not all alike or symmetrical. Sometimes women in the same biological family will have similar genitals, just as there are similarities in their faces. Feasting your eyes on the beauty of your own genitals can go a long way towards increasing your self-acceptance. Other women may also let you look at their genitals. If so, you will see how different yet beautiful, each of us is. Tee A. Corinne has taken some amazing photographs of different women's genitals that are in Joani Blank's book *I Am My Lover*.

I would like to start this description of the different parts that make up our genitals with new information about the clitoris. Up until now, the clitoris has been described as that little button at the top of the vulva between the vagina and the pubic bone. But recently the Federation of Feminist Women's Health Centers has published new research about the clitoris in *A New View of a Woman's Body*. According to this new information, the clitoris is not only the glans, shaft and head usually described. The clitoris also includes two

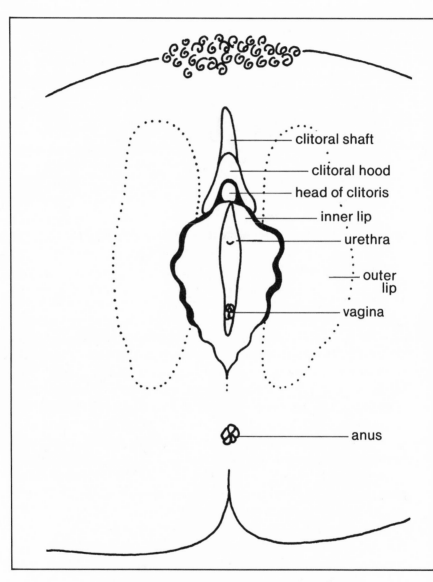

clitoral shaft

clitoral hood

head of clitoris

inner lip

urethra

outer lip

vagina

anus

EXTERNAL VIEW OF A WOMAN'S VULVA

"legs" that separate at the base of the shaft and continue and extend within the pelvic area on either side of the urethra, vagina and anus. Therefore, stimulating any of these parts also stimulates the clitoris. The clitoris is now known to be a much larger and more extensive structure than was previously thought. What was before identified as the clitoris is, in fact, only its visible-to-the-naked-eye part, the tip of the iceberg. The clitoris runs all the way through the pelvic platform from pubic bone to anus. The clitoris is made up of taut wire-like tissue surround by spongy tissue, nerves and blood vessels.

> "Once I heard that there is more to the clitoris than meets the eye I got more excited. I only wish I could see it."

> "Finally an explanation of why when I'm real excited during sex I can't tell whether my ass, cunt or clit is being touched."

The tip of the clitoris is called the head or glans. It rises up out of the pelvic platform on the shaft or stem. It is covered by a piece of skin called the hood. The rays or legs of the clitoris start at the base of the shaft and divide running down either side of the pelvic area. Sexual stimulation causes all parts of the clitoris—legs, shaft, glans, hood—to become engorged and swell. Now we can understand why anal, vaginal or urethral stimulation can lead to "clitoral" orgasm; all of that stimulation also stimulates the clitoral legs.

The glans of the clitoris varies in size, in the amount it protrudes, in shape, and in color. Some women like it touched directly; others find this painful. Often a woman finds one side of the glans and shaft to be more sensitive than the other. Some women like the hood to be retracted; others find that so intense that it's uncomfortable.

> "This is another way that Ioko and I are the same, we both love hard pressure on our clits."

> If Tara comes near my clitoris once we have started making love I go crazy. It really hurts."

The clitoral structure lies in a bed of soft spongy fatty tissues called the outer and inner lips. Books also refer to these lips as labia.

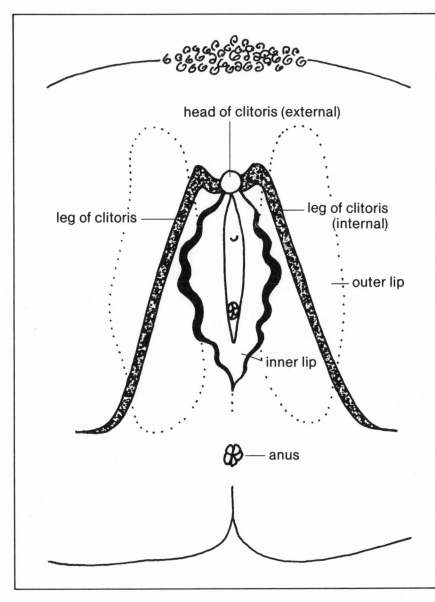

head of clitoris (external)

leg of clitoris

leg of clitoris (internal)

outer lip

inner lip

anus

THE CLITORIS
(Information from *A New View of a Woman's Body* by
The Federation of Feminist Women's Health Centers)

Put your hand down between your own or your partner's legs, the lips are in between the legs and are the fatty tissue covering the whole pubic area. The outer lips are the first set, the inner lips are the next set. In half of all women, the inner lips are longer, in the other half, the outer lips. The outer lips change most as a young woman develops. They vary in size and have an extra layer of fat in them. They are altered by weight changes and pregnancy. Some women can get very excited by having them stroked, squeezed, or kneaded. The inner lips are usually less fatty than the outer ones. They also can vary in size, shape and width. They may or may not attach to the clitoral shaft, hood or glans. Some women's inner lips are so sensitive they do not like to have them touched; others find it very exciting to have them caressed. You might try touching yourself slowly to see what you like. Then the next time you are with a partner, tell her how you like your lips touched.

"I just love it when a woman touches my lips—all sets of lips. But the ones that I love the best are the inside ones. They are so sensitive and slippery once I get turned on. It's almost enough for me to have just that done."

The urethra is a tube that extends from the bladder to the outside of the genital area. It moves the urine (pee) out of the body. The bladder is a holding tank for the urine that's been processed by the kidneys. If bacteria enter the urethra they can be carried up into the bladder and cause infections that can migrate to the kidneys. Wiping away from the urethra toward the anus can help avoid infections. The urethra also carries ejaculate from the Grafenberg spot to the outside.

The paraurethral sponge is a dense concentration of blood vessels wrapped around the urethra with the largest portion under the urethra next to the outer wall of the vagina. Within the sponge is the paraurethral gland. This gland produces a watery fluid which is sometimes called "ejaculate." Little is known about the paraurethral gland while much research has been done on the corresponding prostate gland in the male. Big surprise.

The commonly heard term, Grafenberg, or "G", spot refers to the place inside the vagina where one can stimulate the sponge. It is about two inches up from the entrance to the vagina towards the front of the body. To find it, put your fingers inside your vagina

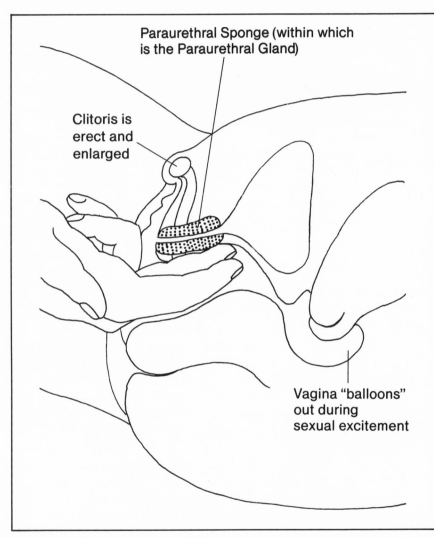

Paraurethral Sponge (within which is the Paraurethral Gland)

Clitoris is erect and enlarged

Vagina "balloons" out during sexual excitement

FINDING THE GRAFENBERG OR "G" SPOT

with the finger tips towards your front and move the fingers up and down. The sponge swells when stimulated, and you may feel like you have to pee, or it may give you a pleasurable sensation. With continued stimulation, a fluid (ejaculate) is produced in the gland and through its ducts in the sponge sometimes is sprayed out of the body via the urethra. It may feel like a lot of liquid, but it is usually a few teaspoonfuls to half a cup. Many women find the fluid coming out of the body exciting.

> "When I first squirted this stuff out of my body
> I was freaked out. I thought sure the woman I was
> with would really flip. Luckily, she knew what this
> was—not pee, but ejaculate. What a trip."

> "Arita ejaculates when we make love and I hate
> it. It seems to drown me if I'm going down on her.
> So I just move to another place on her body and that
> helps."

Ejaculation usually happens at a different time than orgasm. Some women who ejaculate don't have orgasms at all. Others do both, but ejaculation and orgasm are different processes and are not tied to one another. Some women in fact don't even feel it when they do ejaculate.

The pubococcygeus (PC) muscle extends from the pubic bone to the coccyx or tip of the spine. This muscle forms the pelvic platform; it is the muscle that responds when you have spasms or contractions. Keeping this muscle toned can increase your sexual pleasure. To find it, sit on the toilet and start to pee, then stop in mid-flow. You can also find it by contracting your genitals. Now that you know how to contract it, you can exercise it anywhere, anytime. To exercise it, contract it ten times very quickly. Repeat three times a day. Also try contracting and holding to a count of ten. Repeat this twenty times three times a day. You can do this anywhere, anytime—commuting to work, standing in line, watching TV, washing dishes. No one need know you're exercising your PC muscle to increase your sexual pleasure.

The vagina is potential space that only opens when stimulated or when something is put inside it. Otherwise, it lays flat like a deflated ballon. During stimulation, the vagina which is three to four

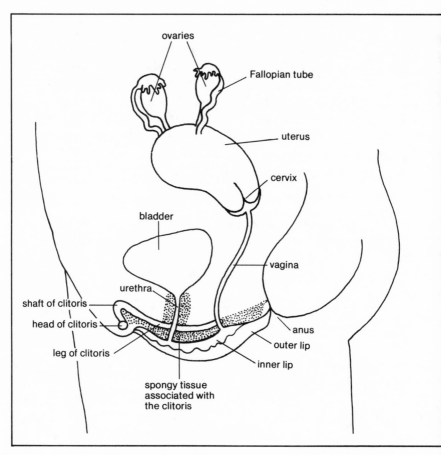

ovaries

Fallopian tube

uterus

cervix

bladder

vagina

urethra

shaft of clitoris

head of clitoris

leg of clitoris

anus

outer lip

inner lip

spongy tissue
associated with
the clitoris

INTERNAL VIEW OF A WOMAN'S PELVIS

inches long, changes shape by ballooning outward. The opening to the outside may increase in diameter and the back two-thirds may balloon out. The first third contains most of the nerve endings and touching there can be very pleasurable. This area can widen or tighten depending upon where you are in the sexual response cycle.

"The vagina is where it's at for me. Unless I have something inside, there is no getting excited. I like to have fingers, vibrators, dildoes, whatever inside me."

The first time I was with Anita, she wanted to put her fingers inside my vagina. It was too personal for me and I wanted none of that. I still don't really like her to put her fingers inside. Maybe I'm old fashioned, but even after seventeen years together it's just not my thing."

The cervix (or os) is the part of the uterus that protrudes into the vagina. It is soft but firm and rounded like the end of a nose. To touch it, put your fingers in your vagina while you are in a squatting position. Move the fingertips towards the back of your vagina. The os is at the top and often enters the vagina at an angle.

If you have never seen your cervix, you can get a plastic speculum from your local women's health center or your doctor. With a light and a mirror, you can view your own cervix. Hold the speculum under hot water until it's warm, then lubricate it with K-Y jelly or vegetable oil. Lie on your back, with your knees up and your legs spread wide. Hold your vaginal lips open and move the closed speculum in slowly. Having a friend watch and help, if needed, can be very reassuring until you've learned how to do it. Open the speculum slowly and clip it so it stays open. Open the speculum only as wide as is comfortable. Have your friend hold a mirror and light so that you can see your cervix. It looks like a little pink doughnut with a collapsed hole. It may have red veins running through it, a drop of blood at its opening, or some clear or milky fluid on it. If you do not find it, take the speculum out, shift your position slightly and try again. Start taking the speculum out slowly, then unclip it, let it collapse, and finish removing it. If you try to close it first, you may pinch your cervix.

The cervix varies in shape and color according to where you are in your menstrual cycle. The small hole in the center of it is the passageway that allows menstrual blood out and sperm into the uterus. During orgasm, the cervix dips into the ballooned portion of the vagina and opens. Therefore, it is helpful to have an orgasm when inseminating to increase your chances of pregnancy.

> "When I first saw my cervix I got faint. It looked like something was rotting inside me—all wet and runny and smashed looking. I decided I had to look at it once a month just to get used to it—after all it was part of me too. I'm glad I did, I like my cervix now."

The uterus is another potential space that is only filled during pregnancy. The uterus grows a lining and sloughs it off every month during menstruation or is the home of the fetus for nine months.

During menstruation many women experience cramps in their uterus. Cramps can be minor and respond to warm, wet heat, to exercises that relax the abdominal muscles, or to having an orgasm. Some women have cramps so severe that they are debilitated for a few days every month. There are many different remedies for cramps that have been found effective throughout the ages. Some women take prescription drugs, others have moved to a dairy, sugar and chemical-free diet, some take calcium and potassium, some have had operations to remove scar tissue formed from various maladies, others have had hysterectomies. Some women experience cramps as a regular, if unwelcome, part of their lives. It is important to remember that cramps are not "all in your head." Menstrual cramps are a physical reaction and respond to physical remedies.

> "My people see our bodies as something completely private. No one ever told me that cramps like I have are common. I felt much better when I found other women suffer too."

> "Forget sex when I am having my period. I'm in pain for almost five days and I can't be touched."

The ovaries store the ova, or egg, that travels down the fallopian tube into the uterus. If the egg doesn't implant in the uterine lining, it, along with the lining, is sloughed off in menstruation. If it does implant, pregnancy ensues. The release of the egg occurs about halfway between two menstrual periods and is often accompanied by some twinges of pain.

The anus is the opening to the rectum. It is small, strong and has numerous nerve endings. It holds the feces in or pushes them out of the body. The anus is quite sensitive, and it can be very pleasurable to have it stroked and touched.

> "I love having Myra touch my asshole. It feels so good. The fact that everyone thinks it's gross makes it even more fun."

The rectum leads to the colon, another potential space that lies flat until filled. It can be very pleasurable to have the rectum filled. Some women do this with enemas, others with fingers or hands. It is important to keep this area clean and not to put fingers or hands that have been around the anus into the vagina. The bacteria that live quite healthily in the rectum can cause serious infections in the vagina.

Our breasts are as individual as our clitorises. They can be fat and full, flat and soft, firm or sagging. They also vary with changes in body weight, pregnancy and age. For most women, breasts are one of the most erogenous areas on their bodies. The type of stroking, caressing, touching, fondling, and cupping that is most pleasurable will be different for each of us and may vary according to the time of our menstrual cycle. Often the breasts are sensitive and cannot tolerate touch right before menstruation.

Our nipples also vary widely. Some nipples are sharp and stick out clearly; others are rounded and soft and almost fade into the areola. The nipples can be very small or so large they almost cover the breasts. Nipples can become erect if stimulated. Stimulation can include rubbing, sucking, manipulating, rolling, twisting, licking—all of which can be very erotic.

> "I love rubbing the nipples of my lover. Her breasts are really big cause she's a really big woman. I just dive into Anna Maria's chest and rub on her nipples—what a turn on."

The areola is the round disc-like area around the nipple. It often is different in color from both the nipple and the breast. Sometimes the areola blends in with the breast and can hardly be discerned, This is more often true in both dark skinned women and very light skinned women. The areola can become engorged during stimulation and is usually responsive to touch.

Sexual Response Cycles

Each woman has her own specific sexual response cycle, although there are common elements. The sexual response cycle was first thoroughly researched by Masters and Johnson, as reported in *Human Sexual Response*. Masters and Johnson divided the continuous response of a woman to sexual stimulation into four different phases.

Stage 1-Excitement: This stage, which can be indefinite in length, is the one in which the body begins to respond to erotic stimuli by sight, smell, taste, touch or fantasy. The nerves, muscles, and tissues of the genitals and breasts begin to react. The vagina begins to secrete fluid. The genital and breast tissue begins to swell and become engorged, get hot and change color.

Stage 2-Plateau: This is the stage of intense sexual excitement. Tissue becomes further engorged; the vagina increases lubrication. The clitoris becomes more erect. The first third of the vagina may tighten and the back balloon out. The cervix and uterus may move up into the pelvis. The nipples may become erect.

Stage 3-Orgasm: This stage is a spasmodic response to the extreme engorgement of the pelvic region. From three to fifteen contractions occur, 4/5 of a second apart, releasing the fluid and blood from the engorged tissues. These spasms are involuntary. At this point, the cervix dips down into the vagina.

Stage 4-Resolution: This is the return of the body to the resting stage. The muscles and nerves relax; blood and fluids return to their normal tissues.

A woman could move from stage 1 to 3, skipping 2; or move through 1, 2 and 4, skipping 3; or move between 1 and 2; or move between 1 and 2 and not move further. After going through all four, she could go back to the beginning and work through them again.

Although Helen Singer Kaplan has made anti-lesbian and anti-homosexual remarks, she has made an important contribution to the sex research field. She uses a three-stage model of sexual response.

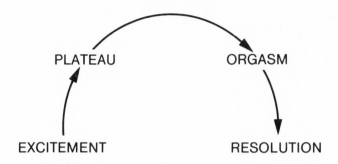

SEXUAL RESPONSE CYCLE - MASTERS & JOHNSON

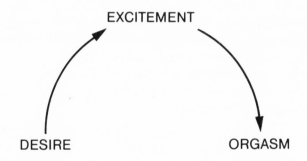

SEXUAL RESPONSE CYCLE - KAPLAN

Stage 1-Desire: Kaplan feels desire is an imperative stage in the sexual response cycle of women. She has identified desire as an area in which many women have problems. Thus, she thought it best to treat desire as a separate stage, so problems specific to it could be identified.

Stage 2-Excitement: This stage combines Masters and Johnson's excitement and plateau stages.

Stage 3-Orgasm: This stage combines Masters and Johnson's orgasm and resolution stages.

Stage three can be skipped. It is also possible to move through all three and start again.

After working with thousands of lesbians around their sexuality, I have developed my own much more complex female sexual response cycle. Look carefully at the diagram below before reading the explanation.

According to my diagram, a woman does not have to begin the sexual response cycle with either desire or excitement. In fact, numerous women report that sex begins for them with willingness. You do not have to feel desire or be excited to have sex. You only have to have the willingness to have sex. You may be willing because you want the intimacy sex creates, because you want to have a fuller sex life, because you know that once you start you enjoy sex, because you want the pleasure sex brings.

Also, as you can see from the diagram, pleasure is the goal of sexual experience. And pleasure can be experienced without any other stage except willingness.

Stage 1-Willingness: This is the decision to have sex for whatever reason. You do not even have to *want* to have sex. You may just be willing to have sex and the reasons can be those listed above. You may also move to this stage because you think you ought to be having more sex. Whatever the reason you are willing, that is the first step of this response cycle. It is not a passive stance. It is not meant to be looked at as "Oh well, I guess I'll lie here and go through with sex." Rather, this is a very active stage, at least in the mind. You are consciously deciding that you do want to have sex and you are willing to do so even if you have no physical or emotional desire. You do not even need a partner who is actively filled with desire. There may be two women who do not experience desire, but are willing to have sex together. This stage can move you

SEXUAL RESPONSE CYCLE
LOULAN

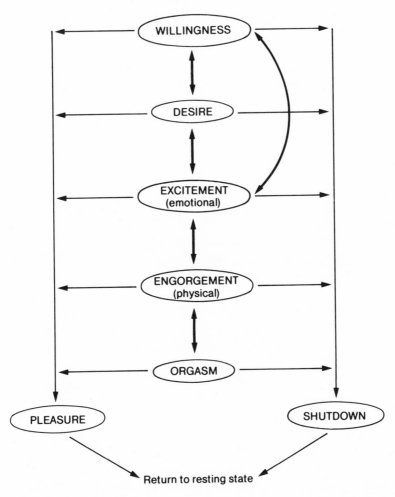

directly to excitement. It can also stimulate desire, shutdown, resting, or pleasure.

Stage 2-Desire: This includes wanting to have sex because it feels good and you're attracted to someone.

There are three areas of desire: intellectual, emotional, and physical. The first is what we experience with our minds. We want to have sex with a partner or ourselves, and we decide that we are going to act on this thought. It does not have to be connected to any body sensations. There is also emotional desire. This could be that we have intense feelings about another woman and want to have sex with her because of the closeness we feel. Physical desire is a lust feeling that we can actually experience in our bodies. This is usually the desire that is shown in the movies as a holy experience. While it can be very exciting; it is not the only way to experience sexual desire.

This stage can move you to excitement, shutdown, resting, or pleasure.

Stage 3-Excitement: This stage is similar to that described by Masters and Johnson or Kaplan. It can include only physical characteristics but it may include emotional ones as well. These physical characteristics vary from woman to woman. It is not something that is predictable. Experiencing this stage does not mean that you love your partner. It is a bodily function. The emotional part of this stage is that of feeling more and more overwhelmed, and connecting deeply to this other person. It is not something that has to occur for connection; it is only one form the connection takes.

From this stage you can go back to stages 1 or 2, forward to 4, or shutdown, resting or pleasure.

Stage 4-Engorgement: This stage is similar to the plateau phase of Masters and Johnson. From it you can go back to stages 3, 2, or 1, or forward to 5. It can also lead to shutdown, resting or pleasure.

Stage 5-Orgasm: This is the same as Masters and Johnson's and Kaplan's orgasm stage. This is not the only reason to have sex. It is only one stage within an extremely varied sexual response cycle. If you experience orgasm, this is not the end of the sexual encounter. Waiting for your partner to have one is not the end of sex. Neither of you could have an orgasm and both could experience extreme pleasure from the experience. From this stage, one can go back to any other stage. One can also move forward to pleasure, shut down or resting. It is important to remember that one can experience pleasure at any point without experiencing this stage.

Stage 6—Pleasure: This is the purpose of sexuality. It is possible to experience any of the other stages and not experience pleasure. In fact, you can have an orgasm and not experience pleasure. And it's possible to experience any of the above stages and experience pleasure. You can leave out any of the stages and still feel pleasure. The orgasm stage or any other is not requisite to feeling pleasure. What is assumed here is an expanded view of pleasure. You may experience pleasure simply from the fact that you were willing to engage in some sort of sexual activity. Even if you shut down immediately after starting. Pleasure is something that only you can define for yourself. Once again, I am going beyond the cultural belief that only an orgasm can bring sexual pleasure.

It is important to note, too, that you can shut down at any point in the cycle. No stage inevitably follows after the other, even with stimulation. "Shut down" can be caused by something very obvious: fatigue, anxiety, depression, a wandering mind that stops on anger, fear of intimacy, or stress. Sometimes our minds wander to some aspect of our life that takes us away from sexual feelings. Loss of feelings can also be activated by unconscious issues that are not apparent to you. Shut down can also be a purely physical response to some sort of stimulation that in fact stops the flow of energy in the body. This can also reverse and you may find that you want to start at some other point in sexual activity and begin the process again.

This stopping of feelings occurs for most women occasionally. In fact, for some women there are periods of time that this is a frequent part of their sexual response cycle. *You may want to try the exercises O-4 and O-5 in the homework chapter.* Whether or not there is something obvious that is prompting your "shut down," if you find that this is something that continues to happen during your sexual activity, you may want to seek some therapy.

Once a woman has started the sexual response cycle with willingness, she can shut down to any further sexual feelings at any point. The next stage or any further stage is never inevitable. She · may also return to a resting state at any point.

I feel that the complexity of my sexual response cycle is much truer to women's sexual experience. By starting with willingness instead of desire or excitement, by including shut down as possible at any point, and by allowing pleasure to follow any stage, each and every woman's experience can be encompassed by this cycle. No woman has to feel that she is different because her experience doesn't match the Masters and Johnson paradigm.

What We Do In Bed

The hardest topic for lesbians to talk about when we discuss sex is what we actually do in bed. We can talk about relationships endlessly, but to specifically tell one another what we do with our tongues, fingers, legs is scary. It is scary partly because there is so much judgment within the lesbian community about what we do. Every possible sexual activity is judged by someone as: not really sex, disgusting, insipid, unsanitary, wrong, male-identified, abnormal, repulsive, silly, too violent, too tame, too aggressive, too passive, too much like heterosexual sex, etc. Some people think that lesbians have to have sex a particular way to be lesbians. Nonsense! Lesbian sex is *anything* two lesbians do together. Monitoring our own and other's sexual behavior is in no one's interest but our oppressors.

I will only cursorily describe what we do in bed as there are entire books on the subject. If you want to know about any particular activity in more depth, see the bibliography. You may not engage in all these activities. That's fine; it means nothing about your lesbianism, how exciting and fulfilling your sex life is, or how good a lover you are. You may find any of the activities unacceptable to you; that's also fine. Do what feels good to you. The following will probably not cover everything you know about having sex with other women. That does not mean that what you do is wrong, abnormal or weird. It simply means I don't know about it or forgot to include it. This is not the definitive list. It's a beginning for all of us to add to throughout our lives.

Massage

Massage can be done with the clothes on or off of either partner. It can include the whole body or only parts of it like the head or feet or hands. Massage can come before other sexual acts or be an end in itself. Massage can be a very enjoyable way to create closeness before sex play. It is relaxing, relieves tension and provides a slow and gentle introduction to greater intimacy.

Creating a private, quiet, uninterrupted setting is important. If you're massaging skin directly, warmed massage oil or vegetable oil is very soothing. *If you are interested in specific uses of massage, see exercises P-5 in the homework chapter.* The bibliography also suggests specific books on sensual massage that can increase your sexual repetoire.

Breathing, Holding, Touching, Kissing, Licking, Sucking

Breathing and blowing on another's skin or various parts of the body can be very thrilling. Breathing on someone's neck, ear, or vulva can be enticing and arousing. Gentle blowing all over the body can be a pleasurable prelude to touching.

The pace and intensity of another's breathing can indicate her level of arousal. Experiencing the quickening of another's breathing can be very exciting. You can increase your partner's excitement when you convey yours by the intensity of your breathing.

Simply holding one another can be both sexually satisfying and stimulating. Standing and holding or hugging, sitting and holding, lying and holding—all are pleasurable and comforting. The simple warmth and closeness of another's body is a universal pleasure that we all seem to crave.

Touching can be done with only the hands and fingers, or with other parts of the body or with the whole body. Lightly touching someone with only the tips of the fingers can be very erotic. The face is especially sensitive to touch. Stroking with the hair, rubbing ones nipples or eyelashes or the palm of the hand over another's body can be especially arousing.

Touching with the entire body is a lesbian favorite. Lying on top of each other, clothes on or naked, lying next to each other, pressing against each other, putting one's leg between another's thighs, wrestling, rolling around, struggling—all emphasize whole-body touch to stimulate sexual desire.

Touching with the breasts, moving them slowly along another's naked body, can be arousing to both of you. Breasts are one of women's most erogenous areas. Many women feel as if their breasts and nipples are directly connected to the clitoris. Some women like gentle touching of their breasts, stroking, kneading, cupping and squeezing. Some like the action to be more intense and harder. Some like very vigorous rubbing and pushing. Nipples can be squeezed, rolled between the thumb and finger, pulled, sucked, licked, manipulated with the tongue or fingers.

Touching another's genitals with the breasts can be quite exciting. Rubbing your breast lightly over her vulva, thrusting your nipple into her vaginal opening, stroking her clitoris with your nipple are ways to use your breasts to fondle another. Some women find they like to put both breasts between another's thighs, or press against each other breast to breast.

There may be times during your menstrual cycle when you can't tolerate your breasts being touched—maybe during ovulation or just before or during your period. If that's the case, be sure to let your partner know.

You may not like to have your breasts touched at all. Or you may not know how you like to have your breasts touched. Masturbating with your breasts as a focus can let you know what feels good to you. Be sure to find out how your partner likes to have her breasts touched, as it may be different from what you like.

If you have had one or two mastectomies, it does not mean your chest cannot have significant sexual feeling for you. There are still nerves in the area. As long as it does not hurt to touch the scar tissue, it can be very exciting to have your breast area touched. You may have to get used to that possibility; go slow and be very gentle with yourself, especially if your fear of cancer has been attached to your breasts and that area of your chest. After a mastectomy, that area of your chest may need the most touching and caressing to help it feel whole and full again.

The mouth is an extremely intimate organ; it's wet and warm and reserved for people you care about. Kissing is a favorite thing to do with mouth and lips. The creative variations women have found in kissing are almost endless. Women have been known to kiss for hours. A lesbian "old wives tale" exhorts new lesbians that good kissers will be good lovers. You can kiss someone on the cheek, neck, breast, clitoris. You can kiss someone's whole body, starting at the top and working down. You can both kiss each other at the same time. You can kiss lightly, kiss teasingly, kiss strongly, kiss passionately. You can touch tongues and put your tongues inside each other's mouths. You can play hide-and-seek with your tongues, explore the other's mouth, teeth and tongue with your tongue. You can touch teeth and bite and nibble.

You can lick any part of another's body or rub your lips over it. Licking ears, face, mouth, breasts, genitals can be very sensuous. Inside the elbows and knees, the insides of thighs, the palms of the hands and insteps of the feet, and the hollow of the neck are very sensitive to licking. Wet tonguing between the fingers and toes can be very exciting. The speed, intensity and wetness with which a woman likes to be licked can vary; be specific about what you like.

Sucking can be done anywhere: you can brush your lips, kiss, or lick. Sucking on breasts and nipples is often satisfying for both partners. Sucking on the fingers and toes is often very erotic. Sucking the clitoris, the vaginal lips, or anywhere around or near the vulva, can be particularly stimulating. Sucking can be strong and powerful or light and playful. It can be done alone or with other forms of touching.

Touching the Genitals and Clitoris

Touching and rubbing the genitals and clitoris is a very common form of lesbian sex. Exploring the genitals slowly, moving around the lips, the clitoris, the hood and shaft of the clitoris, the vagina, the anus, the area between the vagina and anus can be most exciting for both partners. Hands and fingers can be used or tongue, breasts, part of an arm, even toes or legs. Light stroking of the outer or inner lips is often preferred.

Cupping the whole area with your hand or pressing your palm from pubic bone down often feels good. Squeezing your thighs against a whole hand is often stimulating. A rhythmic palming can be matched by the other's moving forward to meet it.

Stimulating the clitoris is one of the most pleasurable parts of lesbian sex. The clitoris is the only human organ that exists solely for pleasure. Touch the hood of the clitoris, pull it back to expose the head. Touch either gently with finger or tongue. Some women may find direct touching of the exposed clitoris painful. Some like the hood rubbed back and forth. Some prefer touch on one side of the shaft rather than the other. Some like the clitoris stimulated by rubbing from the entrance of the vagina towards the clitoris. If the lips attach to the clitoral hood, it may be exciting to have them pulled or tugged, or to have the tongue follow the edges up the clitoris.

Each woman likes to have her clitoris touched in a way special to her. Some like a slow, gentle, lingering touch. Others like a vigorous, active, intense touch. Some like to be rubbed back and forth; others up and down.

Some like to be touched on the clitoris alone without any other body part touching. Some like it combined with something placed in the vagina, or touching of the breasts, or kissing. If you don't know what you prefer, try out various possibilities when masturbating. If your partner isn't stimulating you the way you prefer, let her know.

Due to the extensive internal structure of the clitoris, it can also be stimulated via the vagina or anus. This stimulation will simply feel different than stimulation outside the body.

The Vagina

Many women like to have their vaginas touched. Some like fingers, hands, tongues, or mouths moved around the perimeter of the vagina. Some like to be penetrated with fingers, tongue, vibrator, dildo, vegetables or other objects that are not sharp. The tissue of the vagina is strong but it can be ruptured by sharp things. Having something inside the vagina can be quite pleasurable. The feeling of something moving in and out of the vagina can be extremely exciting.

Make sure the vagina is well lubricated before you put something in it. It is like a deflated balloon when it is not excited. When excited, a lubricating fluid is secreted by the vaginal walls making penetration easier. If more lubrication is needed, use spit or any water soluable commercial lubricant (Vaseline is *not* water soluble.) Move your finger or object inside the vagina at the pace and pressure your partner likes. Some women like an intense thrusting; others a gentle moving in and out. Some like to be penetrated, then have the finger or object slowly removed, dragging it up toward and over the clitoris. Some like their clitoris rubbed or licked while being

51

penetrated. Many lesbians find dildos pleasurable; dildos now come in soft or hard rubber and in various sizes and shapes.

One or more fingers can fit into the vagina. Sometimes the vagina opens to accept four fingers or the whole hand. This experience can be very exciting for both partners. Some women like to have their cervix touched during penetration; others find the sensations intolerable. Let your partner know what you prefer. You may not like penetration; if that's the case, be clear about it.

Oral Sex

Putting your mouth on a woman's genitals—oral sex—is another form of sex play. There are many positions for oral sex: lying on your back with your partner's head between your legs; on your side with her head between your legs; lying with your hips at the edge of the bed and your partner kneeling before you; sitting on the edge of chair with legs spread so you can observe your partner's actions; your partner lying down and you straddling her head and face; standing with your partner kneeling in front of you; or both lying face-to-genitals (commonly called 69, as 6 and 9 are reversals of each other).

Licking each other simultaneously can be done with either on top. The sensations will be slightly different in the top or bottom position. Or you can lie side by side. Many women find simultaneous oral sex too stimulating or distracting. Others find it very exciting but take turns stimulating each other.

During oral sex you can use your tongue, teeth, lips or chin. You can apply direct pressure or rubbing. You can nibble, bite, lick, thrust, or manipulate with your tongue. The clitoris can be licked directly, the shaft can be mouthed, the labia can be sucked, the vagina can be entered with the tongue. The tongue can be used to lightly brush the whole area; it can dart in and out of the vaginal opening; the whole face can be buried in the vulva.

Some women would like to engage in oral sex but are uncomfortable with the taste. You may want to bathe each other first as part of your sexual experience or douche together. Putting a lot of your spit onto the genitals can make the taste more familar. Using other substances like lickable, flavored oils or tasty food can be exciting.

Having fingers inside the vagina or anus during oral sex can be very exciting. Using a dildo or finger penetration of both vagina and anus while being licked can be extremely stimulating.

Anal Sex

Stimulating the anus for sexual pleasure is an important part of many lesbians' sex lives. The anus can be rimmed—the tongue moved around its edge—or stroked with the fingers, or penetrated with the fingers or a dildo. All can be very exciting.

If you feel uncomfortable about the sanitary aspects of anal sex, bathe together and/or give each other enemas. Many find enemas sexually stimulating and incorporate them as part of their sex play.

Anal penetration can be done with a finger, dildo or vegetable. Lubrication is often necessary for anal penetration. Use one of the water-soluble anal lubricants or K-Y jelly. As the anus becomes more excited, it too opens. It may accept more than one finger, up to the whole hand. Many women have very small hands which makes fist-fucking easier. When engaging in anal penetration, be careful not to touch the vagina with the same hand until it's been washed. Bacteria that are very healthy in your colon can cause an infection in your vagina. Usually anal penetration needs to be very slow and careful to allow the sphincter muscle to relax and open. As the anus becomes more excited, speed and pressure can be increased. Let your partner know what you like. For more information read *Anal Pleasure and Health* by Jack Morin.

Anal penetration can be combined with oral sex, with clitoral stimulation or with vaginal penetration. Some women like anal stimulation alone; others like it combined with other touching. Many women like penetration from the rear while on on all fours; others like to lie face down; still others prefer to sit on their legs so they can move up and down on the dildo or fingers.

Tribadism

Rubbing your genitals against someone's body or their genital area is called tribadism. In the nineteenth century lesbians were referred to as "tribades." For years French novels described tribadism as the major form of lesbian sexuality. Many lesbians like this form of sexual play because it involves all-over body contact and a generalized sensuality. Some women find the thrusting and "humping" of tribadism very exciting. Others straddle their partner's leg and rub gently. Some rub the clitoris on their partner's pubic bone or both get into a scissors position and touch and rub genitals.

Tribadism allows your hands and mouth to be free for other stimulation, an exciting alternative for many.

Sado-masochism

Sado-masochism is sex play that involves exchanges of power and using pain as a form of erotic excitement. Bondage and the use of restraints, whips, and paddles can be part of S/M play. Often we may have tried some activity that seemed perfectly normal and enjoyable—holding our partner's arms down, for example, while "humping" her—until we hear it identified as S/M. Then it becomes frightening. Playing with power and pain between consenting adults acceptably includes only activities that both desire and are not dangerous. The actual reality of such playing is usually much less frightening than the images we can conjure up when someone says S/M. Sometimes there is no more pain involved in actual S/M practices than in other types of sexual play. The perception of the line between pleasure and pain varies with different women and with the degree of sexual stimulation.

The consensual exchange of power can be very exciting to some women and can create a highly charged sexual atmosphere. Exchanging power means one partner agrees to give over power and become the "bottom" while the other agrees to accept power and becomes the "top." In order to control the situation, a safe word—totally unrelated to phrases like "please don't" or "stop"—is chosen. The top proceeds to "overpower" the bottom until she has had enough and invokes the "safe word." As you can see, the bottom is really in control since she decides how far to go.

Bondage is one form of S/M. Bondage ranges from lightly tying a partner to the bedposts with silk scarves to using leather wrist and ankle cuffs. Spanking, paddling, and using a riding crop are common forms of S/M discipline. Usually the verbal play that goes along with these activities is an important part of creating desire and excitement.

Stimulating the G-Spot

The G-spot is a recently discovered spot about one-third of the way up the vagina towards the pubic bone. When it is stimulated with direct pressure, intense excitement is experienced, the tissue swells and eventual ejaculation occurs. The ejaculate is a clear fluid emitted through the urethra and varies from a few teaspoonfuls to one-third cup. Ejaculate is not urine. It is a sign you have experienced a very high degree of pleasure. The G-Spot is most commonly stimulated by some form of vaginal penetration.

Sex Toys

Vibrators, dildos, oil, fur, feathers, water, velvet, silk—all can be used as sex toys, aids to increase arousal, excitement and sexual pleasure. Many women have found vibrators to be wonderful additions to partner sex. Some vibrators are designed so they can be used between partners and both can experience the intense, steady, unending, electrical stimulation at the same time.

Others like vibrators used on one area—clitoris, vagina or anus—while hands or tongue stimulates another area. There are vibrators with specially designed sleeves to stimulate the G-Spot, vibrators for vaginal or anal penetration, vibrators that fit on your hand, vibrators that stimulate vagina and anus simultaneously, and vibrators that stimulate both the vagina and the clitoris. Vibrators can have power cords or use batteries.

Dildos come in many shapes and sizes. They can vary from four to ten inches in length and from one-half to three inches in diameter. They can be ribbed, have double ridges, textured dots or French ticklers. Dildos can be of rigid plastic or flexbile latex. They can be strapped on with a pliable harness and used for thrusting, or can be guided by hand. Some dildos are also vibrators and may even have an up-and-down motion.

Double-headed dildos are especially designed for partner sex. They are bendable and long enough to accommodate a variety of positions.

Various flavored oils and creams are available which smell good and taste great when licked off. There are all kinds of materials and textures that heighten sensation and arousal. Silk, satin, fur, feathers and velvet can be used for caressing, stroking and teasing. Black satin blindfolds allow you to anticipate and be surprised by what happens next. A blindfold can also aid you in focusing your attention on the sensations as visual distractions will be excluded.

Many women appreciate the sensuous effects of water. They bathe or shower together as a part of sexual play. They lather each other up, play with bubbles and foam and give each other luxurious caresses in the water. Hot tubs and Jacuzzis are favorite sites for sexual touching. Water-Piks, pulsing shower heads and moveable sprays can increase arousal.

Sex can be delightful when you do it in a lake, pool or ocean. The rhythm of incoming tides can be very sensual, as is water rushing over the skin.

Food can be used as a sensual experience. Eating foods like artichokes and crab while naked in bed can add to sexual arousal. Putting food on each other and licking it off can be a lot of fun. Tasty oils and body paints are now available too.

Having sex in new places—whether on the kitchen counter, on the living room rug after slow dancing together naked, or in the bathroom—can often add an erotic element missing in the bedroom.

Ben-wa balls seem to have been discovered by the Chinese during the early Ming period. It was found that placing small metal balls in the vagina increased both stimulation and pleasure. Now you can buy balls or vibrating plastic eggs, which provide vaginal stimulation while your hands and mouth are free for other pursuits.

Exhibitionism, Voyeurism and Phone Sex

Many women like to engage in verbal or physical sex play while in public or the presence of others. It can be extremely exciting to be doing something that others would find scandalous if they recognized it. Often lesbians touch each other surreptitiously under lap blankets in public places, make out on the beach, have sex in the woods, or in another room at a party or at a friend's house. The idea of "getting caught" or being walked-in on increases sexual excitement and arousal.

Voyeurs enjoy watching others have sex. Or they enjoy listening to others have sex. You may watch yourself masturbate in a mirror, watch your partner masturbate or have mirrors positioned so you can watch yourself having partner sex.

Seeing the growing excitement of others can be very arousing. Some like to masturbate while they watch; others like the feeling of unalleviated sexual tension. Looking at photographs and drawings of sexual activity and watching movies and videos are other forms of voyeurism.

Many women like to engage in phone sex, that is, sexually stimulate each other verbally over the phone. Phone sex can be engaged in while you masturbate, describing in detail what you are doing and would like to be doing to the other. Or it can be engaged in at a public place like work where neither you nor your partner can get release of the building tension. It can be very thrilling to have someone describe what they want to do with you or to you in great detail. The more graphic phone sex is, the better.

Fantasies and Erotic Literature

Acting out fantasies with a partner can be very exciting. Some women go through elaborate costuming and scene setting. Others use verbal exchanges or play roles. The flea market and second-hand stores are wonderful places for getting props. Many women dress up in the bedroom in ways we never would in daily life.

In acting out fantasies, women can be characters or fulfill roles that society has denied us because we're women. We can fulfill female roles that we may have spurned in patriarchy. From the swashbuckling pirate to the black-satin-clad femme fatale, role-playing and dress-up can add spice to sexual life.

We may also want to use fantasies in our masturbation. That means that all urges for that woman who sat in the seat next to us on the bus can be taken care of in our own minds. There are many lesbians who like to make up characters out of their imagination and have wild affairs while being in the comfort of their own beds with their own hands or vibrators as the only witness. Sex with whomever we want, whenever we want — and no one knows!

Erotic literature usually describes other people's fantasies— and sexual experiences. Erotic literature may give you ideas of new ways to do it—new acts, positions, places, etc. Erotic literature can arouse you and when read with a partner, can make sexual experience more exciting. There are far too few pieces of lesbian erotica written by lesbians for lesbians. What is available is listed in the bibliography. An erotic magazine for lesbians is now being published; perhaps it will stimulate more of us to write down our erotic fantasies and experiences. All of us could gain by such sharing.

Who We Do It With

Having sex with yourself is self-stimulation or masturbation. For many of us, this was our first form of sex play. Some lesbians feel masturbation is okay only when you don't have a partner. Others include masturbation as part of their sex life all the time. Still others are not interested in masturbation at all. Masturbation can be a wonderful source of information about what (done where, and how hard) excites you. It can be quite enlightening to look at what masturbation means to you. What were you taught about it? *Try exercises S-1 to S-6 in the homework chapter to learn more about yourself.*

Almost all of the various ways of having sex with a partner are also possible when having sex with yourself. Touching, caressing, fondling, all kinds of vaginal, anal and clitoral stimulation, vibrators, dildos, water, feathers, fur—sex with yourself is only limited by your imagination.

In masturbation you get instant, complete feedback, so you can do, and get done to you, what feels good. Having sex with yourself is available whenever you want it and since you are the partner it can occur how, when and where you best like it.

There are many forms of having sex with women partners: casual sex experienced for the fun and joy of the sensations, having more than one concurrent affair, having one affair after another, having more than one committed relationship, having one committed relationship after another (serial monogamy), having a lifetime relationship, or any combination of the above. Each form of sexual relating has a group in the lesbian community that considers it the only correct or good way to relate sexually.

Those who want to have casual sex may have a very difficult time finding partners. Unlike gay men, we are not experienced at cruising and picking up women. There are no areas where we can go knowing that other women with the same intent will be there. Adding casual sex as a possibility to our community's sexual repertoire will require that many of us withhold the judgments we are so accustomed to making.

Group sex has evolved because many women in our community are looking for ways to relate sexually other than traditional monogamy. Some women love the excitement and intensity of sensation experienced in group sex. Others find it too anonymous, scary, overwhelming, or insecurity-producing.

Group sex can add to your sexual repertoire. It can provide sexual stimulation to stale sex play between you and a long-term partner. It can provide relatively anonymous partners. Sometimes the very taboo of group sex makes it more exciting.

Having sex with men is very controversial for most lesbians. Due to the heterosexist definition of a lesbian as a women who has genital contact with another woman, if we have genital contact with a man we question whether we're really a lesbian. And the entire lesbian community questions it too. Heterosexuals feel sure the wayward sister is coming back to the fold, and the lesbian community is no longer a safe place for her either. Please remember, when you judge, that lesbian identity goes much deeper than our genitals.

Some lesbians have sex with men occasionally or anonymously for variety. Others have fairly regular sexual encounters with a particular man. For some lesbians sex with men is a wonderful adjunct to their on-going sexual relating to women.

When We Do It

Since lesbian sex is not connected to reproduction, we don't have to worry about whether we can have sex while we're ovulating, but whether to have sex during menstruation may be an issue. Some women hate the sight, smell, touch, or taste of blood. Others are turned on by another woman's period or feel an increase in desire before or during their own period. If the amount of blood coming into the vagina is an issue for you, remind yourself that only five tablespoons of blood are sloughed off over the entire cycle. Often careful washing of the genital areas will take care of it. Experiment if you desire to.

There are, of course, thousands of other activities that lesbians engage in. Talk with your lesbian friends and acquaintances. Find out what they do. Get together with four friends and make a list of all of the ways to have sex with a woman that the five of you have ever heard of or tried. See how long that list can grow. Form a rap group that has the sole purpose of talking about sex. See if you can keep the topic on sex each time you meet. There will be a great tendency to talk about relationships and politics. Limit the conversation to the actual doing of sex. How many fingers do you like to have in your vagina? How do you stimulate your lover's clitoris? Ask each other specific questions like that. Imagine what it would be like to learn types of sexual behaviors that you had never even thought of before. Exchanging this kind of information can only enhance our community.

Fantasies

Erotic fantasies are mental pictures of sexual activity. Some of us have them; some of us don't. Some of us have very explicit, sexually direct fantasies. Others of us have romantic, fuzzy, run-through-the-field fantasies. Some of us have both. One of the most exciting things about fantasies is that they often are about forbidden behavior. It seems to be the very forbiddenness of what is imagined that makes it exciting.

> "Finally I understood that fantasies were exciitng because just like any sex, you aren't supposed to do it. It's exciting just because someone would tell you it's bad or impossible. That's why when I used to have sex only with men, I fantasized about women. Now that I have sex with women, I fantasize about men."

> "I just love having fantasies about something I'm not supposed to."

The taboo upon the behavior fantasized can make it very thrilling to imagine. Many of us fantasize situations we would never enact in real life—like having sex in a store window, for example. Fantasies are only ideas; having fantasies is not the same as actually living out those ideas.

Fantasies range from imagining what you would say to the woman you danced with last night, to playing like you're being made love to while you masturbate, to creating an image in your mind of what will happen when your lover comes home. For most of us, certain fantasies are not acceptable. What those are may vary from person to person, but generally they're fantasies that involve coercion, force, men, pain or perhaps another woman besides your lover. Feeling negative about our fantasies often keeps us from talking about them—so we don't realize that many lesbians share the same fantasies we find so awful.

> "Once I thought that having fantasies was bad no matter what they were about. That's when I had fantasies about having sex at the ocean in front of a whole beach full of people. When I started sharing my fantasies with others, I found out my fantasies are tame."

Guilt about fantasies can take up a lot of energy. Accepting ourselves and our fantasies can free us up to more fully fulfill ourselves sexually. Many women need to fantasize to achieve orgasm. If this is the case for you, then you have great company. There is a certain amount of excitement that all of us need to have an orgasmic response. This excitement can be created physically, emotionally, spiritually or intellectually. The mind is a great tool for creating sexual excitement and pleasure and fantasy is one way the mind expresses adventure. Instead of rejecting fantasy because you feel it's wrong, try embracing it as a gift that enhances your sex life.

> "Fantasies about sex with more than one woman at a time are the way I get off. I was able to accept it once I saw that Sumi used a vibrator to get off—my thoughts are no different than her toy."

Some of us fantasize about other women or men while having sex with our partner. This may be upsetting or guilt-producing, but it doesn't have to be. Whether or not you tell your partner is up to you. If you feel it is a barrier in your relationship and indicative of other difficulties, then you need to communicate. If it only makes sex with her more exciting and the fantasy remaining secret is central to that, then perhaps not. Whichever way you go, remember that you are entitled to a secret fantasy life. You need not feel bad and guilty about having one.

> "My fantasy life is about bondage and discipline. Someone tying me up and then telling me what they

were going to do to me sexually. Donna doesn't know and I'm not gonna tell her. Keeping it from her, keeps it hot."

Some of us get scared and defensive when we hear fantasies from our partners that are very different from our own. *Using the exercises in the homework chapter on accepting our partners PL-1, 3, 4 may help with this.*

"When Enid told me about her fantasies of sex with strangers, I was real scared. I thought she wanted to have sex with someone else. I used to judge her and tell her she was sick because of it. We slowly started playing like we didn't know each other once in a while. Now I think it's fun."

Incorporating the scary fantasies into our sex lives can enhance partner sex and defuse the threatening quality of the fantasies. Some of us have expectations that a good sex life precludes fantasies, i.e., if sex were really good, you or your lover wouldn't want or need fantasies. There is no evidence whatsoever that having fantasies says anything about the quality or richness of your present sex life.

"I always thought when I got a good sex life with a partner I wouldn't fantasize anymore. Now I have good sex and I fantasize more than before."

"My fantasies and I are friends. That feels so good after years of seeing them as invaders in my mind."

There has been a psychoanalytic trend towards asserting that fantasies are, in fact, repressed desires that should be acted on. Sometimes this assertion has been used against lesbians who admit their fantasies about men.

"When I told my psychiatrist my fantasies about sex with men, he told me I must want to be heterosexual. I thought he was right for years. Now I know that those are just thoughts and exciting because they will never happen.

Fantasies provide us with the control in sexual situations that we often never had in real life.

> "Sometimes I think I have fantasies of sex with groups in public because I never want to do that in real life. This way I can 'experience' something different and control the whole situation."

We can start our fantasies, stop them, change them, be assertive in them, voluntarily comply in them, etc. Fantasies can be a way of coming to terms with and changing (through visualization) our past experiences.

> "I don't know why my fantasies seem to always turn to thoughts of being overpowered by men. I'm an incest survivor and it seems so awful to get turned on by acts that made my childhood so horrible."

> "It seems to me it will take my whole life to work through being an incest survivor. Some people feel that fantasies are a way of keeping the experience fresh. I feel the experience will never leave, so why not use it to my advantage?"

Using your ability to fantasize to heal yourself can be very liberating.

Some of us may feel that our fantasies are obsessive and not within our control.

> "I'm sick of the 'everything is groovy' syndrome. I hate my fantasies and I feel I can't stop them. No matter what I try I can't have an orgasm or even satisfying sex in any way unless I fantasize about activity that I won't even share with you. It doesn't matter how turned on I am, how much I care about my lover, how good I feel about myself. The thoughts come in just like a drug addiction. I want to stop, but I'm afraid that means stopping having sex altogether."

If you find yourself in this situation, I suggest you work diligently to change the focus of the fantasy to one acceptable to you. Spend a small amount of time each day working with the fantasy. Go slowly and stop when you are frustrated. This process will take time and you will need to be patient with yourself. Start first with changing the face of the person in the fantasy, or, if there is no face, bring an acceptable one into focus. Change the setting, or your position, or the sex of the person—whatever will make the fantasy okay for you. You may feel that you need to replace the fantasy entirely. If so, continue in the same way by replacing each element until you have constructed a new one. As you work with your fantasies, you will find that you are in control of them; they are not in control of you. *You may find some help with doing SL-2 and SL-4 in the homework chapter.*

Sometimes others judge us or we judge ourselves by the types of fantasies we have, thinking that there's a straight line from being primarily submissive in fantasy, for example, to our daily lives. Reality is much more complex than that. Submission is usually seen in the context of sado-masochism, and thus in many circles it's seen as repugnant. In fact, being submissive—surrendering to our partner—can often be the best gift we can give ourselves. There is nothing wrong with giving in to the care and attention of another being. In fact we already do that when we let someone else drive, figure out the bills, choose the movie, or pay for our supper. What is wrong with giving a gift of ourselves to a partner? This does not mean that we want to become a wimpy woman that wants to be dominated by men. It only means that once in a while we give up— let someone else take over. What a relief.

> "I love it when Christina takes over. She lays me down on the bed, takes off my clothes and loves my body. I make decisions all day at work; it feels so good to have someone else make the decisions in bed. In fact, that is what my fantasy life is about — someone else taking over."

The various functions that fantasy serves and its relation to our everyday lives is not understood. And for lesbians, it hasn't even been explored. We need books about our fantasies, and accounts, and visual representations of them. We need to share our fantasies with other lesbians. Start the process by sharing yours.

Let's begin an oral tradition of lesbian fantasy life. The more we exchange stories the sooner we will establish that tradition. The more we tell each other about these fantasies, the more they will stop having such an impact on us. We will more be able to accept ourselves and other women once we get used to hearing and reading about fantasies. It helps us get familiar with one another on a whole different level.

Make a list of how you think sex could be more exciting. If you want to, share it with a friend or a sex partner. See if she is willing to make a list and share it with you. If you are sex partners, try some of the ideas out. Put all the ideas into a hat and see which one you pull out first. This helps diffuse problems like, whose fantasy are we going to do first, and why don't we ever do the ones I come up with? If you want to try acting on the fantasies by yourself, write the list up and then go through them one by one until you have exhausted yourself. Try this again in six months. This can be an exciting way to share your fantasy life.

III. Making Our
Sex Lives Ours:

Common Core Sexual Issues

Tyranny Of Orgasm

Masters and Johnson's research reduced the mythological orgasm to a series of short-lived muscle spasms. But the commonly held attitude toward orgasm is that it's an experience we should do anything to have. No one wants a muscle spasm in her leg, but everyone wants one between her legs. Many women believe that a sexual experience doesn't *count* as fulfilling to both parties unless both women have orgasms. This event often marks the end of sex, and lets each partner know that the other is satisfied. If one is masturbating, an orgasm is presumed to be required—why else have a sexual experience with yourself?

There are many women in this and other cultures who never experience orgasm. According to Kinsey (1953) 29% of women have never had orgasm and only 50% of women have orgasm with any regularity. Women who do not have orgasm when they want to often feel inadequate as lovers and are viewed as "frigid," "nonfeeling," or "uptight." Partners of women who do not have orgasm often label *themselves* inadequate lovers, believing themselves to be insensitive or their lovers to be unresponsive.

Orgasm is highly overrated. Even those of us who usually have orgasms find ourselves tyrannized by this supposed goal of sex. When we constantly work towards having an orgasm, we are unable to experience each sexual encounter for the pleasure it can give us. Our preoccupation with this particular muscle spasm echoes our general approach in a consumer-oriented society: striving for a goal, while disregarding the pleasure (or lack thereof) that we experience in the process. For women who never reach that goal, there often may be little reason to have sex. Many of the lesbians I have worked with reflect this attitude.

"I never felt that I was good enough to be anybody's lover. I have never had an orgasm in my life."

"Erica is very patient, we always think maybe this time I'll come. Now that's all I think about during sex—will I come this time."

"Every lover I ever had left me because I could never reach orgasm with them. I guess I'm just not that open."

Partners of women who never experience orgasm can be just as self-deprecating:

"Sometimes I would cry because I couldn't give Judy an orgasm. It wasn't fair that I had all the fun."

"Mika and I just gave up sex, because I couldn't stand making love to someone who wasn't responding."

"I felt guilty because Wanda never came. I could have orgasm anytime; for her it was an occasion."

Women who are occasionally orgasmic feel guilty about having been orgasmic with another partner or by masturbating. Their partners often become angry, attributing their lack of orgasm to a lack of love.

"Isabella had orgasms with other partners, but not with me. That really hurt my feelings and I began to believe she didn't love me."

"I don't know why I have orgasms sometimes and not other times. It certainly didn't seem that I didn't love Margie when I didn't have orgasms with her, but then I began to question myself."

"I began to really resent Lisa's vibrator. That mechnical toy brought her more pleasure than I did."

We identify orgasm with openness and vulnerability, not realizing that orgasm is only one way to be intimate. However, it is not the only way, the best way, or even a measure of how open and vulnerable we are. Not experiencing orgasm does not make you cold, frigid, or unresponsive. It simply means that you do not experience orgasm, nothing more, nothing less. Thinking we have to have orgasm to experience intimacy and closeness is the problem.

> "I have lots of love and attention from Sue, but what good does that do if she doesn't respond to my lovemaking?"

> "No matter how exciting our sex life was, it wasn't good enough if I didn't have an orgasm."

Our socialization defines all of sex except intercourse as "foreplay." Lesbians replace the word "intercourse" with "orgasm." "Responding" means having an orgasm. The stroking, touching, and excitement prior to, or after, orgasm becomes insignificant, only a vehicle to that magical muscle spasm. If asked to recall sex later, many women cannot even remember the experiences that preceded orgasm.

Women who are sexual partners and have disparate orgasmic patterns often feel a great deal of pressure and blame themselves or their partners for the differences.

> "I take too long to have an orgasm. Sara comes so quickly, I feel embarrassed."

> "I have orgasms too quickly. In fact it's hard to even know if I had one."

> "Angela takes so long to have an orgasm that I just get tired."

Instead of being excited by our differences, we try to make all our experiences the same. My suggestion is to view these differences as wonderful. Who wants to have sex with someone who has responses just like yours? If we can take the pressure off one another, it is suprising how enjoyable our sex lives can become. We are both involved in exchanging sexual energy; we are simply having different

73

reactions. *You may want to explore exercises SL-2 and SL-4 and PL-1, PL-3 and PL-4 in the homework chapter.*

Orgasms: Never the Same

Women have very different ways of experiencing and describing orgasm:

> "It's rhythmic and soft in my genitals."

> "Orgasm is intense and affects my whole body."

> "At some point I feel carried along, as if by a wave. The feelings take over and I go with them."

> "All of a sudden the tension dissolves and I'm totally relaxed.""

Many women who come into treatment to learn to have orgasms only to find that they already have them, but did not now *that* feeling was orgasm.

> "An orgasm to me is a rippling effect that is sometimes intense, sometimes soft, sometimes I don't even feel it."

> "I only have an orgasm with a vibrator. The touch of a hand just isn't enough intensity for me."

There are many of us who do not tell the truth about our orgasms because we are afraid of the ramifications for ourselves or for our partners. In doing so, we continue to hurt both ourselves and our relationships. Often we are more willing to lie than to accept what is true about our responses.

> "I haven't told Theresa that I never had an orgasm while we made love. Now that I've had one, I can't tell her I've lied all this time."

> "I could have orgasms if any of my partners were able to keep going, but I'm sure it's too long for them, so I just say I won't be able to."

"I feel guilty about having orgasms easily when it's so hard for Mickey, so I just say I'm not interested in sex."

We must start telling ourselves, our friends, and our partners the truth about our bodies: how they respond and how we feel about it. If we don't, we will continue to spread the same mythology that has oppressed us for centuries. Telling the truth only becomes easy after we begin and keep practicing. When you first think about it, it will probably seem easier to start next Thursday. But it won't be any easier next Thursday. Start today and see what happens. Start with a small truth whose consequences you feel you'll be able to accept. Graduate up to the secrets you have been most unwilling to reveal. The truth will set you free!

Who Owns Our Orgasms?

Feeling that you need to have orgasms *for* someone else is not uncommon. We often feel obligated not to disappoint our partners so we try real hard to have orgasms or to have the kind of orgasms we think they want. The hidden assumption is that having the right kind of response will make her feel more loved. The other side of this coin is feeling that our partners owe us orgasms, expecting them to "give" us an orgasm. Either way we are relinquishing the claim to our own bodies.

Trying to have an orgasm for someone else, or trying to "give" one to a partner can leave us feeling frustrated, angry at ourselves or our partners, and incomplete. But there are alternatives to feeling obligated to give or experience orgasm. *Exercises O-8 or OP-1 can be helpful.*

Orgasm is not the end or even the goal of sex; pleasure is. If striving for orgasm gives you pleasure, then do it. But if it gets in the way of your experiencing pleasure during sex, then perhaps you should reconsider having orgasms as a goal. Sex can be both fulfilling and pleasurable without orgasm. You can relax and let yourself be flooded by sensations, no longer striving for a goal. Without the tension and pressure of working towards an end, you may enjoy the pleasures of the sexual experience in a way you never have before. Let that happen for you. End the tyranny of orgasm in your bed.

75

Orgasmic Problems
And Concerns

If you haven't read the preceding chapter, "Tyranny of Orgasm," please read it before going on. Changing your orgasmic response is possible; but it is not guaranteed. Systematically working on changing your behavior always helps but it doesn't necessarily bring the exact changes we hope for. Whether you have orgasms the way you want them or not, remember that more pleasure and enjoyment is what you're after. There have been great advances in the field of sex therapy that have helped many women learn to have orgasms. There have been claims in the sex field however, that are being discovered to be unjustified. It is not necessarily easy to change an orgasmic response, though it is a possibility. The body is usually able to follow through with the nerve and muscle reactions. However, women are more than cellular structures, and the emotional and spiritual aspects of our lives direct much of our action. This, combined with many other issues in your life, may cloud the possibility of orgasm for you. Working on this area of your life is enhanced by different exercises specifically mentioned below, and by the whole section on orgasmic response in the homework chapter. The idea is to systematically work on this; just as in bodybuilding, we have to work up to new behavior. Read the homework section first and then decide if you are willing to participate. Work on these exercises when you really are ready, not when your partner or your friends think you should.

You may have stopped focusing on orgasm as the be-all and end-all of sexual pleasure and yet still want to be able to experience orgasm more consistently. If so, this chapter is for you. Before starting any exercises, think carefully about whether you want to tell anyone you're doing them. If we tell our friends we're doing exercises to help us get where we want to go, then we often feel pressure to get there. We may have exchanged the tyranny of orgasm for the tyranny of exercises. If those friends are also sexual partners, they may be very invested in how we're doing. And we may want to prove to them how well we're progressing toward making our sex life work.

> "I realized once I got into sex therapy that I was frantic to make the exercises work. 'Work' meant having orgasms. I kept losing sight of the fact that the process was supposed to make me feel good about myself and my body, not make Toni want to stay with me."

> "My mistake was telling Barbara what went on each time I finished an exercise. I found that I would start to exaggerate just a tiny bit because I knew she wanted me to have orgasms. After a while, I realized I was sometimes out and out lying because I wanted so much to please her. The process that was supposed to help me became an enemy."

Don't let your focus shift from learning about your body and its responses to achieving an end result. If you are doing exercises to improve yourself for your partner, you may end up with a great deal of resentment, which won't help your quest for sexual pleasure at all.

Myths About Orgasm

As I discussed in the preceding chapter, there are many common myths about orgasm. Some of them are: not having an orgasm means you're avoiding intimacy; not having orgasm means you don't love the partner you're with; being in love or wanting intimacy will assure you of orgasm.

These are all myths and it is time for them to be laid to rest. Having orgasm means you were sexually stimulated in a way that led to orgasm for you. That's all.

I've Never Had An Orgasm

If you've never experienced the orgasmic portion of the sexual response cycle, you may feel that your body can't respond orgasmically. Current research indicates that every woman's body is capable of orgasm, although your ability to respond orgasmically at any particular time may be affected by disability, illness, pain, or the use of prescription drugs, street drugs or alcohol. But take heart; you do have a body that can have orgasms.

Maybe your body needs to be stimulated in specific ways you haven't tried yet. Stimulation that is constant at a certain level and lasts up to an hour may be necessary.

> "When my therapist told me I might need to have my clitoris stimulated for an hour or more to have an orgasm, I thought she must be nuts. Then she reminded me about all the things I am willing to do that take an hour—watch T.V., shop, talk on the phone—why wasn't I willing to have my body touched for that long?"

The easiest way to learn to have orgasms is through masturbation. The best book about orgasms and learning to have them is Lonnie Barbach's *For Yourself: Fulfillment of Female Sexuality.* Though written for heterosexual women, lesbians can certainly benefit from reading it. The book has an excellent chapter on masturbation. *Exercises S-1 through S-6 in the homework chapter will be helpful.* A vibrator, a sexual toy you can get in an erotica store, can be useful. The intensity and constancy of a vibrator is wonderful. Don't worry about falling in love with it, getting insensitive to the touch of a person, or not being able to have orgasms any other way. A vibrator is simply a tool to enable you to have more sexual pleasure.

Masturbation with conscious awareness is different than touching yourself in a way that you think ought to make you come. Conscious masturbation is a way to learn about your sexual feelings. It is not intended to be another way to prove to yourself that you are not sexual. Slowly stimulating your genitals, breasts, or other parts of your body allows you to notice that you do have feelings that go through your body. You are indeed a sexual woman. Even if you do not have a response that can be described as orgasmic, it does not mean that you are not a sexual being.

> "Before I made it a part of my ongoing sex life, I thought masturbation was only for times when I was

so desperate to have an orgasm I would try anything—even that. Most of the time that didn't even get me what I thought I wanted. Finally I have just decided that touching myself with great care and love is what I want. It makes me feel like a real woman."

Once you learn what feels good in masturbation, you can integrate it into your sexual life. Masturbate with the intent to explore, not to achieve a goal. Many women find that we have an "edge" we get to, that marks the beginning of the end of sexual feelings. Frustration mounts as we never get beyond this edge. *In the homework chapter, exercise O-5, specifically deals with this "edge."* Eventually, you can discover how much pressure and intensity, done how long and where, creates enough stimulation for you. Enough stimulation of the right kind will saturate your muscles with nerve response until that tension is released in a muscle spasm called orgasm. The feeling generated from experiencing orgasm can vary from a very mild release to intense sudden relaxation. Experiment with yourself. The more time you spend with you, the more you have to offer yourself and partners.

"I never thought not having orgasms could be helped by masturbating. I just thought I wasn't sexual, why try that. I masturbate now and spend time with the frustration of not coming. Sometimes, it feels so good after a while that I forget about orgasm."

"My masturbating seemed like an enemy to Myra until she found that I was able to learn more about myself. Not only that, but it made me feel more like having sex with her, just to know that I have feeling in my body."

I Have Orgasms With Myself, But Not With A Partner

If you have orgasms with yourself but not with a partner, you may simply need to teach your partner to stimulate you in the same way you touch yourself. Sometimes it helps to place your partner's hand on top of yours or vice versa. Then you can show her exactly the type and amount of pressure you use on your clitoris or in your vagina or anus.

> "It was really uncomfortable showing Arneta exactly what I did to my own body to have orgasms. But I discovered that it brought us great relief. Now she knows what to do."

If you use a vibrator during masturbation, you may want to introduce it into partner sex. If your partner doesn't like that, you may need to educate her on the joys of the machine. Such education may include reassurance that it is she you desire not the vibrator. The vibrator is just a toy to increase pleasure.

> "Meg hated the vibrator in bed. That made me nervous because it's the only way I can have orgasms. We had to make a choice. No vibrator, no orgasm that we could count on. Now we alternate: sometimes the vibrator is in bed with us and sometimes it isn't."

> "I just couldn't see bringing a piece of machinery into bed with a lover. So Rachel and I have been practicing other forms of lovemaking. It's great being inventive. We've made it a motto to try anything one of us thinks of at least once to see if we like it. So we rubbed whipping cream all over our bodies and licked it off. We sat in the hot tub with our fingers in each other's vaginas in silence to feel the wonder of it. We have also touched each other's clits at the movies to see if we could get away with it. I don't have orgasms most of the time, but we have fun."

If you don't want to use the vibrator during partner sex, then you can experiment to see if there are other forms of stimulation that will bring you to orgasm. Try different positions. Sometimes squatting or bringing your knees up to your chest helps. This increases the pressure on the nerves in your genitals and increases stimulation. Try having your lover touch your clitoris with an elbow or a leg. The vigorousness of this action may be all you need to have orgasm. Stop and start the action. With the help of your partner bring yourself to an intense feeling level and then stop and start all over again. Do this 1,000 times if you need to. See if alternating stimulation will help. Light touching, fast friction, hard deep touch, then back again to light touching again, alternating one after the other. Experiment for the fun of it; even if you don't find a sure way to have orgasm, you'll have a more enjoyable sex life.

I Have Orgasms Irregularly
Or With Less Frequency Than I Want

If you experience orgasm infrequently, or less often than you'd like, or with less intensity than you'd like, you are in good company. About 80% of women would like to have orgasm more consistently or with more intensity than we do now. Each of us has an idea of what an orgasm should feel like, how long it's supposed to last, how intense it should be. We can either spend our time having sex or spend it seeking this "ideal" orgasm. Either option has its own consequences.

If you let go of having the kind of orgasm you've envisioned, your sex life may become much more relaxed and/or you may never find the particular form of stimulation that brings you to orgasm most consistently. If you choose to pursue your "ideal" orgasm, you may experience a lot of different forms of stimulation that are fun. You may also put yourself under tension and pressure and become goal-oriented rather than being in the "here and now." Either way, if you assume you can't have good sex unless you have orgasm or your "ideal" orgasm, you are working against yourself.

> "To imagine that orgasm does not have to be part of my sex life came as a radical idea. I must admit that once I started to relax, I was able to enjoy what stimulation I received."

Admittedly, being on the edge of orgasm and not having one is a frustrating experience. But feeling that you have to have an orgasm, or a certain kind of orgasm, to have had a fulfilling sexual experience also creates a continual feeling of "not enough". Imagine what your sex life would be like if you decided orgasm wasn't necessary to your feeling good about a sexual encounter. Then when you did have an orgasm, it would come as a wonderful surprise. *Try the exercises on orgasm in the homework chapter, as well as SL-2 and SL-4.*

There may be other reasons you don't have orgasms consistently. When you don't have them: Are you thinking of something else? Are you putting a bit of pressure on yourself to have a "good" sexual experience? Do you feel that if you don't have orgasms, your partner will think you don't love her? Are you angry at your partner?

When you do have orgasms: Are you relaxed? Do you feel your life is going well? Are you willing to accept whatever happens in this particular sexual encounter? Are you not thinking about orgasm at all? Often we get what we want when we stop striving for it. Orgasm is no different.

Partner Differences In Orgasmic Response

You and your partner may have differences in the way your bodies respond to sexual touch. In fact, I'd be surprised if you didn't. All of us are different; those differences can be seen as most exciting, as areas to be explored. But it isn't unusual for us to view our differences as problems instead. Then we have to solve them. And one of us gets to be wrong. This frequently happens in differences in orgasmic response. How about allowing your own and your partner's orgasmic response to be whole and wonderful, no matter what it is?

Imagine that you are from Mars and that you have just met an Earthling and she has a very different way of responding to sex than you do. Ask her to teach you about the response she is having. See if you can suspend your own thoughts about what is right and observe hers as the way of this planet. There is no magic answer that says there is only one real way to have sex. *Try exercises SL-4 and PL-4 in the homework chapter. Also, doing exercises C-3, C-4 and C-5 can help you learn to communicate about differences. They can also help you feel comfortable with sexual activity that is now making you uncomfortable.*

When you are in an actual sexual setting, acknowledge out loud to one another that you have different orgasmic patterns. Say out loud that you are willing to honor your own pattern and that of your partner. Say out loud that you will not judge the other or yourself during this sexual encounter. Saying affirming words out loud before having sex often throws that judgmental part of us off guard.

"When I tried this exercise, it was almost as if someone was saying: 'Hey wait a minute, I thought I could control their sex lives. My judgments have worked in the past, why are they stopping me before they even begin sex?' Angela and I feel so close when we are willing to start sex by saying something that seems so foolish."

"Pam and I always started having sex by silently believing that she wasn't going to have an orgasm and that was going to be a drag. We started changing our beliefs about orgasm with the help of an idea a friend gave us. Before having sex, I say something like: 'Sex with you, Pam, is going to be fun.' She says: 'Juanita, let's have fun with our bodies and have love and respect, not dread.' When we did this out loud, it gave each of us a new framework."

If you or your partner is unwilling to try the suggestions here or others you may come up with, you will need to explore that. Why are you resisting something that might help? Why are you unwilling to try something new that might change the pain in your sex life? Why do you worry more about feeling foolish than about easing the pain? Ask yourself honestly if you or your partner is willing to change—for real. Change is a difficult process. Whether we are changing our expectations or our behavior, the process is difficult. Without willingness, there may be no way to enhance your sexual life.
See if you are willing to love your own and your partner(s)' sexual response regardless of what it is—even if it is different from the response of every other woman you have ever met.

"My whole life I have been trying to be someone different to earn someone else's love. To imagine that I can be loved even if I don't have orgasms seems unreal."

Notice how you have berated your own sexual response in the past. Notice how you have hated your sex life because of your sexual response. Remember how often you have faked or minimized your orgasmic response in order to avoid upsetting your partner.

"I have always had orgasms easily. When I have been with women who do not have orgasms I hide mine. Sometimes I think I was hiding fear that I must have been more involved with them than I thought they were with me. I thought orgasms were love. Sometimes I just didn't want them to feel upset that they didn't come. I ended up hating that I *had* orgasms. Partners would end up hating that they *didn't*. It was crazy."

Imagine starting from the belief that our differences in orgasmic response are beautiful, that we are each learning to be who are.

For Every Woman With Issues About Orgasm

If you are trying to change the experience of orgasm in your life, you will need a great deal of patience with yourself. If your partner (s) is involved, she too will have to be patient. The claims of sex therapy are being shown to have been exaggerated. In this culture, we have treated our sex lives like commodities. If you don't like the one you have, get another. And if you can't get another, feel bad about yourself.

"When my parents were disappointed about my being a lesbian, I told them they couldn't dictate how I was going to be. One day when I was really down on myself for the way I didn't have orgasm, I suddenly thought of my parents. I guess I can't always have life the way I think would make me worthwhile."

"My sex life is not like being able to order a Toyota with a blue roof and four-wheel drive. My sex life is me, and I am different all the time."

How we are sexually is part and parcel of who we are as individuals. We cannot separate our sexual response out from the rest of our being and demand that it change. All we can do is love and accept ourselves for who we are and be willing to explore change if that is what we want. *There is a whole section in the homework chapter on working with orgasmic response (exercises O-1 to O-7 and OP-1 to OP-7). Please look at it and explore the exercises that apply to you.*

Desire Issues

Sex is a physical exchange of energy between two people. Sometimes a lesbian will feel little desire for sex, although that seems almost antithetical to the culture's definition of us as always sexual. Yet in my experience as a sex therapist, I have seen hundreds of lesbians who are experiencing little or no sexual desire, or considerably less than their partners. Lack of sexual desire is the most common sexual problem lesbians come to me with. If you are experiencing lack of sexual desire, you are not unusual.

Many lesbians go their whole lives not having sex; some go for long periods of time. Not desiring sex does not make you not "normal"; it simply means you don't have a desire for sex. Not wanting sex doesn't have to be perceived negatively. You are not cold, frigid, uptight or invulnerable just because you are not wanting sex.

Just as heterosexual culture has defined sex as intercourse, lesbians have tended to define sex as finger-vagina, or tongue-clitoris, interaction, which only counts if there is an orgasm. These are no more "real" sex than intercourse is "real" sex. The physical exchange of energy involved in hugging, kissing, caressing, holding hands, or putting our arms around each other can be very sexual. Sexual desire may be expressed through sensuality. If you have limited your definition of sexual desire to the overpowering need to have genital contact, you may have shortchanged yourself.

Listening To Your Own Desire

Take some time to consider what sexual desire is for you and what you think it ought to be. That difference may be the problem.

Make a list of what you think the culture defines sexual desire to be; beside it list what sexual desire is for you. Is it having a strong feeling or pull in your genitals? Is it imagining yourself being stimulated by a vibrator, finger or someone else's tongue? Is it being "turned on"? Is it being "turned on" to a specific person? What does being "turned on" mean to you? How do you recognize when you're "turned on"?

Sometimes our list of what we think the culture defines as desire is very specific, then if we don't have those specific feelings we decide we don't have desire and feel bad about ourselves. Examples of the culture's definition often include: always acting on being sexual if you have the chance, wanting sex every day, getting excited seeing our partner naked. Don't let others determine what sexual desire is for you. Ask yourself questions until you feel clear about your definition.

> "Once I figured out that sexual desire to me meant being able to snuggle into bed with my lover and have her body touch my body all over. I was so relieved to know that I do have sexual desire."

> "I began to understand that sexual desire was getting excited about having genital contact with another woman about two times a year. That was enough and good for me. I am a sexual person after all."

It may be that you don't have a desire for sex. It may be very hard to know that when your friends, the community, the culture around us is putting such a strong emphasis on sexual expression.

Spend a quiet thirty minutes alone with yourself. In that quiet allow an answer to come—do you want to have sex now? Allow yourself to accept whatever answer comes to you. See what it is like to accept yourself with that answer. If you answered "no" see what it would be like to know that that is the truth for you and to feel nothing wrong about it. *Do exercises SL-2 to SL-4. See if these help your concern about yourself.*

> "Once I accepted that I had no desire for sex, I was greatly relieved. The constant questioning could stop."

"Not wanting to have sex does not mean I am not a warm, loving person. I love to hug, snuggle and be close. I just have no desire to have genital contact."

It can be especially difficult to try and figure out whether you want to have sex if you have a lover who *is* wanting sex.

"Pat is sure that I don't want to have sex with her because I don't love her or because she is fat. Actually I love her size, and loving her has nothing to do with it. I'm not sure why I don't want to have sex, and trying to figure out why is making me crazy."

"All my friends who love sex have lots of reasons to explain why I don't want to have sex. I don't want to have sex and I don't think there are any complicated reasons behind that."

If you are in this situation, it is especially important that you take quiet time alone with yourself to come to know what you want. Once you are clear about what you want, then you can go from there.

Stress

Stress can be a major factor in lack of desire and one we often overlook. Any big changes in your life (changing jobs, moving, having children, the death of someone close, loss of an important relationship, becoming a step-parent, moving in with a lover) affect your feelings and your relationships with others. Feelings of anxiety, sadness and depression can inhibit sexual expression.

"When my mother died, I was surprised that my sex life was so affected. I wasn't in the least bit interested. I felt that a part of me had died, and I did not want to expose something that was alive. When I was over the most intense mourning, my sex drive returned."

"I changed jobs recently. I was preoccupied with doing well. Marissa didn't seem to understand that I had no interest in sex. She kept thinking I was falling out of love with her. When things settled down again, I found I was hungry for her."

If stress is affecting sexual desire and its expression for you, it is important to communicate that to any partners you might have. You need to let others know what is happening to you and how that is affecting you sexually. If you think the stress is inhibiting your activity longer than is warranted, seek some counseling. Stress often has effects on us that we don't expect. *Homework exercises C-1 through C-5 may help.*

There are many women who are in the position of having stress in a relationship which is not going to go away. This may be race, class, age, disability, culture, children, religion, etc. This longterm stress is something that often gets denied after a period of time. Many of us wish to ignore our pain; plus, who wants to go into the same issues for the hundreth time? However, this is exactly what needs to happen if you are going to be able to create a viable relationship. You may be willing to set up an ongoing night each week or once a month to work on the longterm stresses. Making it a specific night and time will give you a forum for your concerns; when the difficulty comes up on a day to day basis, you know there will be some time during the month that you can deal with your concerns in depth. *You may try the exercises C-1 though C-5. Choose one of the exercises each time you get together and see if one is more effective than another. If that's the case, do that exercise with regularity. Also include exercises SL-2, SL-4 and PL-1 through PL-4.*

The truth is that this stress is in the relationship. When we are talking about the types of stress that come from race, class and cultural oppression, these differences are not going away. Patience with yourself and your partner is the goal.

I Want To Change This Lack Of Desire

Perhaps you realize that you are not feeling desire and you want to. You may feel that your definition of desire is so far removed from your experience of it that it is as if you live in Michigan and your feelings are vacationing in Alabama. You may feel you wouldn't recognize sexual desire if it came up and introduced itself to you. You probably also feel overwhelmed and hopeless, thinking that if you don't have desire, you won't ever have it and that there's nothing you can do about it. Well, I am here to tell you that's not true. You need not feel powerless around your lack of desire. Desire can be rekindled and cultivated by intent and practice. Many of us consider it heresy to work at increasing our desire. We want desire to appear magically, to appear naturally of its own accord—a welcome or unwelcome stranger knocking at the door. Of course, this view takes no responsibility for our creation of our feelings. They came to us from the outside, unbidden and uncontrolled, or as in this case, they don't come at all. If we wanted to build arm muscles, we wouldn't wait until the romantic urge hit us. We'd go out and buy weights, make up a schedule, and exercise regularly, building up slowly. Desire is similar; we can build it up. Start with the tiniest and most fleeting desire you experience. Notice it, embellish it, encourage it. Add your fantasies to it. Practice being in touch with your sexual feelings all the time. *Try exercises D-1 through D-7 in the homework chapter.*

"One of the greatest things I have found in working through my lack of desire for sex has been actually going through the paces of sex even if I don't want to. Doing real exercises as if I were trying to change an aspect of myself. These exercises helped me to believe that something really could be done about my lack of desire."

You may feel inadequate as a lover. If that's the case, it's not surprising that you don't feel desire. If you're not good at sewing, when was the last time you had an urge to make a blouse? Sex is no different. Work with your image of yourself as a lover.

Take some alone quiet time. Get comfortable, close your eyes, imagine yourself in a setting that's beautiful to you. See yourself as a very sexual woman who is in great demand as a lover. See yourself being able to have whatever you need. If you have trouble doing this look at the negative pictures you have of yourself. They may be blocking desire. *Try exercises S-1, S-2, and S-4, and G-1, G-2, G-3, G-5, G-6 to help you see yourself as a sexual being.*

You may have had experiences in the past that block your access to your sexual feelings—rape, incest, traumatic homophobic experiences, Catholic school. You may wish to get counseling to help you uncover those experiences. Sometimes working through psychological issues may trigger a period of not having desire. That is not unusual. Be compassionate and patient with yourself if that is the case. Sometimes only time can heal.

> "My partners have not understood that I cannot imagine having sex after dealing with the issues I have about incest. I have chosen to be celibate and that suits me fine."

Periods of lack of desire can also be triggered by menopause, introspection, pregnancy, illness, recovering from alcohol or drug abuse. It is important to know that those periods will not last forever and to remember to love yourself through them.

> "I have been ill for a year. I know that my illness is chronic, and that I will go through long periods of not wanting to have sex. I'm trying to learn patience and to still love myself, but sometimes the despair comes through so sharply."

Couples And Desire Concerns

For those of you in couples, there may be another set of reasons you're not feeling desire. Sometimes lack of desire is indicative of moving to a deeper level of intimacy in relationship. As we become emotionally more bonded, we feel unable to be close sexually too.

> "Sarita and I were having great sex for the year before we moved in together. Since we got an apartment to share, our sex life has been non-existent. She's sure it's cause I'm a Jewish mother and bug her; I'm sure it's because she's so Catholic she can't stand the thought of really acting like a married lesbian."

Once we have made a commitment to become more intimate with another woman, we often stop having sex. There often isn't any fixed reason why our sex lives stop for a while, and our cultural heritages are not to blame. The vulnerability that we can tolerate may have been reached for a time. If that is the case for you, you can be pleased with your growth into intimacy knowing that as you become more comfortable with greater vulnerability, your desire may return. *Once again, try C-1 through C-5 in the homework chapter to help you with this process.*

Often sexual desire is blocked by unrecognized and unexpressed feelings toward your partner. Ask yourself questions to draw out your negative feelings. Are there feelings that you are unwilling to share with her or anyone? Do you feel betrayed by her? Are you angry at her for any reasons? Are you attracted to someone else? Do you feel your attraction to someone else means that you cannot be sexual with your lover? Have you lost respect for her for any reason? Are you jealous of her? Do you feel that she does not find the way you make love satisfactory? Have you begun to dislike different parts of her? Do you feel you can't reconcile who she is with what you want from a partner?

Discussing your feelings with your partner is the first step in dealing with your lack of desire. Sometimes the mere fact of communicating, expressing your feelings and being open, can unblock your access to your desire. *This is a good place for C-1 through C-5, PL-2 through PL-4 in the homework chapter.*

> "I found that I stopped discussing much of anything with Margaret. We began to loose track of why we were even involved with each other. Once we started talking again, I began to see why I was attracted to her in the first place."

You may have concerns about the actual physical activity of sex. What are the limitations you set on sex? Must you meet specific conditions to allow yourself to be sexual? Are you unwilling to compromise on time, setting and activity that you engage in? Do you feel uncomfortable with certain practices that you and your partner engage in? Does oral sex make you upset? Do you feel that if you do not engage in certain activities that you are not a good lesbian? Any of these may lead to anxiety around sex and lack of desire.

> "Once I decided that I really didn't like oral sex, I let Roberta know. I felt at first all lesbians have to have oral sex. I began to accept the way I like to have sex, not the way others thought I should. I worked at setting up time to have sex, and then I slowly saw my

desire for sex return. I made sex something that was fun for me again."

Changing long-term patterns isn't easy. The worst part is that we believe that we cannot do it. Often we believe that, "Oh well, I just don't have desire. I guess that's it for the sex in our relationship, at least we're good companions." This does not have to be the case. In fact, we *can* change the patterns; what we often lack is a willingness to do just that. The work is tedious, slow and often brings little reward along the way. Be willing to set aside time each week. Don't ever give up the time; make this a priority. Make your goal reachable. For instance, decide that you will have sex once a week consistently in a year. "A year?" Well, changing the patterns of one human being takes a long time. Changing the patterns of two that are in a relationship together takes even longer. *Try the exercises D-1 though D-4; DP-1, DP-2, and DP-4, PL-1 though PL-4.*

You and your partner may both have desire, but it may be of different intensity or one of you may feel desire much more often than the other. This is not unusual. Rarely do we find two people who are perfectly matched in the degree and intensity of their desire at all times. As common as this problem is, it is still very painful. Most of us interpret less desire on our partner's part as her loving us less. It is essential to avoid this pitfall or to remind yourself to get up out of this abyss every time you fall into it.

It is very important to look at your differences in an atmosphere of acceptance rather than rejection. Almost every couple will find differences in desire at some point in their relationship. Communicating about those differences is the key. That will help you understand what they are about. Make a list of the ways you are willing to compromise. If you want sex less, are you willing to do it anyway once a month? If you want sex more are you willing to have it even if your partner is only doing it to please you?

Here are some questions for each of you. If you are the woman who wants more sex than your partner, investigate:

1. Do you belive sex is love and believe your partner does not love you if she does not want sex? Have you asked her?

2. Do you refuse to masturbate, believing it to be inferior to partnered sex?

3. Are you willing to masturbate with your partner holding you so that the two of you are participating but she does not have to engage directly in the activity?

4. Have you thought that your sexual needs are a cover-up for not being willing to have intimacy another way?

5. Would you be willing to have your partner make love to you without your making love to her?

6. Have you withheld other forms of affection or intimacy (either physical or verbal) because your partner does not have sex with you?

7. Do you threaten having sex with others to try to increase her desire to have sex with you?

8. Do you refuse to admit that there are times when you really do not want to have sex because she will think she is off the hook?

If you are the woman who does not want to have sex as much as your partner, investigate:

1. Do you believe that you will never want to have sex as often as your partner so there is no reason to try?

2. Have you stopped allowing any physical affection (hugging, kissing) for fear that it will lead to your partner wanting to have sex?

3. Have you withheld your own ways of showing intimacy in retaliation for her insistence that intimacy start with sex?

4. Are you unwilling to make love to her under any circumstances? If you are willing sometimes, have you not told her for fear she will ask for more?

5. Are you assuming your partner is just like someone in your past?

6. Do you believe you will be out of control and have no power around sex?

7. Have you been willing to think of new ways to have sex that would be fun for you and would also satisfy her needs?

8. Do you not admit times when you would like to have sex because you don't want to change your stance?

The answers may not match the picture you have of yourself. They may also not match the picture your partner has of you. Accepting the answers about yourself is the first step. *Working on exercises SL-1 through SL-4 may help with this.* Decide what you are willing to tell your partner. If you aren't willing to tell her anything, that's all right. The important point is that the truth in these matters may indeed be affecting your sexual desire.

You must decide whether dealing with these issues is important to you. Telling your partner may or may not be part of what you consider to be healing. It may be that you are willing to live without desire rather than take the chances that telling the truth or changing yourself requires.

If your partner tells you the truth about some of these questions and it is shocking to you, allow yourself to go through your feelings. Let yourself be hurt, angry, sad. It may be enough to allow the reaction to the information pass through you. If that is not enough for you, you may need to let your partner know what is difficult for you. *Work on exercises PL-1 through PL-4 before you tell her.* See if you are able to incorporate the new information into the image you held of your lover. See if you are willing to accept her for who she is. There may be answers that you just "knew" she felt and she would never tell you before. Instead of saying "I told you so," acknowledge that telling you before now was too difficult. Until we are able to accept one another for who each of us is, there is no way to improve our sexual lives. Make sure you read the chapters on couples to learn more about why we don't accept each other.

Sometimes other differences—class, race, age, physical difference—get expressed as sexual differences. Because those differences are so painful to admit and talk about, we transfer them to sex. Sex is concrete and easy to point to. Those other differences are complex and very hard to tackle. *If you think you've transferred other differences to the area of sexuality, try exercises C-3 to C-5 in the homework chapter. They can help clarify these differences for you.*

When there are differences between us we usually start out denying them and building up resentment. Once we are resentful, we exaggerate the differences until they seem insurmountable. One way to get through this exaggeration is for each of you to privately, without conversation, write down on a piece of paper how often you would ideally like to have sex and how often you think your partner would ideally like to have sex. Then compare them; you might be surprised.

> "I always thought Lonnie wanted to have sex every day—twice if possible. I found out she would like sex twice a week. My ideal would be once a week. The difference doesn't seem so big."

"When I found out Nan really did want to have sex sometimes, I was relieved. I think I pushed for sex because I thought well, if I try every day, maybe she'll give in once in a while. But I really don't want sex every day."

You may also want to look at your belief system around frequency of sex. Often we become entrenched in our belief system without asking whether it's working for us.

"If I didn't push for sex, I thought we'd never have it."

"When I thought about being sexual, I got scared that if I wanted it, and Kit wanted it, we'd be having sex constantly."

If this is something that goes on in your relationship, you get to learn that sex is like any other relational problem. Lesbians in relationship often try to push their partners to be just like them. You can learn more about the dynamics of couples in the chapter on couples. That chapter may shed light on why relationship problems occur and how to work on them.

What happens in sex is not magic; it can be understood, worked on and changed. We do not have to feel powerless around sex as if it were the one area of our lives we can't work on. No longer do you have to say, "Well, I'm just not as sexual as Jane; that's why we broke up." Instead you can work with your sexual dynamic and affect it. Sex can be in your life the way you want it.

We Like Different Things— Now What?

Lesbians have had very few places in which to discuss our sexual practices. Why should we know what lesbians do in bed? The sum of anyone's knowledge is probably what we've done ourselves and some information gleaned from our friends. Since we tend to choose friends like ourselves, our knowledge can be quite limited. Until extremely recently, there were no books to go to, no descriptions of the 969 positions and practices lesbians have been known to use. Our own practices probably originated basically with what our first lover did. And so it has gone.

Usually we assume that our sexual practices are universal and are shocked to hear that another lesbian hasn't even tried them. Many women today assume that lesbian sex is oral sex, yet Judy Grahn reports (in *Another Mother Tongue*) that as late as the 1950's "only the brave engaged in cunnilingus."

When a couple starts being sexual they usually establish patterns rather quickly. Each silently tries moves and different behavior they've tried in other relationships or fantasized about. Usually there is very little talking, very little verbal finding out what the other woman likes and what she is willing to do. Gradually our sex life gets established; some activity becomes very common; some happens occasionally and usually there is a whole group of activities we each know about but never act on.

In this process our likes and dislikes get communicated through our bodies. It is not common for lesbians who are newly sexual to talk out loud about what turns us on. Unfortunately we do not always interpret each other's body signals correctly. Often months or even years later we are surprised to learn that a certain signal (the body stiffening, a finger stopping) taken to mean, "I don't like that" was not intended to mean that at all.

> "Until Estelle and I started talking, I thought she did not want me to put my fingers in her vagina. I always thought she became still when I started that because she hated it. She told me she was trying to concentrate on the feeling and was not even aware she stopped moving."

Changing your sexual patterns once they've gotten established isn't all that easy. First you have to communicate about what you do now and what you might like to do. A finger slowly creeping towards a vagina is not the same as saying "Would you like me to put my finger in your vagina?"

During any discussion of changing your sexual patterns either of you may react with: I'm so glad we're talking about this; this surprises me; I thought something else was wrong; this is frightening me; you are off the wall; I can't deal with this; this totally turns me on; or just silence. Any of these reactions can be the basis for further discussion, further opening up, and eventual closeness.

It's not unusual to find that differences you thought existed between you, don't.

> "When my partner was making love to me, I tried to get in a position to make sure she touched my clitoris with her tongue. I didn't know that for years she thought my moving at that time meant I did not like oral sex."

If this happens to you, great! The two of you can begin introducing activity that each of you had been longing to do but afraid to suggest.

However, you may find that there are real differences between you. When that happens the tendency is to judge someone—either the other person or yourself. One of you ends up depraved and the other uptight. At that point, you need to remind yourselves that you are both on the same team. Neither of you wants to force the other into doing something she doesn't want to. And both of you want to please the other and give her pleasure.

"I finally believed that Gerry wanting to do something new in bed just meant that she wanted our sex life to more interesting, not that she thought I was a jerk. That's when I realized that our sex had become pretty routine and that even I thought something different might be fun."

"What I began to do was look at our differences as a challenge that kept our 28 year relationship alive. It changed my whole perception. I began to come up with ways that I wanted sex that I had not thought of before. It became an effort both of us were working on, not just something June thought we should do."

If you can't get to the idea that you're both on the same team, try exercises C-1, C-3, C-4, C-5 in the homework chapter. Once you get defensive, each of you will decide you have to win this "battle." Try letting go of the battle one time while making love. See what it's like. Imagine letting yourself see your partner's side. Imagine that you won't have to worry about the next ten years, just today. Eventually you may be able to let go of the battle half the time. You may feel that you are giving up too much, but there may be even more to be gained.

Being as specific as possible about the changes you'd like to see is helpful. Then it doesn't seem so overwhelming and frightening.

"Once I was specific with Sue, she saw that I didn't want to have anal sex with a dildo everyday. I just wanted her to put her finger in my anus occasionally when both of us were really excited."

If there is specific activity that you want to do to your partner and she doesn't want you to, you will have to wait for her to feel comfortable. If your partner isn't willing to try, you cannot go ahead with what you want. This may feel frustrating and unfair, but it is the reality. It is her body.

> "Sometimes I want to make love to Angela in ways that she doesn't want me to. It's frustrating because it's not that I want her to do something to me, it's that I want to do it to her. It's her body after all, but I do get upset."

If it's your partner who introduces the ideas of change, your tendency might be to move to a position of refusal. This is especially true if it is something she would like to do to you. Try to avoid automatically refusing by making your own list of sexual activities that you'd like to try. See if any of your activities correspond. Are you interested in any of your partner's suggestions? Are there any that she really wants to try that you would be willing to try even if you don't think you want to?

> "I thought our sex life was great. When Jane said there were some new things she would like to try, I just kept thinking about Jane's last lover and imagined that I was inadequate by comparison. Once I really looked at the situation, I began to see that there were things I would like to do too that we had never tried."

If you feel very resistant, investigate the reasons why. If there's fear behind your resistance, set up boundaries and rules to make the situation safe. Then see if you'd be willing to try something that seemed too scary and wild before. You may be fearful of not having control in the situation, of losing control or of being out of control. Sometimes we are as afraid of losing control and experiencing ecstacy as we are of not losing control and being bored.

> "When my lover suggested we use a dildo when we had sex, I was really upset. I didn't want to have sex with something that reminded me of men. When she made it clear that she just wanted to penetrate my vagina gently with something other than her hand, something that would fill up my whole vagina, I felt easier about it. I made it clear that I would not try a dildo that looked like a penis. I decided I would be willing to have her use something like a zucchini or another item. We found a soft plastic vibrator at a women's vibrator store that didn't look like a penis.

It was something that filled up my vagina, and both of us like using it."

Suggesting ways to alter the activity your lover wants may give you back the control you need. If you're the one introducing change, it's important to be flexible. Allow yourself to let go of how a certain behavior should take place.

"I think I was so afraid of letting Mary know that I would like to pretend I was a man when we made love, that I made my ideas very strong. I insisted that we had to do this, or I would think of leaving the relationship. She, of course, hated the idea when I presented it this way. When we both settled down, she suggested that she would like it if I simply let out my very butch dyke side instead. That appealed to me, and in fact it was a great compromise."

Both of you can clear the air by talking about your sexual prejudices. It's not helpful to pretend we don't have them; all of us do. Try to avoid judging each other's prejudices; work for creating as open and accepting an atmosphere as you can.

"Marit was always so negative about certain sex practices. When we really got down to discussing the exact reasons why, I got a better understanding. We don't agree but I now know her view is serious, not just something she says to be different from me."

"I know that butch and femme is supposed to be a thing only women of another era were into. Well, I see myself as butch. Christa used to think of that as a betrayal of feminism. I don't care what it is, I'm a butch. I think she's a femme. We've worked hard at allowing my identity to be part of our lives. What has helped the most, really, is Christa copping to and working on her homophobia. Believing that women can dress and act any way they please is, after all, feminist belief, right? Well, I dress in what the culture calls 'male' clothes and that's my right, as a woman.

103

It's not something Christa thinks is gross anymore. In
fact, sometimes I really think it turns her on.''

We tend to ignore that sometimes differences spark a friction
that is positive in making our sex lives work. Differences are often
what we crave, but we want to pick and choose the differences. If
you are willing to assume that each of you wants to make your sex
life work, try approaching difference as positive. Work on making
your differences known, obvious, and something you can actively
work on.

Choose a specific area of difference to discuss in depth. Investigate whether there are any compromises that will make the activity acceptable to both of you. If not, let the subject rest. Come
back to it in a month or two. You both may have changed.

It may happen that your partner wants to engage in an activity
that you find unacceptable. If that is the case, you must stand up
for yourself. Even if the whole world considers it lesbian sex, if you
aren't comfortable with it, you needn't participate in it.

"I know all my crowd thinks it's normal to want
to have oral sex. Well, I think it's gross and I won't
do it.''

Your partner then will get to choose how important that particular activity is to her. Is she willing to insist that it be a part of
your sexual repertoire? Would she leave the relationship over it?
Are you willing to lose the relationship over it? How important is
your position to you?

You may get through an impasse like this by discussing the sym-
bolic meaning of the activity. Sex tends to get weighted down with
meaning and once we know the meaning an act has for the other
we may be able to come to a compromise. Using a dildo, for example, may seem to say that a woman without a penis is inadequate.
To the other partner, however, it may just feel good in her vagina.

Let me throw in a little plug here for plurality and diversity.
For too long the lesbian community has tried to consolidate its practices in the face of heterosexual disapproval. It is time we extend
the tolerance to each other we hope to get from the rest of the world.

Sexual Addiction

Women rarely think of "sexual addiction" as a term that could refer to their lives. It seems unthinkable that lesbians, who have so many barriers to sexuality, could be sexually compulsive. Yet I see sexually compulsive lesbians quite frequently in my practice as a lesbian sex therapist.

I describe a sexual addict as someone who engages in sexual behavior that threatens her own self-described goals. A lesbian who wants to keep her long-term relationship, her job, her professional status, her life of emotional sobriety, yet who goes ahead and has sexual relations that put those in jeopardy, is a sexual addict.

If you are not sure whether your behavior fits this description, answer the questions on the Self-Checklist for Alcohol or Drug Abuse in Appendix C. Substitute "sex" for the word "drinking." For example: Are your sexual relationships negatively affecting your reputation? Have you ever felt remorse after having sex? Do you crave sex at particular times? Do you have sex to escape from your worries or troubles? Do you have sex to build up your self-confidence?

I am not talking about single women who like to have a lot of sex, single women who have many partners, women who are in mutually agreed-upon non-monogamous couples, or women who work as prostitutes. I am talking about women who use sex in a compulsive way similar to the way others use drugs or alcohol to create a "high," excitement and danger. Sex outside your relationship, with your boss' wife, with a student, with a client, with someone who's in a relationship with someone else—all these threaten your self-respect, your work, your friendships and your own relationship, and your status in the community. Yet all may provide a "high," a thrilling and exciting sexual encounter.

> "Many times in my life I have felt out of control around sex. If someone is attracted to me, I find it very hard, almost impossible, to say no. The opportunity to be sexual just seems too good to pass up even if it gets me in lots of trouble."

Part of the high may come from the excitement of conquest, of pursuing a partner the community would regard as inappropriate and "winning" her. Sometmes sex becomes a challenge, that when fulfilled keeps self-image and ego intact. Some of us only feel attractive and lovable when we're courting, being courted, or bedding someone. *If this feels familiar, try exercises SL-1 through SL-5 in the homework chapter.*

> "When I'm after someone or she's after me, I feel great. It's a feeling I try to have all the time. I don't think about the complications, just the excitement of knowing there's someone out there who wants me. It hardly even matters who the woman is, as long as I like her and am attracted to her."

Other sexual addicts use sex to shield ourselves from experiencing pain, loneliness, self-hatred or sadness. Sex becomes a distraction from dealing with what's inside. Sexual liasions, getting in and out of relationships, and secret affairs move the focus away from us and our feelings to the outside. Sexual compulsiveness may also be motivated by fears of abandonment, fear of rejection and low self-esteem. Having sex becomes a way of feeling wanted, desirable and worthwhile.

> "I find it very exciting that women fall in love with me all the time. I can't remember a time in my life when I wasn't flirting with someone. That constant exchange of sexual energy is what keeps me feeling alive. I don't think I could do without it."

I see three common patterns of sexual compulsiveness among lesbians. The first pattern occurs among single lesbians who say they want an on-going relationship but are never able to stay with one woman long enough to create one. After the excitement of conquest is over, they are unable to stay around for long-term bonding. New relationships are constantly needed. Sometimes these relationships are with taboo partners—straight women, those much younger or older, or those with much more or less power. Once the other's resistance melts and true intimacy becomes possible, the other loses her charm.

"I've been in four relationships this last year and each one felt like "it" to me. I was in love; the woman was wonderful; I was happy. But after a few weeks the magic went away. I don't know what happened; I just felt deflated and unfeeling. But it wasn't too long before I found someone new."

"Everytime I get involved with someone I feel like I've met the finest woman in the world. I love her totally, buy her presents, bring her flowers, feel like I'm committed for life. But it's never more than a few months before I feel the same way about someone else. I'd really like to settle down but it doesn't seem to happen that way."

In the second pattern, the sexual addict falls in love, creates a "relationship" which may last from three months to two years, then falls out of love and in love with someone else. Falling in and out of love is seen as something over which we have no control. It happens to us, and the strength and passion of our feelings justifies breaking up and starting over. In these situations we do not take responsibility for creating and maintaining relationships. Instead we let "love" with its chance comings and goings determine our sexual lives. Since this form of sexual compulsiveness is disguised in the name of "love," it is rarely recognized as sexual addiction by the lesbian community.

"Sometimes I look around and worry about me and my friends. I've been out ten years and I've had four major relationships. All my friends do the same thing. Each time I'm in love and committed. We live together and are very intense. But after a while it doesn't seem to work and I get attracted to someone else. So I break up and move on, thinking the next one will be better. But it always happens again. At this rate I'll have had twenty primary relationships before I'm old."

"I never really thought my last relationship was forever. But when I met Myrna she was everything I thought a relationship would give me. Within a week, I'd left home. None of my friends will talk to me anymore."

"I met this woman at a conference last month. She was the perfect butch. Even though I hate New York and had to give up a job I loved, she was just too good for me to pass up; so I'm moving in two weeks."

The third pattern occurs in long-term relationships and includes both a sexual addict and a co-addict. The addict begins having affairs while she insists that she wants to maintain her primary relationship. Sometimes she keeps the affairs secret letting the sexuality of the encounters be heightened by their clandestineness. Or she may talk of and act on her "need" for other sexual relationships in an open manner invoking non-monogamy.

"Doreen was too backward sexually. She wouldn't even let me put my fingers in her vagina, but I loved her and didn't want to leave. So I had secret affairs. She would have left me if she'd found out, but I stayed committed to her, so I don't know what the big deal is about."

"Jean made such a fuss when I decided to be non-monogamous. She could never get her jealousy and possessiveness under control. I wasn't in love with any of the women so I don't see why she was so threatened. I just needed my freedom."

Usually this "need" gets expressed in terms of the inadequacy of her present lover. The partner becomes the reason the addict "has" to go out and have sex with another. The partner may not be sexual enough; she may be too rigid sexually; she may not evoke desire any longer; she may not be sexual in the right way. In any case, the partner is seen as the one with the "problem" who causes the addict to have to go out and have sex with another. Of course, this is an excuse on the addict's part for her own behvior. She is blaming her partner for what she is doing and she is not taking responsibility for her own behavior.

> "I know I made Lucy feel terrible. I was intent on having sex with other women, and I didn't want to leave Lucy. I also wanted to make sure I didn't look like the jerk. I was great at making sure everyone we knew was aware of the fact that Lucy didn't have orgasms. Somehow this gave me license to have sex with anyone else. Looking back on it, my friends probably thought I was nuts, but no one ever told me."

If, in fact, there is sexual incompatibility between you and your partner, you can masturbate; you can leave that partner and find someone more compatible; or you can become single again and have sex with more than one partner. If you truly want to stay in the relationship and don't know how, you can both go to therapy and work on creating a satisfactory sexual life between the two of you. Sexual addiction is claiming to stay in a primary relationship, while acting in ways that are destructive to that goal.

The sexual co-addict spends most of her time trying to make herself better to keep the addict. Along with the addict, she blames herself and takes responsibility for the addict's behavior. She feels guilty that the addict is having sex with other women.

> "Kerry was always falling in love with some new woman in town. I felt that I failed her because I never wanted to have sex. So she would go have sex with these new women. I thought it was all my fault and if I just got my sex drive back she would stay home. I got into therapy and the therapist asked me why I would want to have sex with someone who was having sex with every other woman in town. I had never thought that maybe her behavior had something to do with mine."

The co-addict spends all her time trying to get the addict's sexual behavior under "control," trying to "understand," or trying to change the behavior. She may regard the addict as a spoiled child and indulge her behavior while holding a lot of resentment. Often the sex life of the co-addict gets lost in the shuffle as she focuses on the sexuality of the addict. Sometimes in counseling I ask the co-addict what kind of sex life she wants and she doesn't even know.

> "I spent so much time last year obsessing on what Nancy was doing, when, and with whom, that I lost touch with who I was and what I wanted. My wanting sex totally revolved around pleasing her and keeping her; it ended up having nothing to do with me."

She may try to manage their sexual life so the addict doesn't "have" to go outside the relationship (usually with more sex, being sexier, or kinkier sex). Or she may endure with long-suffering nobility her partner's transgressions. Usually such long-suffering degenerates into complaining and punishment. She may stay in the relationship but persecute and abuse the addict about her sexually irresponsible behavior.

> "Mary was certainly hurt by my activity, but she paid me back by saying things to humiliate me in front of our friends. Even to my family. She would call around in the middle of the night looking for me. I know in some way I drove her to it, but she also stayed in the relationship."

> "I don't know why I stayed with Joan through those four affairs in one year. Partly, I guess, because the past had been so good, partly because we'd just bought a house together. A lot of it was that I couldn't believe this was happening to me. So I acted like it wasn't. Now I'm so mad at her I want to kill her. I don't know if we'll ever be friends."

Sometimes sexual compulsiveness shows up when a relationship is under a lot of stress from other places. Instead of, or in addition to, turning to drugs and alcohol, one of the partners turns to sex outside the relationship for relief. Sex provides a soothing, relaxing retreat (just like beer or marijuana) from the stressful situation. Of course, in the long run this behavior simply adds more stress.

> "When we moved to the East Coast together, I started getting turned on to other women and wanting to have sex with them. Our relationship didn't really have much chance after that; it simply caused too much grief added on to the stress of being in a new place."

It is not uncomomon for partners of mothers, once they've become part of the family, to suddenly find themselves creating outside sexual relationships.

> "It all started after I moved in with Martha and the kids. I felt like a fifth wheel, like the real interaction in the house centered on her kids and her relationships with them. Up until then I'd seen her mostly alone, at my apartment. I wanted that feeling again—of being first in someone's life."

If you find yourself in this position, read the chapter on sex and motherhood paying special attention to the sections on jealousy, privacy, and alone time together.

For some women, sexual compulsiveness occurs sporadically throughout their lives. Most of the time they are sexually responsible to themselves and their partners. Then every so often, all hell breaks loose; after which, a long period of responsibility returns. This pattern of compulsiveness is similar to what alcohol counselors call "situational drinking." When a situation occurs in a woman's life that threatens or challenges her view of herself or her self-image, she may turn to extracurricular sex to make herself feel good. Relaxing in the feeling of being wanted or simply escaping into the intensity of desire gets her over the hump for a while—until the next time. Those next times may end up occuring years apart.

> "I'd been 'married' to Judy since college and I'd been feeling a little restless. So when Carol, an old college buddy, called up one night when Judy was out

of town—BINGO. I got in my truck, drove two hundred miles and had sex all night when I got there. That affair lasted two years and Judy never knew. It was five years before I stepped out on her again."

If you recognize any of the above behaviors as your own, you may be a sexual addict or co-addict. If you feel helpless about your compulsion, then you are in a good position to change. Whether you are the addict who is acting out or the co-addict who is victimized, the first step in changing is getting professional counseling help.

Reading the chapter on sex and sobriety can help both of you recognize addict/co-addict patterns. Attending AA and Al-Anon meetings can put you in touch with a program that works with addiction. In this case, your drug of choice is sex, but the process of addiction is the same.

There are those who say that sexual addiction isn't dangerous like drug and alcohol addictions. I disagree; I have seen sexual addiction wreck lesbian lives, causing untold misery for all involved. I urge you to look carefully at your own sexual behavior and see whether you use sex compulsively.

IV. To Learn And Unlearn:

Sexuality And Issues
In Our Lives

Coming Out And Sex

Coming out is a long process and many of us are engaged in it most of our lives. Recognizing our desire to be as fully with women as possible, acting on that desire, and acknowledging that truth to ourselves and others is the coming out process. Although we initiate that process at some definite point in our lives, we have to repeat it over and over again as we meet new people and are in new situations.

There is an old adage in the lesbian community that says, "Stay away from a woman who is coming out." The definition of "coming out" is different for all of us. However, in the wide sense it simply means knowing you are a lesbian and at some time acting on that sexually or emotionally. Since we all "came out" at some point, our reluctance to support each other during this difficult time is self-defeating. It may be painful to re-experience the confusions and turmoil of someone who is coming out, reminding us of all those issues in our own lives, but it is important for our community to support those of us who are trying to become a part of it.

> "When I came out 25 years ago, there was no place to easily find other lesbians in my town. When I finally did, it was next to impossible to get them to befriend me. I think the most important contribution I can make is to talk with women who think they want to come out. Yeah, sometimes they go back to men. The majority stay in the life though, and I feel I have helped just by being a listening ear and kind of a tour guide."

"Sometimes I try and remember what it was like coming out when I talk to a woman who is thinking about lesbianism. I think I get too smug and flip off easy answers like: just go this bar, you'll get used to it; or time will take care of everything. I now try to really give some helpful hints like where lesbians meet in my town. How to get in touch with a local lesbian rap group. Invite her to a party I'm having. It's amazing how much that does for another woman and it makes me feel good too."

Coming out is a two-fold process that will change your life forever but at the same time is simply taking another risk, similar to each one you've taken before.

"At 53 I thought I had done it all, been through every change I was going to do, taken every risk. Now I've discovered I'm a lesbian. I seem to be a freak. My generation certainly won't understand, and all the lesbians I meet are the same generation as my kids. Are there any lesbians my age? This is not like any risk I've ever taken."

"I'm 14 and know I'm a lesbian and I'm trying to come out. The problem is no one takes me seriously. Older lesbians don't want to have anything to do with me because they're afraid they'll be accused of seducing me. I'm afraid to tell girls my age. I just don't know where to go."

Coming to the point of accepting yourself as a lesbian and working toward letting others know about your sexuality is a unique process, one that is not necessarily like any other you have tried. You may want to find out if there are any coming out groups in your town. If there aren't you may want to start one yourself. It is helpful being with other women who are going through the same experiences you are. *You may also want to look at exercise SL-1 in the homework chapter.* Coming out doesn't mean that you're becoming a whole new person, simply that you're letting another part of yourself emerge.

Our changing relationships with close heterosexual friends can be one of the most difficult parts of this transition. Some friendships will continue (or even improve because of the honesty), with a lot of work on our part at helping our friends understand. Some friendships may degenerate to little more than acquaintances. Some may end entirely. Often, one of our straight women friends helped propel us into this process as the depth of feeling we had for her became apparent. If she cannot also accept our coming out, the emotional consequences can be devastating. We might lose a potential lover and our best friend in one blow. You may also lose your sexual feelings in the tension and anxiety that coming out creates.

> "I finally decided I must be in love with Jane, or else I just wouldn't be so jealous of her boyfriends. I think if I told her she would go crazy. When I thought this must mean I'm a lesbian I was afraid."

> "I came out to my best friend and it turned out that she was attracted to me too. The problem was that we just couldn't have sex once we acknowledged that we were attracted to each other. Neither one of us knew what to do about that."

No matter what happens when you come out, you may find that sex becomes an obsession. You may feel that you cannot have enough of it, or that you think of it night and day and yet can't perform when you get an opportunity. Once the newness of the lesbian world wears off, you will find that sex falls into balance in your life. *Try exercises S-5 and S-6, and SL-4 in the homework chapter. If you are very fearful of sex with a partner, try the exercises that fit your needs in sections G, GP, S, and P.* You can go as quickly or as slowly as you like. Just remember that you have all the time you need.

> "Once I came out, that was all I needed. I made love with any woman who was willing. I didn't know what I was doing. I just knew I loved it and wanted to try it as often as I could."

> "Coming out I thought would be the answer to my constantly thinking about and fantasizing about

any woman who came within six feet of me. Well, it just made my fantasy life richer; I didn't have sex with a woman until ten months after I decided I was a lesbian."

Imagining going through such a major transition without the love and support of our closest friends may make us want to hide our sexuality from them. If we do that, though, our friendships diminish as we are unable to nourish them with our most precious gift—ourselves.

"I sometimes can't stop crying because I feel like my world is falling apart. I know I'm lesbian, but my friends can't accept me. I don't really know any lesbians, so I feel very alone."

"Coming out as an Asian lesbian to me meant that I was either going to have to choose between my culture or my lesbianism. I have never fully gotten over that concern. My Asian friends just won't understand. While some homosexuality is tolerated when you're a teenager, an adult woman is supposed to find a husband."

"I'm used to hiding my feelings because I'm already a black woman in a white man's world. But wanting to be sexual with a women is a feeling I can't hide anymore. Who can I tell?"

We cannot control our friendships and what our friends will or will not accept. Just as each of us will, our friends will also have to go through the process of letting go of an old self, a process with stages of denial, fear, anger, despair and acceptance. Because we may still be in that process ourselves, we may have few emotional resources to offer them. The most important ally we have is time. If we can allow the healing effect of time, our friends may accept the changes they experience in us.

Exactly the same issues will have to be gone through with our families. And while we may find new friends, we can't create new families. Our families will always be there and we'll always be dealing with them whether they are "there" for us or not. Responses from families can range from genuine acceptance, to various levels of toleration (It's OK if you don't talk about it, don't bring your lover home, don't dress butch, pretend you're asexual, etc.), to outright rejection. It is that fear of rejection that keeps us from being open and creates deep chasms and shallow relationships—along with great pain.

> "Coming out to my family was the worst experience of my life. My father told me I wasn't welcome in the house ever again. My mother told me I was going against God and would be punished with eternal damnation. My brothers have tolerated knowing I'm gay but won't allow me to be alone with their children. It's all pretty outrageous. I hope it will get better. Other lesbians I know who've had severe reactions by their parents say things do soften over time. But how long? I just hope my parents don't die with this between us."

> "My brother finally told me that he knew I was a lesbian. It was such a relief. I had wanted to tell my family, but after losing my mother to cancer I just couldn't bear losing the rest of them. It has been rough at times, but mostly I know they love me even if they don't always understand."

More and more families are accepting our lesbianism and it is important to acknowledge that. Allowing our families time to adjust and accepting them as they go through their stages is crucial. Remember that they are having to change too, and they didn't initiate the process. Give them time to catch up to your knowledge that coming out is the best thing you've ever done for yourself.

> "It took five years, but finally my family has accepted my lesbianism. This wasn't easy. I had to spend a lot of time educating, even more time waiting for them to come around. I'm glad I spent the time."

"Being Jewish seemed to mean I belonged to a special club that all my family was a part of. The oppression Jews have met all through time created a bond that I thought could never break. Coming out to my family almost seemed to cause that 'break.' They were so disappointed that I wasn't going to be the daughter they had in mind. I told them being gay didn't necessarily mean I wasn't going to have kids. That made them even more upset. I decided to go easy for a while. I kept my mouth shut, but I didn't let them put me down. It's working out better now, it's just that I'm hoping I get to be part of the 'fold' again."

If you are already from an oppressed group, becoming part of another group that is reviled may be almost too much. Finding yourself losing the acceptance of the racial, ethnic or class group that you've always depended upon for support in a hostile culture is shocking. This is not by any means everyone's experience, but if it does happen your self-esteen and your self-image will probably be affected. Remember that there are others like you out there. Hold on until you find them.

"A Latina lesbian? I thought I invented the word. I spent what seemed like years in a sea of white women's faces at concerts and other lesbian activities. I wasn't thrilled. It was hard enough being Latina in a white culture, but at least I had my family. Not having my family totally behind me meant relying on lesbian friends for everything. It was hard when they didn't share my heritage. I almost decided to give up—too much work. Then I joined a political La Raza group and I found some lesbians there. What a difference that made in my life."

"Growing up Chinese in Hong Kong made me one of the crowd. We moved to the United States when I was 12. What a shock to find out what being in a minority felt like. Then to discover that I didn't like dating boys and that in fact I was attracted to my girlfriends. When I found a word that described that—lesbian—I thought I could never fight two sets of prejudices. Well, I have survived, but not without pain. Finding other Asian lesbians saved me."

"I grew up poor. I came out when I was 17 and from then on I felt a tremendouse burden. How was I going to make it in a world that gave me so few choices? I decided when I was 25 that it was too hard, so I married a man, had two kids and tried to make it that way. Well, after ten years I decided that was even harder. So I left him and took the kids and felt great relief. I think the only thing that gets me through sometimes is knowing how hard it was to try and be straight."

Losing the support of our racial, ethnic or religious community is a terrible blow. Added to that is the fact that other lesbians often share the dominant culture's prejudices and stereotypes about people different from us. Not only do we have issues with our communities of origin, but we also have to deal directly with other lesbians' stereotyped expectations about our sex lives.

"When I first got involved with Mae I was sure that because she was Black and I was white that she would always initiate when it came to sex. I was shocked to find that she had a low sex drive. But I guess what really shocked me was my racism."

Our categorizing each other and having sexual expectations based on stereotypes limits all of us. Such categorization keeps us from being able to discover and express our real sexual natures. The sooner we are willing to put aside our prejudices, accept the variety of sexual behaviors in all groups and come to one another without stereotyped expectations, the easier it will be for all of us to come out.

One common result of coming out is that we lose our sexual feelings, the very feelings that motivated us to label ourselves lesbian in the first place. Pressure from family and friends may be added to our own doubts, and surface as loss of sexual desire.

"Now that I am finally out as a lesbian I almost don't want to have sex with anyone. I used to fantasize

about it all the time and even had sex with a roommate in college. Now that I have this label, I'm afraid
that lesbian sex is really wrong."

"Telling my children, who are in their thirties,
that I was a lesbian put a real damper on my sex life.
They were furious and decided my suppressed lesbianism was the reason I hadn't been a perfect mother.
Anyway, my lover and I had terrible fights afterwards.
Jill felt my children had been awful to me; I defended them. We stopped having sex for a long time."

Paying atention to lack of sexual feeling and desire is important. Such feelings do not mean that you should abandon lesbianism;
they simply mean that your fear, doubt and homophobia are surfacing. *Try working on exercises H-1 though H-3 in the homework
chapter. In addition, if you shart to lose sexual feelings, work on
the desire section in the homework chapter. Finally, homework exercises S-5 and S-6 will also be important.* Your sexual needs and
feelings are all right. Just because you live in a culture that does not
openly support them, do not feel like you are the one at fault. Re-
read the chapter on homophobia and give yourself some strokes for
your courage in coming out in a homophobic society.

"My parents got their wish all right. I had been
afraid before I told them I was gay that I stopped having sex with anyone. Then, once I came out to them,
I was so filled with self-hatred that I quit having sex
for months. I almost felt that I had made a mistake and
maybe they were right, that I was just rebelling. My
sex drive did come back and I was still attracted to
women. Now I know I lost it because of what happened with my family."

"Telling people I work with that I wasn't willing
to listen to the 'queer' jokes anymore was the begin-
ing of my coming out to them. It was also the worst
time for sex in my life. Somehow being so vulnerable
to my co-workers made it impossible for me to be
close to Trish. Almost like I could only stand so much

openness. I'm so glad that period passed and now our sex life is back to normal.''

It is true that usually such periods of lack of sexual feelings and desire pass. How long it takes before sexual feelings and desire return varies from woman to woman. Give yourself support for being willing to come out at all. It is a very difficult process. *If you have a partner who is willing, you may want to do some of the exercises for couples in the C and P homework sections.*

Coming out is not a one shot deal. Although there is a primary acknowledgement to ourselves at some point that we are lesbians, we must continually acknowledge that fact to new people and in new situations. Every time we do that we increase our truth-telling capacity and affirm ourselves for who we are. Coming out strengthens our identity, self-acceptance and self-worth. I encourage each of you to engage as fully as possible in that process throughout your lives.

Am I Really A Lesbian?

At some time in life, whether during the coming out process or later, most lesbians question whether they're "real" lesbians. As opposed to heterosexual women who rarely question or even think about their sexual identification, lesbians are constantly encouraged by the culture, friends, family, and even our own children to ask ourselves if we're really lesbians.

> "The most surprising thing for me when I decided I must be a lesbian is how quickly my family and friends assured me I wasn't."

> "I came out and am so concerned about how it affects my job, my family ties, my children's friendships, that every year I question my lesbianism. Maybe I will change and everything can go back to 'normal.'"

Since this culture identifies a lesbian as one who has genital contact with women, often questions of identification come up when we're not being sexual with someone else or are being sexual with men. Being actively sexual with a woman is obviously not all that it means to be a lesbian. Being a lesbian includes identifying with women as a group, finding that your primary emotional attachment is with women, preferring to be around women as people, and perhaps being a part of a woman-identified culture. You may not be having genital contact with another woman and still be a lesbian. Only you know how you feel. If inside yourself, you feel you're a lesbian, then you are. Don't let anyone take that identification away from you or make that decision for you.

> "I came out in graduate school long before I was sexual with a woman. I just knew lesbianism was the life for me and all I needed was a woman to fall in love with."

Even women who have firmly identified as lesbians may find themselves questioning their lesbianism if they go through a period of not having sex. You may wonder if your celibacy means that you aren't really affectionally tied to women.

> "Being celibate for eight years made me really wonder if I was a lesbian. I think that was only because all I ever heard about was lesbians dating, moving in together, etc. Everyone is just assumed to be having sex. I knew that I wasn't heterosexual; I mean, I didn't want to have sex with men, and I couldn't relate to the majority culture. I have always been allied with lesbians. I finally gave up and decided I didn't have to be having sex with another woman to be a lesbian."

It is more than where you put you fingers that makes you a lesbian. Being a lesbian includes sex between women, but there is so much more.

It's hard to be part of an oppressed group; being a lesbian automatically qualifies you as part of one. You receive no rewards from the culture, no special discounts. Being a lesbian has to be its own reward, in and of itself. Giving up that identification, however, because of cultural pressure requires denying a part of yourself and that takes its own toll. *If you are feeling a need to do that, please do the excercises SL-1 through SL-4 in the homework chapter.*

Identifying as a lesbian would be much easier if there were role models for us to follow. Although many of the strong creative women we read about in the paper are lesbians, this fact is well hidden. You can't tell your mother you want to be like Eleanor Roosevelt when everyone's denying Eleanor Roosevelt was a lesbian. Estimates are that at least ten percent of the female population is lesbian. That's a lot of women. If only all of us were able to come out, it would be so much easier on the rest of us.

> "When I found out my second grade teacher was a lesbian I couldn't believe it. Even though I'm an adult

now, that made quite an impact. Somehow being able to say to my mother that she was a lesbian made my identification more legitimate. Just think if all us little second graders had known at the time! Maybe some of us would have been able to make that choice for ourselves as a positive one."

Joining a coming out support group may not be the answer if you're really questioning your identity. Coming out groups are designed to help you get through the process of coming out. They are not designed to help you decide whether you want to come out. Our community really needs "wavering groups" so that those who are questioning have a safe place to deal with those issues. The "wavering groups" could also be available for women who have been lesbians for a long time and are questioning that choice.

"There have been many times in my life I have questioned my lesbianism. I always decide that being with women is the way for me, but deciding would have been much easier if I'd had other women like me to talk to. It's too scary to talk to most lesbians about. It seems a betrayal to them, so I've always had to deal with my questions alone."

Sometimes wavering takes the form of "I'm in love with a woman, but I'm not a lesbian." Other lesbians usually take a very dim view of this response. Some feel that such a woman is taking advantage of the lesbian culture we've all created, often, at some expense to ourselves. If you use that phrase, it could be because you're afraid to come out or it could be that you're primarily oriented towards men and have fallen in love with a particular woman. Only you know the answer to that question and it may take more than one relationship for you to be clear on it.

Wavering can really affect your sex life. You may feel sex with a woman is revolting during this time. Or it may make you ambivalent about having sex with another woman. You may be willing to go ahead and have sex, and then torture yourself with questions about whether you have exploited yourself or your partner. You may lose your desire even though intellectually you think it's okay to go ahead and have sex. You may not respond in the ways you're accustomed to once you do have sex. These reponses can be temporary or last a long time. You are the only one who knows fully how you feel about your sex life. Make sure that you tell the truth to yourself and act from a position of caring about yourself and others. You may feel considerable pressure from all sides to make a choice. Take your time, you have all your life. *Doing exercises R-1, R-2, R-5 and R-6 along with SL-2, and SL-4 in the homework chapter may be helpful.*

> "I know that I still want to have sex with a woman, I just don't know if that really makes me a lesbian in the true sense of the word."

> "I'm terrified of having sex with women while I'm still trying to figure out if I'm a lesbian or not. Sometimes I'm afraid I'll get carried away and not make a clear decision. Then other times, I am worried I'll sleep with someone and she'll fall in love with me and I'll just not be there for her."

Being unable to clearly identify as either heterosexual or lesbian is a very painful place to be in. Standing against both the majority culture and the lesbian sub-culture is truly difficult, let alone unpopular. If your lover proudly identifies as a lesbian, the difference may cause a painful feeling of separateness between you. Acknowledging the differences and sharing the love you have for each other can help you develop a mutual respect that may override the differences. *Try exercises R-7, R-8 and PL-1, PL-3 and PL-4.*

> "Trying to let go of men after being a lesbian for ten years does not seem to be a commonly discussed problem in the lesbian community. Well it's a problem for me and I have a woman lover. I really love her, and we are growing so far apart on this issue. She can't understand."

One of your reactions to the situation may be to insist that you don't want to be labelled.

> "I just don't see the point of calling myself a lesbian. I'm a woman. Actually I'm a person, not just a silly label."

However true that desire may be, it is largely irrelevant in our culture. All of us are labelled; if we don't take on the label of "lesbian," we're assumed to be heterosexual. *Read the chapter on homophobia and try exercises H -1, H-2 and H-3.*

We may also try to deal with our alienation from both cultures by trying to "fix" it. You may try to "act" the part of a lesbian with your friends, a great temptation if you have a lesbian partner who is clear about being a lesbian. Then when you are in the heterosexual world, you may "act" as if you're totally heterosexual. You may want to "fix" your life, to make it fit the expectations of those around you. Unfortunately that doesn't work. Being in your situation, acknowledging it, and going through the pain is the only way to be true to yourself.

> "While I went through the terrible process of deciding whether I was lesbian, I put myself through lots of trouble. I'm from a pretty traditional Jewish family and they loved it that I was questioning my sexual identity. They had all sorts of men lined up for me to meet. I even went out on some dates while I still lived with my woman lover. Then I would come back home and be a dyke. I lost touch with who I was in this whole scene."

You need not be dependent on other's approval; you have the right to the freedom to explore yourself and your needs.

Sometimes, those of us who have seen ourselves as lesbians become sexually involved with men. Almost always this throws our identification into question. Again, the exclusively sexual definition of lesbianism creates problems. Many women who clearly identify as heterosexual have occasional affairs with women without questioning their sexual identity. But both the lesbian and straight communities seem to agree that when a woman has a sexual affair with a man, she is indeed heterosexual.

> "Just because I have occasional casual sex with men seems to make all my friends question whether I'm a lesbian or not. I don't worry about it, and I resent that they do. I feel that all of us should have sexual freedom. Lesbians too."

"I had an affair with a man even though I had been a lesbian for a number of years. This really made me believe I couldn't be gay. It was hard because I didn't want to give up the lesbian culture. After the affair, I had no more problems knowing whether I was lesbian. I'm sure now I was gay all along."

Often we change identities when there are other big changes in our lives, when we're under a lot of stress, or when an identity that includes oppression no longer seems worth continuing. If that happens to you, remember that although other lesbians may judge you harshly, they don't know under what circumstances they might change their identities. Each of us is different and various needs assume varying significance in our lives.

"Going through a child custody fight with my ex-husband made it impossible for me to hang out with my lesbian friends. None of them really understood. Once the case was finished I had cold feet about going back. Now I'm afraid none of them really trust me."

You may feel that being a lesbian no longer works for you. Since most lesbians feel that discovering their lesbianism was a gift, it will probably be very hard for them to hear you. But you must live the life you want. Living a lie is no answer, since sooner or later you will have to face yourself. Whatever position you are in, go out and find the support you need to fulfill yourself.

Going through questions about your sexual identity does not make sexual experience any easier. Such soul searching and questioning can seriously threaten sexual desire. It can also contribute to great anxiety when you approach the possibility of having sex, as well as trigger the flight response. You may stop having orgasms, begin to think masturbation is disgusting, and find the bodies of women to be ugly. You may want to look through the homework chapter and decide if there are exercises that you would be willing to try. If you are ambivalent about having sex, you may not have any interest in working on your actual sex life. However, if you do some of the exercises (in the sex section especially), you may find that your sexual arousal can help you make a decision about your identification. Whatever your responses during a time of questioning, have compassion for yourself and your situation. You can make the difference to yourself.

Being Single
And Sexual

We live in a culture that prefers coupled people to single people. Becoming coupled is stimulating to the economy: it sells weddings, houses and station wagons. Being single is suspect. A single woman may be seen as a loser whom no one wants. Or there's the "swinging single" no one trusts. The lesbian community is as guilty of these prejudices as the world at large. *If you are having a difficult time seeing yourself as a happily single woman, you may try homework exercises SL-2, SL-3, SL-4.* They will help encourage your self-experession.

> "Everyone is always trying to get me fixed up with someone. They see me as the 'old maid.' I like being alone. There is a difference between being alone and being lonely. I get lonely sometimes for sure, but then so do women who're in couples. That's a feeling in our souls that doesn't always go away just cause there are other people around."

Being single encourages assertiveness, independence, and autonomy—all qualities lesbians value. Sometimes it's difficult to get beyond self-consciousness and fear of judgment when you go out alone. Remind yourself that most of us assume we're being judged when that might not be the case at all. Others may secretly admire us for our strength and character in pursuing a single lifestyle.

> "My friends who are in couples think I'm silly, but I know on some level they also envy that the

135

most I have to worry about when I meet a woman is how close to public transportation does she live. I love the freedom of being single.''

After saying all that, it is still the case that most lesbian activities are centered around couples. Many times the single lesbian is left out of invitations to group activities or intimate gatherings. Coupled friends may find it awkward to include us when they go dancing. Not knowing how to express affection to each other without being exclusive, they may prefer to avoid us altogether. If one person in a couple is closer friends with you, the other may get threatened and you may be cut out to insure peace on the home front. Other couples may see all single lesbians as threatening and you may be no exception.

"These women who think that if you're around their lover, you're going to steal her drive me crazy. If their relationship is so shaky, it's not going to survive anyway.''

"I used to be someone who was invited to lots of events, parties, and plays. That was when I was with Johnetta. Now that I've been single for awhile, no one thinks they have to take care of me while I lick my wounds. So they don't ask me to do things with them. I get my feelings hurt; I tell them, yet they still forget me.''

As usual there are many myths about the single woman in the lesbian community. One is that we're emotionally immature and unable to relate at a deep level. Another is that we're heartbreakers who are emotionally insensitive to others' needs. Another is that all the single woman wants is sex without responsibility. The truth is that as single women, we are just as emotionally mature, sensitive, able to relate and responsible as coupled women. We simply are not primarily attached.

Considering that most of us find ourselves single at various times in our lives, it's amazing that we remain prejudiced against the single state rather than being compassionate about its problems. Some of us are single because we find that state suits us tempermentally and socially. Others of us are single while we're seeking an appropriate partner. Some of us are healing from long-term relationships that have ended and aren't ready to take the plunge again.

Others of us are exploring our own identity and sexuality and see sexual diversity as part of that process. Many of us are fascinated by the experience of seeing different sexual sides of ourselves with different partners; we may not want to give that up.

Others of us choose to be single while dealing with therapeutic issues: tendencies toward abusive relationships, anger at a past lover that isn't resolved, and other emotional patterns. And there are those of us who choose to be single while we have other priorities or commitments: a work project, travel, pregnancy, motherhood, caring for an elderly parent, a friendship that constitutes a primary commitment. With so many reasons for being single, it's unfair to make any generalizations about the "type" of woman a single lesbian might be.

Many of us choose to be sexual only with ourselves while we're single. Some of us do not even masturbate. But many of us still want to express our sexuality with another woman. The form that expression takes may vary from casual sex for fun, to serial monogamy, without regarding oneself as coupled. Wanting casual sex is probably the most difficult position a single lesbian can be in. For some women, opportunities for casual sex that come up in chance encounters are adequate.

> "I just leave my sex life to the fates. When I meet a woman who appeals to me and she is turned on to me, maybe we'll end up having sex. If we don't that's okay. I can always have another fantasy for masturbation."

Others want to have casual sex more regularly and pursue encounters for that purpose. Unfortunately, there are absolutely no institutions in our community for casual sex. There are no "swinging singles" bars like heterosexuals have; no cruising areas like gay men have. In fact, pursuing encounters for the purpose of casual sex is regarded by many lesbians as promiscuous.

> "The definition of 'promiscuous' that I love is that a promiscuous woman is someone who is getting more than you. I like sex. I want to have sex

several times a week. I go look for women who have the same wants or needs. Yep, I'm probably getting it more than many other lesbians. If that makes me promiscuous, that's ok. I'm having fun."

Lesbian bars are the only safe place to pursue sexual encounters and if you don't like bars, you're out of luck. If you live in a small town, having anonymous sex is almost impossible.

"Luckily I live in San Francisco. Not only is there a big lesbian community, but there are enough bars to find other women who want to have casual sex. In fact, there is at least one bar that I go to that if you stand in one particular area others know you're interested in casual encounters. I love it. We all know we're there for the same reason.

Standing up to the judgments of other lesbians is a major problem when pursuing sexual encounters. You may be viewed as just "like a man." Identifying this particular behavior as "male" ignores the fact that thousands of lesbians pursue and enjoy casual sex. Others may consider themselves more "evolved" because they accept having sex whenever it comes without pursuing it. The "correct" lesbian etiquette is to meet at a party, connect intellectually or emotionally, and then go home and have sex together. But going out specifically to meet a woman in order to have sex is seen as less pure.

"I feel like my friends think I'm a freak cause I really get a need just to have sex. I'm not relating to any one woman all the time, so I need to have sex with different women. I like anonymous sex."

"I'm too chicken to go to a bar and pick someone up, so I spend a lot of time going to political meetings and making sure I say something clever so the cute woman in the back will notice me. I join the women she's talking with, then I go to the same place for coffee afterwards. It's a lot of effort for sometimes getting to go to bed with someone. But

I love having sex, so I guess I'll keep doing it. It's worked for the fifteen years I've been single."

If you want to learn to initiate sex without developing a relationship, it's certainly possible. The problem is that there are not a lot of us visibly doing just that. We have no role models to teach us how to pick someone up or let others know we want to have sex. Even talk of sex turns into talking about relationships. This is another area in our sexual lives where sharing skills and information can only help all of us.

"Once I met a lesbian who was 55 who was single and loving it. She talked to me about lots of encounters she had had and how to go about picking up women. I had never met anyone like her. It felt great."

"Women are so aware of single men on the 'hunt' for females, that I just don't know who to tell about my dilemmas in finding women. I know they're out there, but where? I have sex with lesbians who say they love being single, then the next morning ask me when we can meet again. I know that next month it'll be talk of a relationship. Where are the lesbians like me? Sex for fun."

Since almost all of us will be single at some point in our lives, it's essential that we provide support for each other to pursue whatever sexual experience we prefer. Part of that is treating each other with respect and trust. Each of us may sooner or later want the freedom to have sex without attachment and a safe place to initiate sexual encounters with each other.

Lesbians, Limerence And Longterm Relationships

Marny Hall

"When we first got together four years ago, we couldn't keep our hands off each other. The only reason we'd get out of bed all weekend would be to let the dog out. All that's changed now. It's hard to remember the last time we made love . . . oh . . . I think it was several months ago."—Jen

Jen's experience is not unusual. A recent extensive survey of heterosexual and gay relationships concluded that lesbian couples have sex less frequently than either gay male or heterosexual couples. The gap between the lovemaking frequency of lesbians and that of heterosexual couples, slight at first, widens dramatically as the relationships continue over time. In the first two years of lesbian relationships, 76% of lesbians reported having sex once a week or more—compared to 83% of heterosexual married couples. After two years, only 37% of lesbian couples still made love at least once a week, compared to 73% of heterosexual couples (Blumstein and Schwartz).

What accounts for the third year plunge in sexual frequency among lesbians?

The Limits of Limerence

"Limerence," a word coined by psychologist Dorothy Tennov in her book *Love and Limerence,* means the state of being in love. It is limerence which propels us into love relationships and ultimately helps us define our sexual orientations. Erotic feelings distinguish limerence from friendship, but there are other symptoms frequently reported by those in a limerent state. Dr. Tennov's smitten subjects were unable to stop thinking about their loved ones. Euphoria often alternated with despair when their intense feelings weren't reciprocated; this intensity tended to flourish under adverse conditions.

There are few lesbians who don't recognize the signs of limerence and most of us are all too familiar with the types of adversity which fuel it. Applying Tennov's formulation, adversity in the form of social resistance to our sexual preferences may account for the high voltage which often charges our relationships initially. The tension generated by our forbidden preference, combined with the special "gender empathy" unique to same sex relationships, makes the initial limerence period memorable for many lesbians. Unfortunately, it doesn't last.

The two year point found by the Blumstein study to mark the beginning of the decline of lesbian sexuality corresponds to Tennov's findings about the outer limit for feelings of limerence. From interviews with her subjects over time, Tennov concluded that the limerent state rarely lasts more than two years. She goes on to say that "if a relationship does persist after limerence . . . has ended, it is because some other bonding has taken place or because circumstances make it difficult to disengage."

Many of our relationships do endure after the initial limerence period. What keeps us together is not family pressure—usually our families are delighted when our unions dissolve—nor shared mortgages or join parenting responsibilities, but bonding. The problem, it seems, is that the bonding necessary to keep our relationships together in a hostile culture is precisely the sort of relentless us-against-the-world stance which makes sex infrequent in our longterm relationships.

The Trouble With Bonding

Our relationships form in a society which restricts choices, forces lesbian/gay communities underground and inward, and alienates us from colleagues and relatives. It is not surprising that our bonding processes, which occur in this inimical environment, result in relationships which change quickly from intense romances to havens—havens from the ingrown lesbian community, from an often hostile work world, and from families who frequently exclude our lovers.

Indeed, data collected from several studies suggest that in the process of defending ourselves against the homophobic culture, we have gone beyond bonding—into mergers where we sacrifice our individuality:

—Only one third of the approximately 1000 lesbians interviewed in the Blumstein/Schwartz survey pursued activities independently of their lovers. This is in contrast to almost two thirds of their heterosexual female counterparts.

—Of 24 lesbian couples interviewed in depth in another study, (Tanner), all went through an initial insulation period in their relationship, where "time and space were deliberately put between 'them' as a couple and the outside world."

—"My desire to be independent" was listed by over half of the coupled lesbians in yet another study as a factor likely to lead to some difficulty in their relationships.

This retreat from the world has a profound effect on the sexual aspect of our relationships.

In order to present a united front to the insistent heterosexual world, we must draw a tight circle around our unions—and eliminate any potential divisiveness. Such purging often includes censoring differences between us, particularly those which might lead to conflict. Under siege by the dominant culture, we feel we cannot afford anything but security, mutual validation, and predictability within the private world of our relationships. By following this code of confinement and denial of our differences, we may keep our relationships intact. But the price is high.

Confinement does not obliterate the outside world. Denial does not dissolve differences. After overlooking a myriad of small disagreements, we are still left with the ones too big to ignore.

Whether suppressed differences erupt into irreconcilable conflict or whether their suppression is "successful" and conflict never surfaces, the outcome is usually the same. Sexual expression declines.

Sex and the Shapes of Denial

According to brain-mapping studies, centers in the brain for sexuality and aggressive responses are close, perhaps overlapping. In fact, many physiological responses to anger and sexual arousal—increased heart rate, breathing, muscular tension and adrenaline secretion—are identical. Research on brain physiology coincides with Tennov's observations: sexual arousal is connected to some measure of adversity, frustration, or anxiety. Those emotions are exactly the ones we want to banish when (in response to homophobia) we try to iron out every wrinkle of uncertainty, every possible source of conflict in our relationships.

The research linking sex to dissonant feelings does not mean that sexual expression is contingent upon open, chronic warfare in relationships. The implication is, rather, that if we succeed in our attempts to suppress feelings that are not entirely pleasant, we may also inadvertently suppress another not so serene feeling—sexual passion.

There are three specific relationship patterns which seem to result in the decline of sexual expression. In each of the patterns, the partners have, over time, denied important differences between them.

Close Close Relationships

In close/close relationships, in which both partners feel affectionate and companionable, the rekindling of sexual desire may not seem worth the discomfort generated by some feelings of uncertainty. There are risks, however, in avoiding risk. There is no such thing as peril-proof relationships. When we try to construct them, we create partnerships which are actually more vulnerable to the disruptive effect of conflict.

Far/Far Relationships

For the first year of their relationship, Sammi's and Lucy's personal differences in taste and housekeeping, preferences in pets, and even their friends were sacrificed for the harmony of the relationship. All seemed small concessions to make in exchange for the security and pleasure their relationship provided. At holiday time, Sammi's family, unaware of her lesbianism and her new relationship, invited her home for two weeks. Lucy had expected to spend the holidays with Sammi. Sammi's acceptance of her parents' invitation was, to Lucy, nothing less than a repudiation of their relationship. She was angry and accusative. Sammi, in turn, was alienated. Lucy's lack of understanding seemed shocking after the year of mutual accomodation. Both retreated behind barriers of anger. Barely civil to each other, sex became non-existent.

If our differences do emerge after a period of suppression, chances are they will burst out with a vehemence which precludes mutual sexuality. Each person will be barricaded behind resentments which make intimacy unthinkable.

Far/far relationships resemble armed camps. Such stalemates may come after a blow-up like Sammi's and Lucy's, or can evolve imperceptibly over time. Whatever the pace, the result is the same. There is often little physical contact, and no sexual intimacy.

Close/Far Polarization

Reinforcing our tendency to bond with our lovers is our socialization as women. Straight and gay, we have been trained to be sensitive to interpersonal cues, to nurture, and to consider relationships to be our primary sources of gratification.

No two partners, however, focus exactly the same amount of attention on their relationship. That slight variation in relationship focus may turn into a chasm when other differences between partners are denied. Instead of mirroring each other, as do lovers in the close/close and far/far relationships, the partners in close/far relationships polarize. The slightly less intimate partner assumes a distant stance, while the other partner becomes the standard bearer for closeness. The closeness/distance drama is also likely to occur in the bedroom. There, all the unspoken disagreements from other areas of our relationship are expressed. And the form this expression often takes is sexual polarity. The "distant" partner will respond to her lover's desire for sex with a resounding "No!" As with close/close pairings and far/far configurations, the result of the close/far split is the same: a sharp decline in sexual contact.

Relationships may shift back and forth between close/close, far/far and close/far patterns. They may be a blend of all three. Or, they may fit exclusively into one profile. Since the patterns have more to do with what is going on (or not going on) outside the bedroom, attempts to solve the problem by trying harder sexually are usually unproductive. The remedy is better communication—not with one's partner, but with the sides of ourselves we have excluded from the relationship in order to preserve an island of peace within a homophobic society.

In longterm relationships, sexual expression is bound to wax and wane. But continued sexual vitality over time depends on the continued expression of difference, of individuality inside and outside the relationship.

Autonomy: The Liberation of Ourselves

Autonomy is independence or freedom of choice, of action. Acting autonomously means exploring new territory, ignoring old social maps which insist that our role as women (gay or straight) is custodian of the hearth. Developing autonomy means risking the meager ration of security we can create for ourselves within this homophobic society—the predictability of being in an ongoing relationship (whatever its quality). Autonomy for most of us is both novel and frightening.

Describing her own evolving independence, one woman said, "I'd go out and be with friends . . . it was the first time my lover and I had done separate things in years. And I'd be having a good time and all of a sudden I would wonder, what's Doris doing? Is she falling in love with someone else? Then I'd lose it. I'd have to remember all over again that I was with friends, having a good time. And if Doris was having a good time, great. It was like nothing I remember except learning to ride a two-wheeled bike when I was a kid. I'd be going okay, then I'd start wobbling and have to put my feet down—start over again. It was really learning something new. A new way of being."

Honoring our autonomous selves requires our willingness to try new behaviors—behaviors we have not been taught as women or seen modeled in our own communities.

The first step toward autonomy is refurbishing the rusty parts of ourselves, the parts stowed away when we met our partners.

Making dates with old friends, pursuing special interests, hiking, meditating, are ways of regenerating our forgotten selves. Here are a few more ways.

Special Attention

We are taught as children that wanting special attention is indulgent—and this is another lesson to unlearn. If we are in longterm relationships, it is essential that we get attention outside our primary partnerships—attention which is loving and consistent.

Counselors and healers of different persuasions are the most likely sources of such single-minded focus. It worked best for one woman to piece the parts of her life together like a puzzle in traditional psychotherapy; another preferred psychic healings and regular astrology readings.

Another woman felt most validated in an adult children of alcoholics group. It highlighted growing-up experiences which her lover hadn't shared. Yet another woman started a group to explore working class orientation—also a perspective which her lover didn't share. Yet another preferred participating in a feminist theatre group. In each of these cases the effect was the same. The partners came back to their primary relationships with a heightened sense of self, a feeling of separateness within the primary bond.

Enacting Our Own Privacy of Information Act

Participating in special groups and having separate friends are activities which probably don't clash with our notions of ideal primary relationships. We may be less nonchalant, however, about separateness in another zone. We have been taught as women that private thoughts are incompatible with real intimacy. Unshared information, therefore, may appear to threaten our bonding processes.

Information, like friends or activities, can be pooled—the boundaries between our thoughts and those of our lover erased. In fact, it is easy to avoid private thoughts when both partners, exquistely sensitive to each other's nuances of expression, the gestures which signal some preoccupation, quiz each other relentlessly about the source of the distraction.

Noting this attunement in gay couples, one psychologist writes, "The heterosexual [couple] tends to be rich in stimulating contrasts and short on rapport . . . By comparison, homosexual relationships are overclose, fatigue-prone, and are often adjusted to . . . narrow, trigger-sensitive tolerances . . . "

Posing as intimacy, such hair-trigger sensitivity often leads us to believe that we can read each other's thoughts. We can not. With this idea, though, comes the corollary conviction that we are somehow guilty of dishonesty if we don't confide all. We are not. Such convictions sabotage the independent expressions of ourselves which lead to genuine intimacy. Keeping separate information, like taking a solitary walk, or pursuing a separate activity may not be comfortable, but it is a small way of acting autonomously.

There are many ways to keep information separate. One couple subjected their relationship to rigorous scrutiny after a secret affair of one of the partners came to light. Both decided that after years of describing every moment of their days, each random mental notation or imagined misdemeanor to each other, they had both created the need for a big secret.

After a recommitment to a monogamous relationship, they decided to keep regular, small secrets. They instituted a regular "unaccountable" evening. One night a week, they simply refrained from reporting their activities. The privacy was difficult for both at first. The woman who had had the affair wanted to assure her partner that her evening out had been innocent. Her partner, in turn, had to resist her urge to solicit reassurance. The arrangement, difficult as it felt at times, provided a feeling of latitude which heightened the sense that their relationship was freely chosen.

One woman, sensitive to her lover's frequent bouts of moodiness, realized her interrogation about "what was wrong" only started fights. She tried a change of phrasing. "Do you feel like talking?" often drew an emphatic "No!" from her partner, but did not provoke a skirmish.

Observing information boundaries obviates the necessity for BIG secrets—affairs, or other violations which really damage the relationship. Private oases in our lives and the lives of our lovers, underscore our individuality within our relationships.

Emphasizing Differences Within The Relationship

Karen and Marla went to couples therapy because they had polarized around sex, when one said yes, the other said no. The therapist asked about other differences in their relationship. Both partners assured the counselor that, aside from sex, there was no area of incompatibility in the relationship. Eventually it emerged that Karen had recently been promoted and now earned twice as much as Marla did. Both were reluctant to admit the discrepancy. The therapist asked the women to go shopping together. She advised Karen to buy something for herself that Marla simply could not afford, and not to offer to buy the equivalent item for Marla. At home, later, the women were to talk about the experience together.

Both partners found the experience extremely painful. Both also felt tremendously relieved by their discussion. By continuing to focus on this difference in their relationship and the feelings it evoked, the yes/no polarity about sexuality eventually dissolved.

It is important to think about the ways in which we are different from our partners. The charged areas—often those areas which violate egalitarian principles—are particularly difficult for most of us to contemplate. Differences in money, power, class, race, or family background are important to consider and talk about, painful and unfair as we may believe such differences to be.

Sleeping Apart

A great deal happens when we sleep. We dream, pass through different levels of consciousness, sense our bodies in different ways. There are no two people whose sleeping patterns coincide; yet frequently partners will try to alter their patterns to be more compatible with those of their partners.

Jess liked to stay up late but went to bed early to be with her lover, then tossed and turned for several hours trying to sleep. The next morning, her lover Rachel woke up refreshed. Eager to get going, she forced herself to lie quietly so she wouldn't disturb her sleeping partner.

When Rachel went on a business trip, both partners had the unexpected experience of sleeping alone for the first time in years.

Neither had realized how much she had been compromising and how much she had been missing. When they got back together, Rachel brought up the possibility of sleeping apart from time to time. Despite the positive experience she'd had during Rachel's absence, the suggestion frightened Jess. She remembered that her parents' move to separate bedrooms had heralded their divorce. She was willing to experiment, however, as long as she could crawl in bed with Rachel early in the morning.

They began to take turns sleeping on the previously unused sofabed in the living room once or twice a week. During Rachel's trip, they hadn't had a choice. Under the same roof, sleeping apart seemed artificial at first. Though the strangeness never entirely disappeared, the coming together in the mornings, both decided, made the nights apart well worth it.

Describing lesbian relationships, one author wrote that in contrast to the heterosexual pair which "operates in an energy field of centripetal forces," the lesbian couple "operates in a field of centrifugal force." Or as JoAnn says succinctly "our relationships need less teflon and more velcro."

Because our relationships often provide our only refuge, our lover is often the only other person who provides our social reflection. And as anyone knows who has stared in the same mirror for a long time—eventually the reflection blurs. Interactions with others constitute new mirrors where we see parts of ourselves not clearly visible in our primary relationships. These new visions of ourselves are important ways to find balance in primary relationships.

The greatest challenge facing us as lesbian couples is to put our selves—the selves closeted even from our partners—back into our relationships. If we can honor our differences, we innoculate our partnerships against stress and prevent the intrusion of truly devastating conflicts.

Permission for the full range of each partner's personality to emerge in the relationship, rather than any particular sexual technique, is the best aphrodisiac for longterm lesbian relationships.

Sex and Disability

Jill Lessing

At the beginning of this chapter on sex and disability, it makes sense to define the term disabled. This is easier said than done. It is, in a way, like trying to define your class background. For some it will be clear cut, while for others it is a mixed bag. Problems are compounded when we try to delineate differences between disability and illness. While there are similarities in experience there are also differences. In this chapter we are trying to look at a broad spectrum of physical differences. You may already define yourself as disabled or you may never have considered yourself in this way before. Perhaps you have thought you simply have "back pain." In this chapter we are speaking to women, and their friends and partners, who are experiencing physical limitations and loss to any degree that either consistently or intermittently affects your functioning, your self-esteem and the quality of your life. This may be temporary or permanent. This may be from a broken leg that has never been quite the same, to a quadriplegic in a wheelchair. From someone with environmental allergies to someone with cancer. From chronic back pain to an undiagnosed illness. What is important here is that you are experiencing the quality of your life affected adversely by your physical limits. That you experience yourself as physically different.

Being physically disabled creates an emotional as well as a physical context within which our sexuality must be viewed. Many people will be able to understand and relate to much of this because we as women have so much in common. However, it is important to remember that when one's differences and limitations are pervasive, it sets up a dynamic in our lives that must be understood and dealt with from that perspective. In other words, we, as disabled lesbians, are dealing with many of the same issues as able-bodied women are, but we are dealing with them in a much more pervasive way and with many far-reaching implications. For example, how we are seen and accepted in the world does so much to shape and mold our own view of ourselves which affects our sexuality greatly.

I want to speak a little about what I see as a somewhat common experience among disabled lesbians, that is external and internalized oppression, some common ways of trying to deal with that, and some suggestions of ideas that might be of value in the future.

First I want to address some experiences common to lesbians with visible differences. Debra Kelly articulated our dilemma very well when she said, "It's as if we're always on center stage and yet invisible." If there were no other dynamics to deal with, this alone would be enough to create issues to work through for a lifetime. We are stared at as a curiosity on the street, and yet are very rarely met by people's eyes or given a friendly greeting. What's the message here? Your body is to be objectified and your feelings ignored. This is how we have learned to put on various forms of protective layers. One common form looks like: "I'm tough and don't need anything from anybody." This works great on the street. But, when one is at home with a lover and wants to be able to be open about vulnerabilities, look out. It doesn't work. We often compensate for our limitations in a sometimes hostile world by having to hide those limitations, our differentness, our vulnerability and pain. We must be so damn good at what we do that not only will we compete and succeed but maybe no one will even notice that we're not really like them.

The problem is that we do want to be noticed. We want to be appreciated and understood, like most people. So, we go home to our lovers and friends and now we want to interact and relate from a more whole place inside ourselves. We want to be able to ask for what we want and receive it. But to even know what we want and to have permission inside to go after it, is quite a task for the disabled woman. This is especially important because to have a good sexual relationship, it is essential to work toward good communication. We are told over and over again to talk with our partner about what we want, feel, need, can and can't do. But if you are disabled, you have a body that not only causes you distress but you and your body are put down, feared and rejected in the world at large. This makes it even more difficult to accept your own body and her needs. As we all know, to accept love from another, we must love ourselves. If you look different, or you are in pain, or your body and the way you feel is unpredictable or fluctuates, you may be struggling to resolve the conflict between self-rejection and accepting sexual and loving attention from others. Whether you are disabled from childhood or have had an adult onset, whether hidden or visible, it might be helpful to try the exercise on self-love included in this chapter. This may enhance your own level of acceptance of your body with her differences. You can adapt this same exercise to use with your partner and it will facilitate acceptance together.

We all fear what is different. We all want to run from life's inevitable losses. However, the disabled woman must be allowed to leave her role as "symbol of loss" for everyone else and take her long overdue place among the desirable and attractive. In fact, a common myth is that the disabled woman is not even sexual at all. This is expressed throughout the culture, by doctors, teachers, counselors, friends and it is decidedly untrue!

If you have a hidden disability or illness you have many difficult issues to face. One common experience making it difficult to accept your own body is that you may hear over and over again that you are not really disabled. You are faking it or making it up. It is difficult to believe what we do not readily see or experience. However, this kind of mistrust is an extremely damaging attitude. There is an enormous amount of pain and loss of privilege in the life of a disabled woman and I have never known anyone who actually wanted to take that on. If someone says that she is disabled, believe her and let her know that you are interested in hearing what her experience of life is like and how disability affects her.

It is also extremely important to remember what you hear. If you do not notice her experience you will not have this obvious and constant reminder, so it is easy to forget. Remembering will be an act of validation and caring. This begins to set up trust wherein that good communication mentioned earlier can begin and flourish.

Another barrier to self-esteem and a good sex life can also be pain. Pain is hard to live with and it carries with it a kind of psychic pain. The pain of feeling that there is something wrong with me. For the disabled woman this message is pervasive and all too easily internalized. The truth is that what is wrong is that you are hurting. For even though pain is a part of everyone's life, the vast amounts of constant or intermittent pain suffered by disabled women often seems like way more than our share. Sometimes the anger over this gets misdirected or it is the easiest emotion to express. Easier than the sadness and frustration.

The constant message in life to the disabled woman is to hide. Hide your pain because no one really wants to deal with it. It reminds people of their own pain. So, not wanting to turn people off, we try to give them an image of who we are as happy, cheerful and above all, okay. It's even difficult to tell your lover when you are in pain. Perhaps sex is the last thing you want. Or, maybe sex is the only time you really feel good in your body. Or, perhaps, as is the case with some diabetic women, the intense high of sexual excitement and orgasm may be reminiscent or indistinguishable from low-blood sugar and may be frightening. The key here is, that no matter what you feel, it is important to really allow yourself to be just exactly where you are and to share this with your partner. Going through the sadness and disappointment together can be a real gift of closer intimacy and can again help create more trust.

If you are in pain and your partner wants to be sexual, perhaps finding creative alternatives such as ways to be physically close would be a happy compromise until you are both feeling sexual again. Perhaps asking for a massage from your partner, followed by holding her while she masturbates. If you must defer all pleasure until later, then honor that even though it is difficult. Waiting until later is hard. However, this is not anyone's fault and can be dealt with more easily if both partners can talk openly about the frustration. Remember, no one is to blame. As allies you can help each other through these hard times. The meditation on pain in Steven Levine's book, *Who Dies,* will be helpful to you in this process.

I want to stress something everyone of us needs to be aware of and to remember. It takes an enormous amount of energy to be disabled. There is the physical energy required to deal with your limitation. There is the energy of trying to get along in an often hostile or pitying world, competing and needing to do "twice as well as anyone else to be thought of as half as good." And, there is the energy it takes to save energy. No one has to plan their life out so much in advance for their needs so constantly as the disabled. We often experience this as being done automatically. So, we are not aware of just how much energy it really does cost. The point is, one can never leave their disability behind. It is constantly there and constantly demanding something from us. It is exhausting! This will affect our sexuality, of course, and needs to be dealt with as a reality. The good news is that when we make room for what we are struggling with explicitly, there is more room for pleasure.

If your physical difference is due to the loss of a limb, mastectomy, or looking quite different physically, you will also be dealing with your own and society's ideas about how you "should" look. It is very difficult to leave behind our stereotypes about looks and learn to appreciate our bodies the way they are. You might spend time with a lover going over every part of your body together. Introduce her to the different parts of your body. Have her greet them with openness, love and playful affection. If you are the partner, remember that the areas on your lover's body that are different are the places that need your loving touch the very most. Ask her explicitly where it is not comfortable to touch and where it is the best. Also, what "kind" of touch does that area like. Experiment together. Ask her to tell you her "stories" about those places on her body that are different as if she is the hero with scars from the wars to tell about, which she is.

If you need to rely on appliances for your daily functioning, such as a catheter or illiostomy or colostomy bags, then many of the same issues that other disabled women face will also be yours, in addition to other difficulties. The first thing to know is that a rewarding sex life is certainly in no way prohibited to you. It may take some getting used to. A major concern here is often the fear that you will be a "turn-off" to a sexual partner. Again, this may be the case with some people as with other physical differences; however, as you are able to accept yourself, it will be that much easier to find acceptance with a partner. Another cause for concern is how to be sexy, wear sexy clothes, worry about sounding bad and smelling bad. There are the right foods and products available to you to help in this area (a good place for information is the National Foundation for Illiatus and Collitus in San Francisco). It is also extremely helpful to find and get advice from a good enterostomal therapist who, with their experience, will help you develop skills to master your appliance as well as finding the right ones for you. It is important to pay this kind of special attention to yourself in developing a self-accepting attitude. If you are the partner of someone who needs an appliance, check inside yourself to discover what your responses are to the imperfections of others. Spend some time figuring out what you would need if that imperfection were your own in order to accept it. Now try giving that to your partner.

If you have an illness such as cancer, heart disease or a degenerative disease you are dealing with many difficult issues, not the least of which is "not knowing." Will it come again? Will it get worse? When? How? Not knowing is hard for all of us. It means giving up control in the most profound and basic way. Not having control over your own body and the ultimate loss of control and power, of course, which is death. Sharing your fears and loss together with your partner will keep you close and break the isolation. Sharing the pain and sadness together can make a tremendous difference in living each day with quality. I highly recommend support groups for women with these issues in order to sit together through not knowing and to not be alone in whatever way that is possible.

Very fat women experience oppressions along the same lines as any woman with another disability. If your fat contributes to a body size or shape very physically different than society's standards, the information in this chapter is appropriate for you. Further information is in the chapter on Barriers To Our Sexuality.

As with the rest of life, all the disabilities mentioned here do not exist in isolation. Many of us experience several disabilities simultaneously. Obviously, this compounds our problems. It's important not to blame ourselves for these problems, and instead seek our own understanding and the understanding of others.

Self-Love Exercise

Tools needed are uninterrupted time and space to be alone for about an hour, a comfy spot to relax, a mirror, paper and pen, and a cassette recorder.

Sit comfortably and relaxed with eyes closed. Allow all tension to drain away and simply notice your breathing or pay attention to the gentle rising and falling in your abdomen with each breath.

Now, thank your body and appreciate her for allowing you to be here, to be alive and to be experiencing life. Consider for a moment how you are connected to all other living things and how this makes you feel. Let yourself notice and appreciate the nature of all living things, the repeated cycles of existence and the wide range of variabilities of all things in life. Notice and appreciate how the differences of form in nature just simply exist without judgments about good and bad, right or wrong. Allow your own judgments to melt away for a few minutes and notice how easy it is to appreciate the beauty and gifts of the earth no matter what their shape. There is no such thing as imperfection in nature. The gnarled tree is all the more beautiful for her interesting and different shape. Imagine for a moment how wonderful it would be if we all appreciated ourselves and each other in this way—free from the mental constraints of false ideas about perfection. We could just be.

Start to create that world right now. Imagine that you are already free from those constraints, that you appreciate yourself and others fully without reservation. Take a deep breath. Now take a few minutes to get in touch with your own body's limitations. Think about and let yourself feel your losses. Your pain. The wishes you have to be different. Give yourself complete permission for a few minutes to feel your sadness, your tears, your grief about the difficulties you face each day. Really experience this. Relax.

Now take another deep breath and feel yourself moving back from sadness. Breathe. Ask yourself what you have learned through your struggles. Really notice and appreciate yourself for this learning, for your survival, for your compassion, for your ingenuity in facing your challenges. Take this in deeply. Breathe. You are now ready to continue creating an experience of self-acceptance without reservation.

Imagine for a moment that someone you love is in front of you and that they are appreciating you for the wonderful, unique being that you are. Hear them telling you all the things you've always wanted to hear. You are beautiful, desirable, sexy, intelligent, clever. Your good qualities abound. Make a mental list of these appreciations in detail. Deep breath. Now pick up the mirror and look into it. Look deeply into your eyes in the mirror and say, "I love you, (your name)," say it again and then repeat your lists of appreciations only this time, saying them to yourself into the mirror.

It is difficult for many of us to look into the mirror, either due to disability, or past abuse issues, or because of internalized self-hatred of any kind. Alternative to the mirror could be to write a letter or make a cassette recording of yourself. The goal is to work toward giving yourself love, acceptance and appreciation.

Take another deep breath. Get in touch with and experience your whole body through your thoughts, feelings and by touch. Touch yourself all over. Slowly, carefully, lovingly. Get in touch with the places that are physically different and experience them as if for the first time. Experience these places one by one as if they were each your own small child. Experience this child's need from you for love and acceptance, compassion for her struggle and hard work. Tell her that you are sorry that it's hard for her and that you will always be there for her, that you will never leave her and that you love her. Listen to her needs. Find the needs you didn't know were there before. Reassure her that you will work to meet those needs now and on-goingly in the future. Tell her again that you love her.

Sex And Motherhood

This chapter is for all women who are trying to create a sex life while they are also trying to raise children or to have them. It is also for the partners of mothers, friends of mothers, and those who are co-parenting. I believe that motherhood and active lesbian sexuality are not incompatible. This chapter is aimed at helping them become more compatible in your life.

Pregnancy And Sex

Getting pregnant is not easy for a lesbian. There are many questions to be answered. Am I doing this alone or with a lover or friend? Would I be willing to continue trying to get pregnant even if my partner backed out? How will I find a donor? Will he be someone I know, someone else's acquaintance, or from a sperm bank? Should I wait until I have more time and money? Will that ever happen? How will I figure out when I'm fertile? How will I arrange to get the sperm? If I am alone, what will I do about morning sickness? Who will go through birthing classes and the birth itself with me? How will I tell my biological family? What will people say at work? All these questions and many more face the lesbian who wants to get pregnant and does not want to have intercourse with a man to do it.

Whether you are single or with an ongoing lover, your sex life will also be affected by your pregnancy. You will have to face the issues of body image and the physiological and psychological changes that occur with pregnancy. Remember that you are engaging in a radical act in this culture—having children without men.

And I mean *really* without men: without the expectation of a man, the hope of getting a man, the desire to rely on a man. That fact alone puts you in a vulnerable position and may make pregnancy, which can be difficult for any woman to deal with in ideal circumstances, even more stressful.

"Just the words 'artificial insemination' made it seem like my method for conceiving a child was wrong somehow. I feel that being a lesbian mother is hard enough, but I also am not doing this pregnancy with any man involved. The world doesn't recognize me at all."

"I was never a radical in college, I never even demonstrated. Somehow having a child on my own as a lesbian has become this bizarre act that is very political. I just want to be a mother, this extra stress is awful for me."

It takes a heterosexual couple an average of six to twelve months to get pregnant. So it is not surprising that it often takes lesbians even longer than that. I have known lesbians who have been trying for years to get pregnant. Once you've made the decision, repeatedly inseminating, waiting in suspense every month, then trying again is emotionally exhausting and draining. Feeling disappointed, frustrated, defeated, and inadequate is not unusual. Sometimes in this process we get alienated from our bodies; we feel that they have betrayed us and see them as objects outside ourselves that refuse to do what we want. Feeling frustrated with and alienated by our bodies, it is not surprising that many lesbians find themselves not wanting to be sexual.

Added to the frustration is the preoccupation with bodily processes that occurs when trying to conceive. "When will I ovulate? Am I inseminating at the right time? Am I pregnant?" Although lesbian sexuality is, in fact, separated from reproduction, we may feel fearful of causing a miscarriage by having sex in the two weeks after we've inseminated. Even though we know that sex doesn't cause miscarriage, our feelings of fear may inhibit our sexuality.

"Getting pregnant through insemination seemed like an impossible task. I was always nervous that

I didn't inseminate at the right time. I was sure I was too late or too early for my ovulation. Not only that, but I would worry about whether my donor would think I was a flake and stop giving sperm. I felt like a beggar.''

"It seemed that the first two weeks of my cycle were spent worrying about whether I was pregnant or not. Then I'd get my period and I would be concerned with when I was ovulating. Forget a sex life. Lucille was as uptight as I was and we just never could get it together to have sex."

Once you do become pregnant, the physical and psychological changes you go through also influence your sex life. The first trimester brings any number of symptoms: nausea, extreme fatigue, enlarging breasts, weight gain, changes in stomach and waist, sometimes total loss of libido. The psychological issues raised in this period loom large: What have I done? Why have I done it? Depression and euphoria can alternate without a break. The first twinges of "mother guilt' about eating, drinking, and smoking are felt. The natural fear of the awesome responsibility of becoming a mother surfaces. The necessary process of turning inward, of becoming preoccupied with the life within, concurrent with loss of interest in outside issues, begins.

The second trimester brings still more changes. Your body is in the midst of gaining ten to forty pounds. Your breasts continue to enlarge; the waist disappears. Face, arms, and legs often become puffy as the body produces and stores more fluids. It begins to be difficult to get a full night's rest. Some women still have extreme fatigue and nausea. Other women find in this period a reprieve from the extreme symptoms of the first and last trimesters. Eating regularly and wisely becomes very important at this time. The psychological issues begin to increase, there is no going back. Now women begin to concentrate on what they want from mothering and how they will fit that into their current economic and emotional lives.

Changes during the second trimester again affect sex. Many women find their bodily changes so disturbing or overwhelming that they do not feel a desire for sex. Some women find their partners are not as attracted to them as they once were. Others feel so overwhelmed by the prospects of their new position in life that sex seems irrelevant. Yet still other women find that their sex drive increases.

The last trimester is usually the most physically difficult. The breasts are enlarged, the abdomen has stretched to what seems unreal proportions. Fatigue is a constant companion and poor circulation may make support stockings necessary. Activity that once seemed normal (tying shoes, vacuuming, lifting laundry, climbing stairs) is difficult and tiring. No one really knows what this period will be like until they've experienced it. Regardless of how much you think you've prepared, the way your body actually feels during this period comes as a shock.

Now the psychological issues around pregnancy become prominent. Suddenly there's not enough time to complete the arrangements. Where is this baby going to sleep? How can I get all my work done before my maternity leave? How will I make ends meet until I can go back to work? You will often get sick of your own preoccupation with the coming event and your friends and lover(s) may be crazy from it. Anxiety, fear, and even depression often increase as the birth date draws near.

During the third trimester, sex may become the last item on a long list of priorities. If there have been any extraordinary physical difficulties during pregnancy, sex may already have been given up for long periods of time. Having enough energy for food preparation, eating, sleeping, working and cleaning is often all the very pregnant woman can muster. During this time you need, above all, to take care of yourself and be clear about your sexual desires.

"When I was pregnant, it was all I could do to concentrate long enough to have a conversation with another person. I was so inside myself that it was like I was having a primary relationship with this little being who wasn't quite on the planet yet."

"I felt terrible during my whole pregnancy. It seemed that I was nauseated the entire nine months. Samantha finally was sick of me. She felt that not only had I tuned out and spaced out, but also been so physically debilitated that she was in a relationship with someone who wasn't there."

Going through pregnancy with a partner introduces particular strains. We've all heard that pregnancy is supposed to be one of the happiest times of our lives. Yet both partners may find it the most difficult time they've gone through. There is no reason to feel guilty if that's the case for you. It is a period of tremendous stress.

As the partner, you may find yourself feeling left out. The pregnant woman gets all the attention, gets her belly touched and oohed and ahhed over. You often do not get credit for going through the trials and tribulations with her. You get awakened at night when she's restless; you worry about the impending responsibility; you often deal with her and/or your families. You may feel obligated to limit your activities to what she can physically do.

Both of you may find yourselves increasingly isolated from your friends and support group as you gravitate toward other women with children. Just as likely, your friends may slowly move away, fearful of being asked to be responsible in some way for a new baby or uncomfortable with the thought of being around a child. You may find yourself feeling disillusioned with other lesbians who thought it was great when you got pregnant but have now faded into the woodwork. During this time, increased isolation and increased need for support, for both the pregnant woman and her partner, can create tremendous stress on the relationship. Each may expect the other to provide all she needs. Such an expectation is unrealistic and leads inevitably to resentment on both sides. The fact of the matter is that there is not enough support available in the culture for a pregnant lesbian and her partner. The two of you cannot make up for the fact that there is literally not enough to go around.

> "Tammy and I are trying desperately to be happy about being pregnant and having a child. It's just that she is having the baby; she's the one who is preoccupied and needs help from me. Also I am the one who doesn't get all the strokes of everyone around us. I'm sort of extra baggage. But when it comes to needing support, I'm the only one who is always there. Where am I supposed to get my needs met?"

> "This child who is coming seems to be the whole focus of our relationship. I feel that is all we

talk about and sometimes it seems that that is the only reason we stay together—to have a family. Seems that we lost our relationship."

If you and your partner are having such difficulties, exercises C-1, C-3, C-4 and R-8 in the homework chapter may help. Getting in touch with why you chose each other as partners, why you chose to have a child together, why you are important to each other can help you get through a painful period. Often this pain gets expressed through moving away from each other sexually. *You each may want to look through the exercises on sex with a partner (P-1 through P-7) and see if any of these help to improve your sexual relating.* If sex is something one or both of you is unwilling to engage in, and if it has been an important way of increasing intimacy in your relationship, you will have to create other ways of getting the intimacy and closeness you need.

Pregnancy As A Single Woman

Almost everything discussed so far applies to the pregnant single woman, but there are other issues which only she may have to deal with. These include her increased dependence on her peers, the responsibility of becoming a single parent, and issues around dating and having a sex life.

Friends and their support become more and more important to the single pregnant woman. She becomes dependent on them in a way she never was before pregnancy. They become her family, her security, her support group—the only people to whom she can express her fears and misgivings. If all of your friends are non-mothers, you may find they have no experience from which to give you advice. Or they may have difficulty in identifying with your concerns. You may feel that you don't have the capacity to accept rejection at this time, and so begin to isolate yourself for protection. If at all possible, avoid this. You need all the support you can get.

"Right now I am so vulnerable. Having a child is something I want to do. It's just that none of my friends have had kids, and they don't understand how frightening it is. I feel very alone."

"I am just too tired from this pregnancy to get together with my friends. I'm afraid to ask for them to always come see me. I really don't have much to offer them."

The single mother is the sole person responsible for the coming baby. Being in this position is an intense experience; it is important that it be acknowledged and not minimized. Again, it is a position almost impossible to imagine unless you've been there. To be the one person a child looks to for the fulfillment of every need; to be the person ultimately responsible for the child's life; to have no one to share that ultimate responsibility with is both overwhelming and terrifying. Find other single mothers who know what this experience is like; seek out women who will validate your courage and strength. The positive part is that you are having a child by yourself without having to compromise with another person who has her own viewpoint. You don't have to worry about a lover who is not getting enough attention from your pregnant self. You can make decisions according to what you feel is right and good. At a time in your life where there are so many decisions to be made, it is wonderful to make them without another adult's needs in mind.

"I love being single during this pregnancy. I see other lesbians having such struggle with their lovers over who is going to do what and how they are going to handle this or that. I just make a decision and then go to the next one."

Just because you are about to become a mother does not mean you cannot have the sex life you want; however, being pregnant and single may make it more difficult. You may have your sex life interrupted because of physical difficulties; you may lose interest in sex altogether due to anxieties around your present situation and coming responsibilities. You may find that some women want to have sex with you for the novelty of having sex with a pregnant woman. You may be too insecure about your body and its shape to want to expose it to possible rejection. You may respond to your forthcoming loss of freedom by wanting to have a lot of sex with a lot of different partners. Whatever your sexual needs are, allow yourself the freedom to pursue them. *Look at exercises*

SL-2, SL-4 and SL-5 in the homework chapter which may help with your concerns.

"Having sex with a new date when I was six months pregnant seemed to be sacrilegious somehow. On the other hand, it was also some of the best sex I've had. I guess I was real swollen 'down there', which made all kinds of sensations feel great."

"When my friends stopped trying to fix me up for dates I asked them why and they told me they didn't think I'd want to go on a date since I'm 'showing.' It reminded me of the fifties. I have had a great sex life while I've been pregnant with lots of different women and I love it."

Miscarriage And Sex

The lesbian who has decided to get pregnant, has inseminated repeatedly, and then has a miscarriage finds herself subject to severe depression. If you are in that position, do not suffer alone. Talk to other women; you'll be surprised at the number who have miscarried.

Statistics show that 40-50% of all pregnancies end in miscarriage. Most result from a "blighted ovum"—an egg that is fertilized but dies soon after conception. However, the egg attaches to the uterine wall and is only miscarried when the body belatedly realizes it's not viable.

Part of the depression of miscarriage comes from the radical hormonal changes. One minute you are pregnant and the body is pumping hormones into your blood stream. The next minute you are not and the body is reversing itself. Do not be surprised if you need to spend days in bed from the physical depression of miscarriage. The psychological pain of having gotten pregnant, been pregnant, and then having nothing to look forward to is extreme and will need to be expressed.

"When I miscarried, I felt that the world had come to an end. I was never depressed like that except when a good friend of mine died. It was like that, a good friend had died."

"To be planning my whole life for the coming baby and then have it not be there was too much for me. I almost don't want to try to get pregnant again."

The thought of going through the tedious and time-consuming insemination process again may be overwhelming. Facing your friends and community who were looking forward to a baby may be difficult. You may feel like you've let yourself and others down, that you're inadequate, that your body has betrayed you. You may be fearful of telling your family, afraid that they'll breathe a sigh of relief rather than support you. Your own homophobia may creep in, making you doubt whether lesbians should get pregnant.

"My mother is a very political woman and has even thought that we Blacks should have lots of children because we are being systematically wiped out by the white powers that be. When I miscarried, she told me I was being punished for my lifestyle. I was devastated. The worst part was that I began to believe her. Luckily my dyke friends helped me remember the love that I have and how a child would be privileged to be mine."

Your partner(s) will be very affected by your miscarriage but may feel unsupported in their own loss. After all, they're not the father or the mother; they didn't experience the actual pregnancy. Still, whether they are living with you or planning to co-parent, they have also experienced a loss and need a period of mourning.

"There seems to be a lot of sympathy in the world for Carol who had the miscarriage. They forget that as her lover, I have had my future changed instantly too. I am very depressed and almost feel I have no right."

"We both believe that we contributed to my miscarriage. Vivian feels that she was too angry at me for not keeping up my end of the chores around the house. I feel that I didn't eat right. Hearing that

lots of pregnancies end in miscarriage helps some,
but we are both left with questions and guilt."

Both you and your partner(s) may get into feeling guilty or
blaming each other. You may each question whether you did
something wrong or whether your partner did. Such feelings are
natural, but accusations are not helpful. Healing is most needed
at this time. It may be difficult to experience the closeness and
intimacy of sex now when you most need it. You both may be
alienated from the body that brought you loss. *Exercises R-8; P-3,
and P-5 in the homework chapter can help you heal the rift so
that loving sex can return to your lives.*

Not So Loud, Honey, The Kids Might Hear

Everyone knows "mothers don't have sex"; we know "*our*"
mothers certainly didn't.   This attitude has stifled the sex lives
of many lesbian mothers. Sex *may* be okay for the monogamous-
ly coupled lesbian mother, but it is definitely off limits for the
single parent. If you have too many partners, your friends will start
to wonder and your family will lecture you on the effects on your
children. Remember, mothers need sex too; you have the right
to act on your sexual needs.

> "Letting my children know that I am a sexual
> being is so hard for me. I guess it's because of my
> family who never let anyone know anything that
> was going on sexually. I have this idea that 'nice
> girls' don't have sex and if they do, they certainly
> don't let their kids know about it."

It is important to remember that most children don't like to
think about their parents' sex life. In fact, they mostly wish that
their parents didn't have sex. Many of them can't believe that their
parents have sex and when they find out they do, it is a major ad-
justment. We tend to believe that our children (especially
teenagers) hate our sex life because we are lesbians. Ask your
straight friends. Their teenagers hate their sex lives too. All kids
react to the sexuality of their parents. It's normal; it's healthy; it's
a way for them to learn that you are a human being with sensual
needs just like them.

"My teenage daughters hated it when I had dates with women and they stayed overnight. I think that they were struggling with their own impulses to have sex and were feeling conflicted about it. They are just as oppressed by the culture as I was. Girls aren't supposed to have sex. Then their mother had sex on top of it all. It was too much. The great thing was when I saw that all their friends felt the same way about their parents—gay or straight."

Major factors that affect a mother's sexual relationships while she has children living with her are: jealousy between children and lovers, time, privacy and the homophobia of the mother and children. Different issues exist for the single mother and the mother who is part of a couple. The single mother also addresses issues like: How can I date with a child? How many casual affairs are too many? The coupled mother addresses: How do I make this group a family? How do I get out of the middle? You may want to use the communication exercises in the homework chapter for you and your children. Choose the ones that would work in your family and try to learn more positive ways to communicate.

Jealousy

Jealousy is the major cause of stress in lesbian families that include children. Children do not want to share their mothers with anyone, no matter who that person is. Lesbians generally do not want to share their lovers either. Having a relationship with someone who has a primary relationship with someone else is not easy. There is no such thing as a monogamous relationship with a mother. The problems of jealousy will be compounded by the lover's lack of status and authority, by power struggles around different ideas of how to raise children, and by the mother's protectiveness. If two lesbians have chosen to have and raise a child together, many of these problems may be minimized. The simple fact of their both being with and bonded to the child since infancy will forestall many problems. But that is not the case for most lesbian mothers whose lovers entered the picture after the child is older. In fact it seems that the later the lesbian partner comes into the picture the less the children regard her as a co-mother.

In addition, the partner often does not see herself as a mother if the children are older. Sometimes there are almost two family units living under one roof.

If step-parenting for heterosexuals is not easy, it is doubly difficult for lesbians. The society at large, the grandparents, even the children themselves refuse to recognize the mother's lover as a parent. There is no hope she can ever become a "stepfather." The children see their biological mother as their "real" mother and often recognize only her authority. Even if the lover has chosen to co-parent, often only she and her partner accord her the status of that role.

> "No matter what I do, these are not my kids. I am their mother's lover. I will never be their 'stepmother'. They have a mother in the house. So it feels like we are in adversary positions."

When jealousy on the part of the lover and protectiveness on the part of the mother combine, the two may feel they are on opposite sides.

> "I know that when I tell one of the kids that they have to do what I told them to, if they don't like it, they will just tell their mother. And I'm afraid that she'll side with them. If she doesn't I am pleasantly surprised."

> "Sometimes I find myself siding with my children against my lover even if I don't want to. I think I'm trying to protect them from her. She and I have different ideas about childraising and I feel she is so jealous of them, she is hard on them on purpose."

It can be very painful for the lover to realize and accept that the mother's children are her primary commitment and always will be. This can be especially painful for a lover who never wanted to have children of her own. Not only does she have the responsibility of children, which she never wanted, but she has a lover with a primary relationship with someone else.

"The truth is that I would choose my children over my lover when it gets right down to it. That's the way it should be."

When the mother and her lover live together, the jealousy occurs daily in large and small ways: from who is Mom going to watch television with, to who will Mom go on vacation with, to who does Mom love most?

"I know I'm being selfish when I ask Laura to go to a movie with me, but I just can't stomach another Snoopy special."

"I'm always in the middle between Julie and my kids. Each feels I'm abandoning them if I spend time with one and not the other."

There are few solutions to the jealousy that occurs between a partner and the children. This is often just a type of stress that has to be accepted in the relationship. No one is to blame. It is the nature of loving someone that we want that person all to ourselves. That is what sibling rivalry is all about. If we can accept sibling rivalry as natural, perhaps we can also accept partner-children jealousy. Because the partner is an adult does not make the jealousy any less likely. Often the partner is dealing with the loss of having a primary relationship with her lover, who is a mother. Finding a wonderful lover then seeing her give her primary love to her children is difficult.

Mothers get a lot of physical affection and touching from their children that partners do not get. Nursing mothers, especially, have a close connection that gives them lots of loving with their child. That touching may diminish the mother's needs for physical attention from her partner. The partner, who is not receiving that level of physical intimacy needs it and may feel resentful or jealous.

"Mamie felt I gave all of myself to the children and there was nothing left for her. I felt she was unwilling to create separate relationships with my kids. We have just agreed to disagree. And when jealousy surfaces, we try to be clear about it and set aside time for just the two of us. That really helps."

171

Making sure that you and partner get time alone and you and your children get time alone may be one of the best solutions to the problem. The important thing for the moms to remember is that you cannot do it all for anyone. Your partner and your children will expect it, but that does not mean you will be capable of delivering. You are not inadequate; you are human and cannot take care of everyone's needs. *All members of the family could benefit by exercises SL-2, SL-3 and SL-4.*

If the mother is single, she may feel guilty at bringing new, not permanent relationships into her children's lives. Out of guilt, she may side with her children when there is conflict, especially if she is not particularly invested in her lover.

> "When my children complain about my dates, I immediately feel guilty. Maybe I have too many sexual encounters with other women. Maybe I should wait until the kids are out on their own."

> "I have purposefully avoided getting into a committed relationship with another woman—my kids have been through too many. There are different problems now though—do I go out on a date when my kids are jealous of any time I spend away from them?"

You have to remember to keep your needs high on your list of priorities. You have a need for and a right to sexual experience whether you are in a committed relationship or not. Recognize your children's jealousy for what it is; don't allow it to edge into criticism of your single lifestyle. It is no more "moral" to limit the number of women you see or bring home to have sex with.

It is important to educate your children as much as you can about the right of women to have their sexual needs met. Children are often dominated by the values of their peers and the culture does not encourage single mothers to assert their sexuality. You can do your best to set an example of getting your sexual needs met. Ask them to read the chapter on homophobia. See if that helps them to think differently about your sexuality. *Once again, exercises SL-2 and SL-4 in the homework chapter can help.*

Time

How to support yourself and your children, have a relationship with your child(ren), have relationships with your lover(s) and friends, get your housework done and still have sex—that is the dilemma of the lesbian mother. There is never enough time. If your child gets up at six, how can you stay up until midnight like you used to? How do you make sure you have sex between the hours of 8:00 and 10:30? When do you have sex at all? How do you get enough energy to have sex?

"There is no way I could ever get enough time for myself, my child, my lover and my work. I have to choose one at a time. That's why doing things together as a family helps me. Then I am taking care of three things at once."

"I don't have time for sex. At least I don't feel like I do. When would I do it? With what energy?

Priorities about how to use time shift with children in the household. If there is an infant, or when a child is sick, emotionally needy, or needs help, time is funneled in that direction. Time becomes a precious commodity there is never enough of.

Life with children requires lack of spontaneity. Everything has to be plannned out. Not only is this disappointing to the mother, but it can be a real irritant to the lover if she hasn't accepted it. Without some kind of schedule though, there is no way to get work, school, eating and loving all accomplished.

"I feel like a police officer. My kids think that if one of them doesn't brush their teeth on time, I get upset that my day will be thrown off. My worry is that if I don't keep everything moving, I will have no time with Andrea. Then when we have sex, I have a schedule there—if I don't get to sleep by 11:00, I won't be fit to live with the next day."

"When we were first together, Georgia was willing to be spontaneous all the time. Now that we

173

have settled into the relationship, I feel like I'm in the army. Realistically, though, there is no way we can just get up and go the movies if we feel like it. Not with two kids."

If both partners can accept the structure of a schedule as allowing them some spontaneity, then a way can be worked out to meet everyone's needs. Relief comes when everyone knows what to expect and knows that their needs will be met as well as possible.

"We made a schedule of events in the house. I spend time with the kids from 6:30 to 8:00. Nothing interrupts that time. Gladys and I spend 8:30 to 10:30 together. Nothing takes the place of this time. I've had to give up lots of extra activities in my life. I just can't do everything. I made choices and for now, this is how my time makes the most sense."

"Roberta used to let her kids stay up until 10:00. There just was no time for the two of us. When she finally told the kids that they had to be in bed by 8:30, I was relieved. I get her alone too."

Private time with your lover may get lost in the scramble to take care of the immediate needs of your household. But letting that happen can sabotage your relationship and teach your children that a woman's need for love and sex can always be put aside. Let your relationship with your lover take priority some part of each day. Let them see that when your partnering and sexual needs are met, you have more to give them. Let them know that having love in one's life is a wonderful gift.

Not only do you need private time each day, but you also need "alone time" together out of the house each week. That does not mean time together grocery shopping. It means time together to remember why you became lovers in the first place, time to renew your relationship. Since getting child care will be necessary, arrange this time in advance, perhaps setting aside the same night each week; that will give you both something to look forward to.

If you are single, you still have rights to have time with your peers. Although you do not have an ongoing lover with whom you "should" spend time, having time away from your children is important. Spend time doing whatever you want to, but spend time out of your home, having fun without your children.

As mothers, we often hide behind the needs of our children, fulfilling the expectation of our role as women—as if we have no independent needs of our own. Sit quietly with yourself and ask whether you are fulfilling your own needs for quiet "alone time" and for time with your peers. Allow yourself the stimulus of a relationship with yourself and with other adults without your children.

> "It is hard for me to make time for anyone but my children. I feel guilty all the time I am not with them. I have to work, but I don't have to socialize."

> "When my son was three I realized that I would go stark, raving, mad if I didn't get a lover into my life. Someone for me to relate to in a peer way. At first, dating was difficult. Once I saw it was imperative for me, I just kept making myself do it."

> "Carmen and I broke up after three years together. I know it was not so much because of her kids, it was because we didn't make our relationship as important as being parents. Kids won't be whole human beings unless they see their parents acting like whole human beings."

Having kids is hard work. Having relationships with friends and lovers is hard work. The two are not incompatible; they are just hard work. There are rewards. Having a fulfilling sex life (whatever that means to you) is important, and having time alone with your lover(s) is the only way to have sex. Let time for sex become something valuable to you. *Make a decision to work on one of the sex exercises in the sex section with a partner (P-1 through P-7).* Decide to do this once a month at first, then gradually increase to the level that feels good to you. If you don't want to have sex, make sure that you have some time together with a partner away from the kids doing something intimate and loving.

Privacy

Privacy is an important factor in any woman's sex life. Privacy is often missing for the woman with children at home. As the mother, you must remember that your needs are important too, and your child must learn that adults have a right to privacy. Make clear boundaries with your children, i.e., "You can come into my room when the door is open; when it is closed, you must knock first."

> "When Sheena and I got together we were so excited because we were both from poor families and we thought all would be great. We had very different views of privacy. Her family always had lots of people and relatives around partying and having fun. My family was isolated in the country and we didn't have any intruders. So we have real different ways with children too. The best thing for us was fighting it out until we reached a liveable compromise. The kids now know we have private time every day. The rest of the time, the house is like a circus. Both of us get some of what we need."

If your partner and you have different ideas about privacy, try exercises C-1, C-3, C-4 and C-5 in the homework section making privacy the topic of the work.

To create a sex life that is fulfilling, you must have a space that is your own, even if only for a short period of time. You need to be able to count on some consistency. It is possible, if you are willing to put yourself first some of the time. This sets a wonderful role model for your children. They get to learn that each of us is entitled to our own space.

Homophobia

Parenting has been under severe scrutiny by male psychologists and sociologists for years. Instead of men doing parenting themselves, they tend to complain about the way women are doing it. As a result, women have become extremely self-critical and guilty about how we are raising and have raised our children. When the question of homosexuality comes up, our guilt rises to new heights.

> "I have no problem being gay myself, but I don't want my children exposed. You know, in the 40's and 50's lesbians sent their children to boarding school to keep them away from the lifestyle. I don't think that was a bad idea."

> "If my children turn out to be gay, I just know my family, their father, the society will say it was my fault. I don't think being gay is a problem, but everyone else out there does. So I'm afraid of the effect my lesbianism will have on my children."

Having a lesbian parent is no more responsible for a child's choice of sexuality than is having heterosexual parents. Most of us had heterosexual parents and you can see what that did for us. The real question is, why will you be upset if your child is gay? If you are proud of your own lifestyle, then you can allow your children to choose their own sexuality also. At least they won't have to worry about being disowned—whatever they choose.

Some argue that it's not fair to bring children into a life that includes oppression. "It's okay if you're gay, but it's not right to bring children into a situation in which they might be ostracized." Following this reasoning to its extreme, Black people, disabled people, and poor people should not have children because of the oppression their children might encounter. The obvious though more difficult solution is to change society, not to give up our right to have children.

For single mothers, often the concern about how many partners have passed through your home is simple homophobia in disguise. Only you now the quality of your mothering, and it is not determined by the number of your sexual encounters.

Dealing with the homophobia of your children can be very painful; their denial is even more painful than rejection by our parents. Children's homophobia can range from a refusal to bring friends home to deliberate snubbing of your lover. Children, too, pick up the homophobia of the culture around them and must be educated away from it. Sometimes it's our own homophobia that influences them.

"I used to leave my lesbianism out of my home. My lovers never lived with me. I always went out to experience any of 'the life.' When I discovered that my adult children knew nothing good about lesbians I was shocked. When I brought my lesbianism into my home, the negative attitudes about lesbians were greatly reduced. They began to see me as more like them—having lovers, friends, etc."

Integrating our children fully into our lives and lesbian culture will allow them to see the joy and love that exists among lesbians.

Remember that you and your children are not enemies—if there *is* an enemy it is a culture that fears and hates us for being gay. Being on the same side with your children allows you to talk about your fears and work out compromises that everyone can feel good with.

"My guilt over my children hating that I was a lesbian was so great, I did everything I could to compensate. I finally realized that doing any sort of apologizing was only encouraging the thought that I was doing something 'wrong.' Now they don't like my lesbianism any better, but at least I don't feel responsible for that."

"In our home we decided to try a new approach. We decided to be on the same team so to speak. I would not threaten what they felt they needed in order to keep their friends, and they would not threaten what I felt I needed to keep a lover. We worked hard at compromising on different issues. For instance, I didn't kiss my lover in front of their friends. They didn't insult my lover with words or with silence."

Regardless of all the difficulties lesbian mothers face in creating a fulfilling sexual life, it is possible. The first and most important feeling must come from inside you; you must know that you have the right to have sex. *Work on the exercises in the homework that make sense to you, especially H-1 through H-3.* Motherhood and lesbian sexuality are not incompatible, simply difficult.

Sex And Sobriety

During my therapeutic work with lesbians, at any one time, at least half of my clientele are self-described as: 1) an addict in recovery, 2) the adult child of an addict (one or both of her parent figures was an addict), 3) a woman just discovering she is an addict, or 4) a woman who is learning that her partner is an addict.

Research has shown that thirty percent of the lesbian and gay male community is addicted to alcohol (Rofes, 1983). This percentage does not include those of us who abuse drugs such as cocaine, marijuana, speed, downers and hallucinogens. If, as is estimated, for every person who abuses alcohol or drugs, there are six more people—family, friends, co-workers, neighbors—whose lives are affected by this abuse, then most of us in the lesbian community must have our lives touched in some way by alcohol and/or drug abuse.

In the last few years most large cities have seen the start of gay Alcoholics Anonymous and Al-Anon (the AA associated Family Groups). In some places there are even lesbian AA and Al-Anon meetings, as well as treatment programs for women. If you or a loved one is affected by alcohol or drug abuse, there are places to get help.

If you are not sure whether alcohol or drug abuse is a problem for you, check out the two ways of knowing described in Appendix B. Abuse is not determined by the amount you ingest, but by your relationship to the substance or your relationship to someone who abuses the substance. You owe it to yourself to discover whether your chemical of choice *is* a choice or a habit.

If you think there has been little written on women's sexuality from our point of view, try to find information on the effect of addiction on women's sex lives. There is almost none. If you are a sober lesbian and have been looking for information on how your past addiction could be affecting your sex life now, probably you have been unable to find anything. Over the past eight years I have done much informal research on lesbians, sex and sobriety. In 1983, I conducted a formal survey of 274 sober lesbians who identified themselves as having been alcoholics or addicts at one time. Although the results of that survey have not been completely analyzed yet, much of what follows is taken from my own informal and formal research.

This chapter is applicable to any woman who is addicted to alcohol, street drugs, prescription drugs or food and to those of us addicted to addicts and the adrenalin high created by the drama of those relationships. Regardless of your "chemical" of choice, the process of addiction and sobriety is the same. Lesbians who are or have been associated with drug abuse or alcoholism often have specific sexual problems related to chemical use. The following covers some of the more common issues.

In an unpublished dissertation, Mickey Apter-Marsh (1982) studied sixty-one recovering alcoholic women with a minimum of one year continuous sobriety. During the first year of sobriety, most women experienced less ability to achieve orgasm than they had during their period of drinking. Anxiety over apparent "loss of sexuality" was common, but orgasmic function increased gradually over time. Apter-Marsh's findings seem further verified by the results of my own research with recovering alcoholic women. *Ninety-five percent of my sample reported changes in their sexual functioning as a result of sobriety.*

Few women going into recovery are prepared for the changes in their sex lives. In fact, there is no available information for the newly sober lesbian—or her partner(s)—on what changes will happen and how long they'll take. Although there is a general trend for sexual satisfaction to improve over the course of recovery, many of the women in my study experienced significant difficulties in their sex lives, especially in early sobriety. As we learn more about sexuality in the sober period and especially in new sobriety, we will know better how to support each other through this time.

The Body, Sex And Recovery

The effects of alcoholism on humans have been well documented. For in-depth information please see the bibliography (especially Forrest, 1983). Every organ system is damaged by the habitual ingestion of alcohol, as is the ability of the organ systems to interact in an effective and appropriate manner. Damage has been documented down to the cellular level in practicing alcoholics (Bennett, et al., 1983).

In our Western medical system, the central nervous system is considered the primary sex organ. It receives sensory input from genital or other stimulation and produces excitement, intense feelings and orgasm. Adequate functioning of the central nervous system, as well as the muscle and circulatory systems, are essential to sexual pleasure. For those of us who have been addicts, all these systems suffer function damage. Other physical problems may appear as well. Stomach and intestinal upsets, nausea, vomiting, diarrhea, ulcers, swollen liver, and pancreatitis are all common consequences of alcoholism. Our bodies are more susceptible to respiratory infections; our skin has low resistance to trauma and infection; our body's supply of calcium and magnesium is greatly depleted resulting in interference with muscle contractions, soreness, cramps, and more fragile bones; and the adrenal glands lose much of their normal functioning resulting in fatigue. Our sexual pleasure, interest and desire are not increased by any or all of these physical problems.

In recovery, there seems to be a gradual healing over the course of time. Healing may take years and, depending on the extent of original damage, full functioning may never be restored. The woman in recovery may first feel the effects of organ damage many months into sobriety and then begin to experience difficulties in sexual functioning.

In Chinese medicine, the kidneys and the adrenal glands, rather than the central nervous system, are the source of a person's life force and sex drive. And they are the two organs most affected by alcoholism. The alcoholic's kidneys and adrenals are weakened by poor general nutrition. The kidneys have had to filter increased toxins introduced by alcohol. The adrenal glands have been producing extra adrenalin in response to the stimulation of alcohol toxins. The entire system is under stress (Kushi, 1978).

Regardless of which system of medicine/health you follow, sexual functioning clearly suffers for all of us as a result of addiction. There may be no sexual desire because of general fatigue, lack of nerve function, decreased adrenalin, upset hormone balance or physical pain. Or you may find changes in your regular responses including lack of orgasms, slowed production of vaginal secretions, insensitivity to soft touching, or extreme discomfort upon physical contact.

Emotions, Sex And Recovery

When we begin recovery from alcoholism, we do so in the midst of a culture obsessed with sex. Personal status and self-esteem are connected with our view of our own sexual attractiveness and skill. At the same time, honest talk about sex is limited. Sex is usually discussed in the form of joking and "dirty" stories. As recovering addicts, we are surrounded by many fables and few facts about our own and others' sexuality.

Added to this confusion about sexuality is the general lack of interest in and support of sobriety. Your co-workers do not avidly listen while you describe a party where there was no alcohol or drug use. You, as a newly sober lesbian, may listen to hours of other people's drinking stories and then be criticized for "talking about nothing but sobriety." And you're probably not able to get more information about the long-term effects of sobriety—there is little. There is one book that is especially for lesbians in recovery and has some information on the long term effects, *Out From Under,* edited by Jean Swallow.

Most newly sober women have rarely or never had sex without the use of alcohol or drugs. Facing sex sober for the first time raises tremendous fear and anxiety. Fears of incompetence, inadequacy, intimacy and lack of control are common and frequently continue throughout the first year. The fear of losing your partner, losing your own sobriety, or never regaining an absent sex drive may be constant. The changing power dynamics in relationships brought about by sobriety can be confusing and anxiety producing. Experiencing genital intimacy without the use of a chemical "aid" may create so much anxiety that being sexual becomes an unpleasant or even impossible task. As a recovering addict, you may feel unable to perform sexually, unable to receive sexual attentions, or simply have no sexual desire at all. *There are many exercises in the homework chapter that may apply to your situation. SL-2 to SL-5 will address self-esteem. Relaxation can be helped by exercises R-1 thorugh R-6. The sections on desire and having sex should be explored and appropriate exercises tried.*

> "I almost wish my lover and I would break up. I'm so afraid she will want to have sex that I'd rather leave her than try."

> "Whenever I find myself going to bed at night, I break into cold sweats. I'm terrified of having sex."

> "I don't really remember the last years of having sex with partners. That feels so weird to say. I'm afraid some woman will question me about what sex has been like for me, so I just don't go out on dates."

Frequently the newly sober woman, frustrated by the difficulty of sober sexual intimacy, recounts the pleasant and exciting sexual experiences of her days of using drugs. If asked to examine the sexual encounters of that period closely, she often finds herself unable to remember specific details or individual incidents. Those she does recall may well have been unpleasant or unsatisfying . Regardless of the myths of our culture, habitual use of chemicals is simply not compatible with full sexual responsiveness.

The major street and prescription drugs that are expected to stimulate sexual activity can in fact do just the opposite. Alcohol, barbituates (downers), amphetamines (uppers), amyl nitrate (poppers), cocaine, marijuana—all may enhance sexual arousal or response under some conditions. But continued or excessive use of them creates sexual problems.

As a depressant, alcohol reduces physical responses to sexual activity and creates emotional depression. Barbituates are also depressants and reduce physical response, as well as cause depression and other more serious consequences. Amphetamines stimulate the central nervous system, eventually destroying nerves crucial to sexual response. Amyl nitrate opens blood vessels in the brain and the heart, causing dizziness and headaches. Taken excessively, it can actually cause heart failure. Cocaine stimulates the central nervous system, causing depression, irritability, and anxiety. Marijuana produces a a false sense of time, distorting one's view of sexual response and orgasm.

In addition to facing sex without chemical aids, many recovering women experience the resurfacing of memories previously lost to consciousness due to chemical use or as a psychological defense in childhood. In sobriety, it is common to remember earlier experiences of incest, sexual assault and rape. Incest seems to be especially prevalent in the alcoholic homes in which many of us who become adult alcoholics were raised (Meiselman, 1978). In sobriety, we have no numbing of the pain, powerlessness, and sense of violation that sexual intimacy often raises for the survivor of incest and sexual assault. Faced with this pain, we may consciously or unconsciously choose to pursue no sex life at all. *Work on exercises SL-2 and SL-4; also try working with yourself on G-1 through G-5 and S-1 through S-6.* Re-learning your own body's responses may be helpful in learning how to be sexual in sobriety.

> "When I drank, I never got freaked out when I was having sex. Now I have flashbacks to the times my father molested me. Sometimes I wish I could take one drink to stop my mind. But I know that might be the drink that would kill me so I don't."

> "I get too angry when I have sex sober. I keep thinking of the time I was raped. I never worked that experience through. I just used more drugs. Now five years later I have to go through it."

Clearer memories of past sexual behavior may also interfere with sexuality. During the period of alcoholic drinking, you may have engaged in sexual activities which in sobriety are no longer comfortable. Any variety of practices—oral sex, non-monogamy, s/m, casual sex—might be included here, as well as a particular choice of sexual partner or setting. Sex in the present, unrelated to these activities, may stimulate memories and bring up guilt and shame. You may find yourself avoiding past partners and not trusting new partners. There is sometimes a sense that your sexual partner can almost "mind-read" your "shameful" sexual history. In recovery, you may be uncertain about what activities *are* acceptable to you, may feel unable to pursue any sexual practice, or be confused by your aversion to activities that intellectually seem quite acceptable.

Whenever you are in a sexual situation which is frightening to you, stop the action. Simply tell your partner that you cannot go on. You may need to take your re-entry into sex slowly. *Read the section in the homework chapter on relaxation, sex alone or with a partner, and the one for incest and rape survivors (sections R, S, P, A, and AP).* Even if you are not a sexual abuse survivor, you may need the gradual movement into sex that is suggested in section A. Section P, sex with a partner, also provides some exercises to help you move slowly into partner genital contact. Go as slowly as you need to. You are healing from self-abuse and need recovery in all areas, including sex.

> "When I think about what I did when I was drinking and who I did it with—I guess I'm ashamed."

> "My biggest problem is that I don't really remember what I did with the last two women I was with when I was using drugs. I avoid them at community functions because I'm afraid what I did was awful."

Many newly sober women transfer their addictive energy to some other realm. One of the most common is compulsive sexual behavior. You may create the same kind of danger and risks by sexual behavior as you did through alcoholism. Sexual feelings may be seen as "out of your control;" they may just "happen to you;" you may feel you "have to act on them." I have seen newly sober women threaten their relationships with their lovers, their AA sponsors, and their support group by pursuing sexual attractions that seem totally inappropriate. Risking a job, school, attendance at AA meetings and emotional sobriety is common with sexual compulsiveness. Usually sexually obsessive feelings become identified with "love", which is used to justify all kinds of imprudent behavior. Often so much stress is created that the person returns to drinking to "cope". If your recovery is being hampered by sexual compulsiveness, it is important to look at the transfer of addictive energy and deal with it directly. There is an entire chapter in this book that deals with sexual addiction in more detail.

> "I know I'm on a run just like when I used drugs, but I have to get this woman out of my mind."

> "I know they tell you not to get involved the first year of recovery, but I am falling in love with my sponsor and I cannot stop myself from having sex."

> "If my lover waits while I have affairs, that will be great. If she can't take it, I'll just have to lose her. I want to have sex with this woman I just met. I know this isn't the last time I'll want to do that."

Our sexual and emotional growth stops at the age we started using. If you started using at sixteen, for example, then you probably have not developed any new sexual skills since then. Although chronologically you may be thirty-five, sexually and emotionally you have the skills of a sixteen-year-old. Lesbians in recovery must now pursue personal explorations of sexuality that others did in adolescence. Most of us feel that we should have finished our sexual explorations as teenagers; going through it as adults often feels like failure. While sexual changes occur throughout our lives (it's just that no one talks about them), it's also true that chemical abuse has cut you off from sexual experiences for a number of years. *Once again, work on exercise SL-4 in the homework chapter, then try S-1 through S-8.*

> "I feel like a jerk. I don't even really know where my clitoris is, let alone someone else's. I'm not about to tell that to a woman I go to bed with. I avoid sex."

> "Everyone says I was such a great lover while I used drugs. Well, what do I do now when I feel like I'm starting over?"

> "I feel like a kid. I don't know how to ask a woman out. I really don't know much what to do in bed. Or at least I don't think I do—maybe this is all I ever did."

Your sexual activity in sobriety may cease simply because there is so little acceptance for the kind of exploration necessary to become familiar with yourself as a sexual person. If you find yourself in that position, take courage and find partner(s) who are comfortable with your exploration. *Then work on exercises R-7 and R-8 and P-1 through P-7 in the homework chapter.*

The Co-Addict

People who choose addicts as partners are often themselves addicts, come from addicted homes, or need to be needed by someone worse off. Such people are called co-addicts. They enable the addict's addiction to continue by assuming their responsibilities and picking up the pieces. The lover who acts like a "mother" is caretaking another adult in an inappropriate manner. This, in turn, can take over the life of the co-addict.

Between women who are truly peers, mothering each other is an activity commonly passed back and forth. But mothering becomes a problem when the same person in the couple is always doing it or is doing it in inappropriate ways. For example, always doing her laundry because you've decided she won't get to it. Such a situation creates tremendous resentment. No one likes to be treated like a child most of the time nor does anyone like having to be responsible all the time.

> "I know that Violet hates for me to get her up in the morning. But I'm afraid that if she doesn't get to work on time I'll be left paying the rent again."

> "If Zoe asks me to do the dishes one more time, I'll throw them at her. Doesn't she get that I see the dishes need doing? I just don't do them on her time schedule."

In a martyr-like fashion, the co-addict "gives up her life" for the addict, getting "nothing in return" yet she keeps on doing the same behavior over and over again. She usually feels tied to her situation as if there were no way out. The anger that builds in both parties is enormous. When the addict refuses to go beyond the call of duty as the martyr has done so many times, the co-addict is furious. Meanwhile, the addict is faced with someone who will always sacrifice *more* no matter what; she feels defeated even before she begins.

> "I just want Hannah to notice one time all that I do for her. Is that too much to ask?"

> "I know that Joan has this notion that I'm lazy. I get paranoid that it's her racism coming out because I'm black and she's white. What's real is that I can't keep up with her. I swear she beats me home to do the housework so that she can complain that I didn't do it."

In yet another role, the co-addict as "manager" works out the addict's life for her. Regardless of the way her partner wants to plan her career, her clothing, even housework, the manager has a better way. Eventually the two are in an untenable situation with the addict feeling discounted and the manager feeling she has the only effective way of running a life that works.

> "Let's face it, my bills are always paid on time and Suzanne's aren't. I hate to put her down, but I do have a better system of saving."

> "Shawn even plans out my time for me, where we're going when and reminds me that I haven't seen a friend this week. I wish she would let me live my own life."

The common trait in all of these roles—mother, martyr, manager—is focusing on someone's life other than your own. The co-addict chooses, creates, and perpetuates a situation in which she is necessary. She becomes preoccupied with someone else's problems so she doesn't have to solve her own. In so doing, she gets validated by others as a wonderful, caring human being.

If you are a co-addict, you may find little support in the lesbian community for changing your behavior. Mothers, Martyrs and Managers are appreciated by community organizations and political action groups, as well as by friends. But even though co-addiction is so much more supported by the community than addiction, it doesn't make the behavior any healthier.

"Once I figured out that I was taking care of Linda so that I would look like a wonderful wife, I couldn't believe it. I thought I was so needed. Well, she left me and lives on her own and as far as I know she isn't starving to death. Sometimes I think I'm only here to care for someone else."

"I'd been brought up to be the perfect woman. I didn't know what my needs were, so it was easier to second guess what I thought Habiba needed. I just wish someone was giving me all I was giving them. Actually, I wish I could give me all that."

In our culture there is not much difference between the socially approved roles for women and the roles of the co-addict. Women are trained in, encouraged, and approved of for being co-addicts. Lesbians are no exception. It is important, however, to consider the sexism of assuming that all of this behavior is negative. We must find a balance between when the traditional work of a woman is negative for her and debilitating to those around her and when a woman is being the loving, caring person that we are indeed attracted to. We can, of course, support our womanness, but only to the extent that it does not disable us or those we're involved with.

Being sexual partners with a co-addict puts a negative mood on any couple's sexual life. Who wants to be sexual with someone who is treating you like a child, a villian or an idiot? Unwinding the thread that binds the co-addict and addict together can be very difficult and complicated. If you are half of such a relationship, hopefully the next section will help.

Sexual Issues With Addict/Co-Addict Couples

Addict/Co-Addict relationships can be changed, but doing so is a difficult, time-consuming and patience-exhausting project.

Both of you must want the relationship to continue, must want to change your patterns, and must want to take responsibility for your part in the working of the relationship. Even with desire and effort, many couples do not survive the first two years of recovery. Without work on our addictive/co-addictive behaviors, most of us are likely to move on to the next relationship and repeat the same patterns. Giving up the ways of the past is necessary to creating a healthy relationship.

Often the first order of business for the addict/co-addict couple is to learn to survive sober. When survival is the main issue, sexual issues often do not come up for at least six months. If the recovering addict has lost her desire for sex, it makes no sense to work on sexual issues until her desire has returned. It is important for both of you to remember that during the first two years of sobriety, many women have a period of not feeling sexual at all as well as losing the ability to have orgasms.

Although survival is the first order of business, anger and resentment will also need to be expressed and dealt with. Often, sex becomes the focal point through which anger gets expressed.

> "I just hate the way she comes after me all the time. She keeps thinking that if we have sex, I'll forget all the nights she was out and making me worry sick."

> "Now that I'm sober, she just thinks I ought to want to have sex all the time. I'm sick of sex. In fact, I'm just plain sick; sex is the last thing I want."

> "Our sex life reminds me of what our relationship was like when she was shooting dope. I do all the giving and she does all the taking. She says it's because I take too long to have an orgasm. She's too tired now that she's sober."

Learning to live sober involves learning how to have sex sober, learning how to allow an intimacy that chemicals formerly protected you from, and learning how to wait through the recovery period. *Exercise P-5 in the homework section may be helpful in this process.*

"The first year of her recovery I found that I was just gritting my teeth saying 'I just need to hang on.' I wanted our sex life to be better, but I was sick of waiting—always waiting—for her."

"After being sober for one year, I finally had the nerve to go to bed with someone. Sex was scary, but I was *there* for one of the first times in my life."

"Our sex life as a couple improved after we were both able to look at our different sides of recovery. I had to learn to take responsibility for being an adult. She had to learn to stop living my life for me. It took us both a while, but having sex with an equal is wonderful."

Recovery is made more difficult by the fact that both partners are physically and emotionally exhausted by the dramatic lifestyle of addiction. Both parties have worn out their adrenal glands whether through the use of chemicals or by running two lives. At a time when both parties need each other most, each has very little to give and a lot of resentment and anger built up. Changing patterns requires the belief that there is something to be gained by living differently. *Exercises PL-1, PL-3, and PL-4 can help you with these changes.*

"Because I never did pay the bills I was afraid I wouldn't be able to do it right. I had visions of the electricity being turned off. I just had to bite the bullet and say I would do it anyway."

"I had to learn to say no to my lover when she asked if I would mind doing her chores around the house. I had done her chores too often in the past. I always felt bad though, every time I said no."

Low self-esteem and guilt often get in the way of change. Taking responsibility for creating a new relationship without the addict/co-addictive dynamic is frightening but it can also be very exciting. Changes in your sex life can be quite positive. Sobriety can bring a new you to your sexual experience—a you who is more conscious, has more sensitivity and is a more willing participant. Changes like that are worth it!

Sex And Aging

Despite the very real evidence that women live full lives well into their nineties, our culture still believes that women over forty are "over the hill." Our concept of aging is an entirely negative one which is reflected in our language. Derogatory phrases such as, "little old lady," "she's too old to understand," "I can't believe someone her age can do that" indicate younger people's ageism, with its devaluation of older women. It's impossible for us not to have internalized these messages, which are repeated constantly in younger women's actions.

> "My lover is 60 and I am 75 and when young women talk to us, they only look at my lover. She's seen almost as my caretaker, as if I can't hold my own or don't have anything to contribute because of my age."

> "When I look at women in their sixties, all I think of is my mother. I don't swear in front of them; I don't ask their opinions. I actually know it's not true, but I act like I know more than they do and can do more 'cause I'm 30."

The time frame when "older" occurs seems to depend upon how old you are. To teenagers twenty-five seems old; when we hit twenty-five, old gets pushed to forty; and when we're forty, it's those sixty-year-olds who are old. This way of thinking can continue well after our sixties, an indication of the general denial of aging in our culture. None of us thinks we're aging; only those who are ten or twenty years older than we are, are aging. Actually the process of aging is as personal as the process of starting to menstruate and begins when we are born.

The typical identification of becoming the older woman at the scary age of forty, along with the cessation of menstruation, generally has less effect on lesbians. Most lesbians are not so identified with their childbearing ability or with the end of the primary mothering role as heterosexual women are.

It is definitely possible to view aging as positive rather than negative. As we begin to age, we have more experience to bring to bear on the challenges of living. Very few of us would have any interest in repeating an age we've already passed. Most of us recognize that the more we live, the more full we are. Aging can be seen as the gift of time, not an enemy. If we don't listen to society's messages about us, our lives are no less vital and compelling as we age.

Aging definitely has an effect on sex and it's usually positive. As you have more experience with sex you get better at it. You know more what pleases you. Simply having sex more times gives us more knowledge about our bodies and the processes they go through. We also know better how to please our partners as there has been more experience with lovemaking. Whether we have learned this with one partner or with a series of partners, the sheer fact of experience contributes to your knowledge of how to have a good sex life.

In 1978, Marcy Adelman conducted a study of twenty-five women over sixty who identified as lesbian. She matched them in age, occupation, education, etc. with twenty-five heterosexual women. All of the lesbians were serially monogamous and three distinct relationship patterns emerged. One third of the lesbian women regularly had relationships that lasted two to three years. Another third regularly had relationships that lasted seven to ten years. And the rest of the women had relationships of twenty to thirty years.

None of the women had casual sex partners after she became sixty. For all the lesbians, sex became less important and less frequent as they aged. However, all the lesbians still masturbated and were still sexually active with partners. Most had sex an average of three times a month, which is comparable to, or more frequent than, sex reported by lesbian couples of all ages. Whatever pattern of sex life each had, the women over 60 all reported very high satisfaction.

As far as I know this is the only study on older lesbians that asked direct sexual questions. Very little is known about the sexual functioning of older lesbians. Here's another area of knowledge in which the contributions of those of us who are older are needed.

Being a lesbian before 1970 was significantly different than it has been for those of us who came out in the last fifteen years. The difference has been created by the feminist movement, which has gone a long way towards making lesbian relationships legitimate.

> "Those 'in the life' always were gathered in ugly bars and terrible parts of town. We were arrested sometimes for not wearing 'female' clothes. We were constantly hiding and feeling like there was something wrong with us."

> "Sex was a difficult proposition. You had to find someone who you were attracted to in this secret society. I sometimes just had sex with a woman because she and I were both available, not because we were really attracted to each other. Sex wasn't always the greatest."

> "Hiding passion was so painful. It was difficult to drop that hiding even in the safety of your own bedroom."

Although our relationships are still viewed as unacceptable, we do not endure the kind of oppression that existed in the forties and fifties.

> "I was from the era when no one ever told their families about their lesbianism. It was very painful for Lucy and me. When she went into a nursing home, her family kept me from seeing her. I never got over leaving her there by herself."

Obviously, such intense repression created severe sexual stress. Seeking each other out was dangerous.

"Even finding each other in the 1940's and 50's was next to impossible. Once we did, getting into a sexual scene was often very frightening. You never knew who would find out."

Even though the era was repressive, women still came out and lesbians still had relationships. Obviously, there was a great deal that was positive in the "life" and in lesbian relationships. Women still felt lesbianism worth risking repression for.

"Being a lesbian in the 40's was such an exciting proposition. We were a true underground, hiding from the straight world. No one thought it could ever be different, so we didn't really lament it. Leading a double life was thought of as superior—straight people couldn't have survived what we survived."

"Even though it was hard being a lesbian before the 70's there was no other way to be for most of us. We loved being with women and we would go through anything to be able to do just that."

Although not all pre-1970 lesbians were into roles, "butch/femme" roles were one way lesbians created to recognize each other and facilitiate their relating. Whether you were part of a butch/femme scene was affected by when and where you came out, and to what racial, class or social grouping you belonged.

For butch/femme lesbians, the butch role was the more active and often included giving pleasure to the femme by making love *to* her, without being made love to. As women moved to new areas or changed in other ways, they sometimes moved into the other role. If you happened to fall in love with someone more butch than you, you might turn femme. If women did not identify as either butch or femme, they used the word "ki-ki" to label themselves.

Often those of us who didn't live through the butch/femme era don't see the survival value of roles. We forget that butch women didn't want to be men; they wanted to be allowed as women to have characteristics arbitrarily assigned to men. Femmes didn't want to be with men, but they still wanted to develop the side arbitrarily assigned to women.

"The first time I went into a gay bar, I was asked if I was butch or femme. I didn't really know what that meant, so I said butch. Luckily I liked that role although I'm sure I could have pleaded ignorance if I wanted to change."

"Having roles made everything easy. No one had to worry about who should ask who to dance. The butches asked the femmes. No one had to worry about who initiated sex. The butches took care or that. Actually, I don't know how it's done today, it must not go very smoothly."

"I have always been a femme and I feel like I am a terrible lesbian to the younger generation. I feel very comfortable in this position and don't like being told I should be out learning how to be both roles now. I'm sixty-three years old. I've been with my roommate for thirty years, and I have no intention of changing."

Butch/femme was not the only way that women, prior to 1970, related to one another. There were many lesbians who saw themselves as androgynous. They both shared all household tasks, worked many types of jobs, and dressed however they pleased. Often, the lifestyle you were engaged in as a lesbian was primarily determined by the group of people you came out with.

"Ada and I have lived together for 25 years. We always wore each other's clothes, worked at the same kind of job and shared the housework. I think it's ageist to assume all women over 50 were 'into' roles. There are plenty of young women into roles in 1984. Plenty of women before 1970 were not."

Whatever has been your form of sexual activity through the years, age brings its own particular influence to sex. Many women

197

find that as we age, sex becomes more pleasurable. We don't feel as rushed, we are able to relax into the activity and have more fun. We are not as ego involved as when we were younger; we have learned that we are more than our sex lives. We are often not so driven around our sexuality; we don't need to be on "the make" anymore. Sex finally becomes what it is: pleasurable body contact, not so fraught with symbolism. You know that one night of bad sex does not break a romance. You also are experienced at making your sex life and that of your partner a joyous occasion. If you do not find yourself having the sex life you want, make a commitment to yourself that you're going to have an active sex life. "Active" can mean whatever you want it to mean. Once a year, once a month, once a week, once a day. How often is up to you. Whether you create this "active" sex life with yourself, with partners or both is not important. Not how often, but that it's chosen and acted upon is essential. An active sex life is possible when you find the motivation within yourself and when you decide that you're an important enough person to make a commitment to.

The most dramatic changes in your body after forty occur with menopause. As less estrogen and progesterone are produced, the menstrual cycle stops and you go through concurrent physical and emotional changes. Emotional effects for some women can include mood swings, hot flashes, depression, irritability and anxiety. Your physical and emotional discomfort may equal your worst-ever period. And added to this, you never know when to expect these symptoms, as they occur irregularly. Sometimes spotting or bleeding starts up again after months of cessation; you may suddenly get depressed without having the physical signs of a period. Having sexual experience can be pretty scary if you can't predict how you're going to feel. The challenge of menopause is learning to live with a body that frequently is out of your control.

> "I never know where I'll be when I break out in a sweat. I wish I knew when a hot flash or mood swing was coming. It makes me want to hide until this whole process is over."

> "When I had periods, I hated them. Now I hate the process of menopause worse. I can't wait until

my body has adjusted and then I can predict my behavior again."

Both physical and emotional symptoms may keep you from having sex whenever you want it. Letting a possible sexual partner know what specific symptoms, if any, your menopause has caused can greatly alleviate your tension. Let her know possible symptoms and how they affect you and your behavior.

"Women my age don't even have to be told when I'm having a hot flash. They understand. I feel embarrassed with younger women; often, they won't even meet my eye. That's one of the reasons I stay with women my age."

"I've found that practically making a formal announcement on a first date that I am going through menopause creates such freedom. If the woman I am with hasn't gone through it, I'm happy to answer any questions. If she has gone through it, we get to exchange stories. There is some point of conversation created right from the start."

There are many women who go through menopause with no physical or emotional symptoms at all or very few. They breeze through feeling relief at not having periods anymore.

"I love menopause. I have never felt better in my life. I don't worry about bleeding, I don't worry about cramps; I don't worry about when I can have sex. I feel like a free woman."

"Menopause is one of the greatest bonuses of growing older."

Many women experience a stopping of sexual desire during menopause. They simply do not feel the urge to have sex. Desire may take some time to return. But once your body becomes adjusted to hormonal changes, desire will come back.

"I was so afraid when I went through menopause and wanted to have nothing sexually to do with Gretta after 37 years. I just thought: 'ok now we're old ladies and we'll get separate bedrooms.' Well, I hung in there and my sex drive did come back. It took almost three years though. A long three years. We kept having sex, but it wasn't fun for me like it had been.''

If you're glad to have sex out of your life, honor that in yourself. If you want to have sex in your life, try exercises D-1, D-3, and D-4. If you have a partner, try DP-1, DP-2 and DP-3. Remember, you do not have to be physically excited to have sex. You can engage in sexual activity solely because of your willingness to do so.

As your hormone levels taper off, you may experience a change in your vaginal walls. The natural lubrication will decrease; the tissue may become more brittle, delicate and thin. Using a lubricant can be very helpful. Vegetable oil, unscented massage oil, or K-Y jelly are fine; don't use anything with a scent or a vaseline base. Adding lubrication can also remedy the problem of inserted objects sticking to the walls of your vagina. You will have to let go of gauging your arousal by how "wet" your vagina is and let your partner(s) know to do the same. For some women, greater lubrication returns after menopause.

"If you don't want to lose it, use it" applies to continuing to have an active sex life. The longer you go without having sex, the harder it is to initiate sex the next time. Also, it's more difficult for your brain, nerves and muscles to respond. As in all physical responses, exercise makes the response easier. It is never too late to become more sexually responsive.

"What I found with aging is that I have become sensitive in places that I never thought would be erogenous zones. Having my neck touched is amazingly erotic now.''

"Having oral sex with no teeth is incredible, both for me and for Sonia. I never thought I would love to have false teeth. But better sex makes a great consolation prize.''

A woman of any age can think about improving or changing her sex life. If you have found that you want to expand or change any of your usual sexual activities, this next section deals with that process. Remember that changing your sex life does not have to mean changing your whole self and relearning how to live. Often it can simply mean changing how you stimulate your own or your partner's clitoris. It may mean wanting to have oral sex for the first time or being more active or having a more varied repertoire. Changing patterns of long standing is difficult regardless of our age, but it's not impossible. Do not assume you can't do it; all of us are changing all the time. Make sure you read the chapter on couple dynamics, as there is great information there if you're in a couple.

> "When Kip and I got together in 1955, it was clear I was a femme. Now I want to be more aggressive sexually, but Kip won't hear of it."

> "I was raised in a time when women were not supposed to deal consciously with sex. I want to change some of my sex activity, and I'm not sure how to do that."

Begin by discussing sex with your partner in a non-sexual setting. Let her know what you're feeling, what you'd like to change, what you'd like to move toward. Ask her if she'd be willing to embark on a sexual adventure with you.

If your partner is a longterm one, she may react with defensiveness, as if you're criticizing her sexual practices. Defensiveness around changing sexual patterns can occur in any longterm relationship, not just the relationships of older women. Let your partner know that at one time the sex you had together was fulfilling, but that you need a change. Assure her that wanting something different does not reflect negatively on her. Speak of what you need in positive terms.

Try homework exercises C-1, C-4 and C-5, using how you each feel about your sex life as the topic. Try relaxation exercises R-1, R-2, R-5, R-6 and R-7. If any of the other exercises feel especially appropriate, try them. Look through the homework section on genitals together and do all the exercises you both feel comfortable with. PG-2 is especially important, then try P-1 through P-5, and any after that that are applicable.

Working on changing sexual patterns without a longterm partner can be more difficult. If, like most lesbians, you aren't comfortable talking about sex, don't have casual sex, and aren't assertive about getting sex, you may feel overwhelmed trying to change with a new partner. Changing the way you have sex with yourself can be the first step. *Work on homework sections G-1 through G-9 S-1 through S-6, R-1 through R-4, O-1 through O-7.* If you see any other homework sections that apply to you, try them.

Sex and Youth

The most important information you can have about being a lesbian under twenty-one is that you are not alone. There are hundreds of thousands of us out here, recognizing ourselves as lesbian. And it's important for us to remember we are sane; we are sexually normal and healthy and that we don't need to fear a lifetime of loneliness. What has been true for most lesbians is also true for us; we will find a good life only if we follow our hearts. Trying to force ourselves to be with men will not create a loving life for us, while improving our loving connection with women of all ages *will* help. Being a lesbian isn't strange; it's the ideas that the mainstream society has made up about us that are strange.

One of the most difficult facts about being a lesbian under twenty-one is that no one considers us adults—not the legal system, our parents, employers or schools. Our rights are severely curtailed because of our age. In addition, we are invisible as sexual people. Most other people our age are heterosexual and their homophobia usually prevents them from recognizing or supporting our lesbianism.

In reality there are many girls who recognized our own lesbianism (even if we didn't have a word for it) from the time we were very young. Certainly by the time we got to be teenagers, we started learning what makes us feel good sexually. Those people who say that a young woman cannot figure out her sexual preference are just plain wrong. Those who waited until they were adults to come out have said they just never had the courage, awareness or support to recognize their attraction to girls and to call it what it was.

"I thought I would go crazy every time my
friends at school started talking about boys they love.

It's not that I thought they were creepy, it's just that
I couldn't say what I felt about Susan."

But even if we are out, or if others do recognize our lesbianism,
we are usually under intense pressure from others our age to
conform.

"Everyone knows I'm a lesbian. I'm put down
all the time. School is like going to hell everyday and
I can't tell my parents why I hate it so much."

The pressure to conform is overriding in every area of our lives,
but for most of us, it's most intense around sexuality. Whether you
find yourself ignored or ostracized, maintaining your sexual identity will take a lot of courage.

Unfortunately, turning to parents or other straight adults for
support and guidance may be less than helpful. Parents are notorious-
ly well-known for trying to insure that their children grow up happy. And being different in any way is often seen as a barrier to hap-
piness. Living with people who do not approve of your sexuality
can vary from tense to a living hell. Some parents have sent their
daughters in for psychological counseling to therapize us out of our
orientation.

"My parents forced me to go to this male shrink
because they thought I was nuts. It was just because
I wanted to date another girl—not boys. The shrink
gave me medicine that was supposed to calm my
nerves. I wasn't nervous. My parents were. I told them
they should go to the shrink. They didn't like that
much."

If this has happened to you or is happening to you, just
rememeber that it doesn't work. Changing people's sexual orientation is very difficult, almost impossible, and many studies have
documented a high failure rate for this type of therapy (see *The
Homosexual Matrix*). Try to hold onto your self-respect and self-
esteem although they may take a lot of battering from an unsym-
pathetic counselor.

Some parents may try to directly intimidate or harrass you into being heterosexual. They may lie to you about the lesbian lifestyle,

about lesbian sexuality, about the degradation inherent in your future. They may even threaten you.

> "My parents told me they would have me arrested if I kept seeing my lover. We have lots of fights over my being a lesbian."

Sometimes both counseling and intimidation are combined. This would be true for those of us confined to a mental institution or given shock treatments.

> "When I was 16, my parents sent me to a shrink and I even had shock treatment. It never changed my mind about my being a lesbian. If anything, it made me even stronger."

In all of these situations it takes tremendous courage to follow your heart. Give yourself credit for persevering through a very difficult situation.

On the other hand, parents and/or other adults are sometimes completely oblivious to our sexuality. Such obliviousness probably includes elements of homophobia, sexism and ageism. It may never occur to adults that we could possibly be lesbians. All of their homophobia, prejudice and stereotypes get in the way. "A nice girl like you!" They probably also assume women have no sexuality apart from men, so if we're not seeing men, well—. And certainly not least of all, they probably think that sexuality automatically appears sometime *after* twenty-one, when we're "really ready for it and able to handle it."

The frustration and pain of not having our parents and other adults see us for who we are is sometimes offset by the sexual freedom some of us experience by being ignored.

> "If sex between me and Kathy got any hotter we would burn the sheets. My straight girlfriends don't know what they're missing. For one thing, we get to spend the night together and no one even suspects that we have sex."

There are some of us who enjoy the support of our peers, parents and schools. This may seem impossible to you, but it can happen. In San Francisco, there is a high school that has a teenage lesbian/gay group as a recognized school-sponsored activity. The gay students often speak at other high schools to educate teachers, students and parents about their lifestyle. There are many young women who have come out to their parents and after a period of problems, the parents see that nothing is going to change and try to accept their daughter.

> "I know I'm lucky. I have parents who love me no matter what. I am a lesbian and they know it. At first they were scared I'd be hurt. I told them what would hurt me most was if they stopped loving me. They have stood by me all the way."

> "My school has a club for young gays. I know this is special because of where I live. Just having that group to go to once a week gives me courage to sneak around my parents and straight friends to keep doing what makes me feel good—loving Betsy."

Your next attempt to find support and validation will probably be in the lesbian community. After attempts with heterosexual friends, parents, and other adults, the lesbian community may appear to be your saving grace. Unfortunately, the lesbian community is as riddled with ageism, sexism and homophobia as the world at large. Ageism in the lesbian community may start with women expressing their fear of corrupting a minor. The assumption here is that we do not know ourselves or our sexuality, that we can be seduced, misled or "changed" by an older, more experienced lesbian.

This assumption relates to a number of sexual myths about younger women. Even though they are contradictory, all of these myths seem to be prevalent in the lesbian community at the same time. One is that a teenage lesbian is just going through a phase, that we won't *really* know whether we're lesbians until we are twenty-one. According to this myth, it's impossible to "come out" before you're twenty-one; before then we're considered too young to have any sure knowledge of our desires.

> "When I told my mom that I thought my teacher in eighth grade was the most gorgeous person I had

ever seen, she didn't realize I meant I was in love with a woman. I'm in high school now, and I am in love with my best girlfriend. I guess that makes me a lesbian. I always thought other girls were cuter than boys."

Many of us recognized our sexual attraction to girls as soon as we were old enough to notice other people. All of us are sexual from birth and can identify who we are attracted to throughout our lives. There is no magic age at which you "become" a lesbian.

Other myths say that young women are hyper-sexual. First we're seen as devoid of sexuality, then we're seen as more sexual than older women. This is the way myths work.

"I'm a 13-year-old lesbian. I read all the time about how teenagers have sex all the time. Well, I don't know who the newspaper knows, but none of my friends are having sex."

In fact, there is as much variation in sexual practice among younger women as among any other women. Some of us are very regularly sexual; some are not. Generalizations based on age can't be supported.

The effect of these myths is to separate us from other women. The sexuality of young women is seen as different, not understandable, a mystery.

"Sometimes I get really mad listening to all this stuff about lesbian community. I feel totally left out. No woman wants to even know me because I'm 'only' 16. I can't help it that I'm a teenager. What I need is support. I'm not looking for another mother. I'm looking for other lesbians."

Some of these attitudes are a reflection of the ageist mainstream attitude that younger is littler—and less: less wise, less responsible, less experienced. But like most sterotypes, it cuts both ways: the mainstream also glorifies younger people (especially younger boys/men). In part, some of the attitudes can be seen as a reaction to the glorification of boys by the heterosexual and gay male communities. It's as if lesbians have seen the over-emphasis on being young in the rest of the culture and have done just the opposite—placed a negative value on being young. But regardless of the reason, it is especially painful not to be valued by our lesbian community.

In addition to the stereotypes, there are some other considerations for lesbians over 21 being sexually involved with those of us who are younger. In most states, there are laws which consider adults having sex with someone under the age of 18 to be statutory rape. And since it is generally (wrongly) believed that lesbians increase our "ranks" by soliciting and seducing young women, many lesbians are wary of incurring homophobic reprisals (economic and legal) for "seduction." The fact is, that most of us who are having sex with women older than ourselves are doing so because we really want to. The culture certainly makes it hard enough to be a lesbian at all, so unless we are highly motivated from the inside, it is hard to be sexual with women over any length of time. But because women over twenty-one are legally seen as the "responsible" one, many wait to be sexual with women who are of "legal" age.

In addition to these legal concerns, we younger women have some concerns too. There may be a marked power imbalance in sexual relationships with a big age difference. These are real considerations that complicate the possible sexual relationships between women of different ages.

This leads to one of the main problems for those of us who are younger. How do we find each other? Because we are not of legal age to go to the bars, most socializing is inaccessible. Bars are often the only (or at least primary) place where women have traditionally met, danced, flirted and made sexual overtures. Although there are beginning to be other places to congregate—bookstores, coffeehouses, poetry readings, concerts, etc—none of these situations is overtly sexual, so your sexuality will again be minimized. Even aside from bars, lesbian organizations often discourage us from joining out of fear or ageism.

What we can do is seek out groups for lesbians under twenty-one. March in the under twenty-one contingent of your Gay Pride Parade. Look for announcements of groups activities like softball teams in co-ops, health clinics and on community bulletin boards. Attend women's concerts, readings and sports events. You have a right to express your sexuality and to be a part of the lesbian community.

Most of us meet one another through school and community activities. But tentatively approaching peers you think might be lesbian is pretty frightening.

> "I just knew Abigail was into girls too. I don't know how I knew, it was just a feeling. When she never had a date with a boy, I got even more convinced. Well, I finally asked her to go to a concert with me. I just kept making remarks about how boys made me sick. She got the picture and put her hand on my knee. I was so thrilled I could hardly breathe. Then we went driving around after the concert and went and parked and started to make out. It was a dream come true!"

> "Somehow we found each other. I don't really know how it happened, but I found myself in a group of teenagers who were all gay. We got the guys to take us out once in a while to please our parents, then we would meet up with another couple and the girls would go with the girls and the boys with the boys. It was great."

> "I love having Becky spend the night. Our parents don't get it, and she and I have fun all night sometimes."

For those of us able to find a lover—so far, so good, but obviously, the pressure, tension and frustration we experience with our peer group, our parents and the lesbian community doesn't bode well for good, relaxed, uninhibited sex. It is hard to be open when disapproval is lurking around every corner.

Where to have sex is a major problem for most teenagers and even more so for us. Whether in the car, in our parents' house, or in a park or secluded place, there is always the fear of being caught. Sneaking around, being secretive and having to be very quiet isn't always conducive to good sex. Privacy may be one of the biggest obstacles in our sexual lives.

> "Trying to have sex in a car all the time is awful. Especially because Mary and I can't go where all the

other teenagers do. When the cops find my straight friends they just sort of laugh. If they found us, we'd probably be arrested."

Being sexual at home often isn't a much better alternative.

> "No way can I totally relax while I am doing it with Lisa. I'm always afraid my mom is going to walk in on us."

Lack of privacy may also affect your ability to talk to each other openly about what you like, how it feels, what you want now. Coupled with the disapproval you may feel from all sides, communication about sex can be very problematic. "Doing it" in the dark, as quickly as possible, with as little movement or noise as possible may carry over to the daytime.

> "Adelle and I never made a sound when we had sex. I couldn't tell what felt good to her and what didn't. When it was daylight, I felt too embarrassed to ask. She left me for another girl and I never have known if it was because she didn't like how we made love."

Don't give up; even though our situation is discouraging, it's not impossible and parts of it are great. And, as opposed to our heterosexual friends, we never have to worry about getting pregnant.

> "When I hear my dad's footsteps down the hall I'm sure Patty's mom found some love note from me, called him and he's coming to bust us. That just gets us turned on more. We even make up fantasies about what it would be like if they told us we couldn't see each other again. Like doing it in the girls' restroom at school."

> "I love having sex with my girlfriend. I'll tell you it beats having to go out with boys."

A final note to this chapter, all of the information about sex in this book is applicable to us. Our age doesn't make us different sexually from any other women. The only verified difference is that it seems easier for women to have orgasms the older they get. We don't know the reasons why. *If that's the case for you, work with the exercises in the homework chapter O-1 through O-7 and OP-1 through OP-7.* The orgasm chapters and Lonnie Barbach's *For Yourself: Fulfillment of Female Sexuality* can also help.

You have a right to full, satisfying sexual experience and to clear, informative sexual literature. Don't let the age oppression of this culture deter you.

V. Be Your Own Camp Director:

The Homework Section

The Homework Exercises

Homework

The homework exercises described in this chapter are powerful and effective tools. I have used them in various combinations with hundreds of lesbians and have seen remarkable changes in expressions of sexuality. All of us have issues around communicating with a lover, or around sexual concerns at various times in our lives. Some of these exercises may be useful to you at one time, some at another. But the exercises alone provide no solutions and they most certainly will not "cure" you of sexual distress. They do provide a framework within which you can begin to look at your own individual needs around sexuality; a better understanding of your needs can lead towards significant changes in your feelings and behavior. The task of making these changes involves some hard work, however, and that work will be your responsibility.

Some History

In the 1950's, when pioneer sex therapists William Masters and Virginia Johnson first began their work, they were looked at with some dismay by members of the professional community. They shocked physicians, therapists and people in general with their exacting methods of research, which included observation of many heterosexual couples engaging in acts of sexual intercourse. Their significant contributions included the concept of behaviorally oriented exercises ("homework") designed to improve sexual functioning, and many of these exercises continue in wide use today. There were problems with their methods, however, not the least of which was their exclusivity: Masters and Johnson worked only with heterosexual couples who could afford to spend two full weeks at their clinic in St. Louis, pay hotel and food costs, and meet the high fees of their elaborate treatment program.

Helen Singer Kaplan, a sex therapist at Cornell University, working in East Harlem, developed a somewhat different approach to treatment. She worked with many working class and poor people and saw couples weekly (or less often) over a longer period of time. Since husbands were often working and unable to attend sessions, or were disinterested in the therapy altogether, she frequently saw women alone. She continued to use behavioral techniques in her exercises, but also looked to deeper personal issues when the behavioral approaches did not work. She has done considerable work with what she calls "disorders of sexual desire" and was the first major sex therapist to promote therapy addresssing the issues of people who simply were not interested in sex. She unfortunately has a very traditional psychological attitude towards lesbians and her treatments are certainly not designed to enhance lesbian sexuality.

Lonnie Barbach, coming into the sex therapy field more recently, worked specifically with pre-orgasmic women. She broke significantly from the traditions of previous therapists by working with women in women-only groups and seeing many women who were not in committed couples or relationships. She emphasizes the necessity of women getting in touch with their own sexual needs (rather than those of their partners) and taking responsibility for their own sexual fulfillment. She has had a remarkably high success rate.

Therapy for Lesbians

All of the major sex therapists have designed treatments for heterosexuals. They have not considered the unique needs of lesbians in sex therapy.

There are a few concerns that I consider are imperative:

1.) The first is to consider the sexual problems in the political and social context of society. That is, there must be some knowledge on the part of the therapist that the homophobia of the culture, in and of itself, creates tremendous pressure on lesbians and thus affects our sex lives.

2.) The therapist her (or him) self must not believe that the basic problem is lesbianism.

3.) The therapist must understand that two women having a sexual life together have a different rhythm and pattern than gay or heterosexual couples. Their own definition of a good sex life must be explored in detail, and the pressure lesbians feel from the culture to conform to male sexual standards must be acknowledged.

4.) Female standards of erotica and sexual attraction must be accepted.

5.) If there is a lesbian sexual counselor in your area I urge you to see her. There are, of course, heterosexual counselors that can deal with lesbian sexual issues very well. It is important that the women involved interview whomever they choose as a counselor, to find out what she (or he) sees as potential issues that may come up because the clients are lesbians. Ask the therapist if she is willing to consider the questions above. You may also want to refer to *The Lavender Couch*, a book by Marny Hall that addresses the issue of gays choosing a therapist.

The exercises that follow are designed specifically for use by lesbians. Many of them are adaptations of exercises used by other sex therapists. Some I have developed personally over years of working with lesbians. All have been successful in my experience when they are properly practiced.

How To Do The Exercises

This chapter is to be used in conjunction with the other chapters in the book. The following exercises are suggestions that you may want to try to help you with any particular sexual problem that you have. You may want to look through these in an attempt to find something that will relate to what you are feeling upset with in your own life. Or you may rather go back to a chapter that addresses those issues and from the reading discover which "homework" assignments may be suggested.

The reason the following is called "homework" is because it is exactly that. Work that is to be done in your home. Work that only you can do. This section is written so that you may take concrete action with problems you face. You will not have to just read the facts and information written in the rest of the text. You will be able to take a shot at lifting the frustration you feel towards your sexual concerns.

These are just suggestions. They are not the answer to every sexual problem. They may need to be altered to your specifications. Do not let the fact that they are written down keep you from altering them in a manner that works for you. If we were talking, we would work out something tailored to your surroundings, your lifestyle and your particular problem. We would together alter the homework exercises according to how they work for you. Make sure that you know what you feel as you are doing the work. Do not try to second guess how it should be coming out.

The Exercises

Communication Between Lovers:
Exercises C-1 to C-5

Do not make any of these exercises into a marathon. Work at it for only twenty minutes. Just as your muscles get tired, so will your mind and emotions from exercising them too much. It can set up a negative attachment ("I don't want to do that again, last time we did, I was up until three in the morning."). Make sure after the exercise that you take a break from one another and that you do not discuss the material when you are physically back together.

Also, do not do the work just before you are going to bed. This can help to set up negative feelings about bed. You may want to process a lot after the actual time of the exercise, and bed is not always the best place. This can make later sexual encounters there difficult. The purpose of any of these exercises is to enhance your relationships to friends and lovers, and to make your sexual life more full.

C-1: Equal Time
If you are having an argument, use this exercise. Because most relationships have one member who talks easily and one who does not talk as well, it is often important to make sure each has equal time. Sit down with a clock in plain view. Flip a coin to establish which of you goes first. The woman with tails talks first and talks for a pre-established period of time. This can be five to fifteen minutes. Afterwards, the other woman talks for the same amount of time.

The woman who goes second would benefit by saying what she had wanted to in the first place. Often in an argument, the second woman will argue with what the first woman has said. It's difficult not to do this, but in the long run it is counterproductive to do so. Each of you has something to say and if you're spending your time arguing with what your partner is saying, you have wasted the time. You have not been able to say what your view is of the entire situation.

After each of you has talked, take time out. Leave the physical presence of one another. Spend some time with yourself reflecting on the situation. The length of this time period should also be pre-arranged. At the end of it, both of you come back together and you do not talk about the problem that came up during the talk. If you want to talk about it again, you have to arrange for another meeting at least two hours from the one just finished.

Usually one of the two of you feels more afraid or angry when there is distance. The other partner is usually a woman who cannot stand to be intruded upon. She feels smothered by constant pressure and contact. This exercise has something for each woman. The time together is structured so each will have a time to talk and a time to be silent. The time apart will give some distance but has a specific time when it will end. The more you practice it, the better you will be able to carry it off. Do not get discouraged, just keep doing it.

C-2: Talk About Sex

Spend a specific amount of time each day talking about sex. I usually recommend that this time be short. That is, talk about sex five minutes each morning. Anyone can find five minutes. You may each want to agree to do the talking for fifteen minutes every day. Do not agree to more than that, because it may become a burden rather than a way to becoming more comfortable with your sexual life.

Talking about sex can be done any way. You can talk about your sexual response cycle. You can talk about anything you read in this book. You can talk about what you like about your sex life, or what you do not like about your sex life. The purpose of the exercise is simply to allow you to become more comfortable. Include sex as part of your everyday life rather than something you bring out of the closet when you feel very safe. Sex can become a very ordinary part of us.

C-3: "My life would be better if you would only..."

This is an exerise developed by Betty Fuller. I have adapted it somewhat for this book.

Step 1: Create a prearranged time together with your partner. Make a list that would finish the sentence: "My life would be better if you (meaning your partner) would only..." Fill in the blank with whatever comes into your mind. Each of you does this. Include all the things that irritate you about your partner. For instance, "My life would be better if you would only do your share of the housework."

Step 2: Read your list to each other. You may want to choose the top five to allow the exercise to have impact and not just get lost in a long list. Partner A reads to partner B: "My life would be better if you would only do your share of the housework, pay your bills and have sex with me, etc." Partner B responds to the list by repeating it, not by arguing with it or taking offense. She simply repeats it to let partner A know she has heard what the complaints are.

Partner B takes the next step and reads her list to partner A : "My life would be better if you would only stop nagging me, stop spending so much money and stay home with me more." Then partner A responds by repeating the list to let partner B know she has heard.

Step 3: Exchange lists. Partner A now has partner B's list, and vice versa. Partner A begins by explaining the list of partner B's complaints. That is, she tries to establish in her own words why B has these complaints. A does this by using her own words and reading the list as if it is her own. For instance, partner B had complained about A nagging her. When A takes B's list, she explains as sincerely as she can about why nagging is so irritating to her. "I hate the way you nag because I always feel like an idiot. It seems as though you don't know how to say anything nice to me anymore." A tries to take B's position.

The point of the exercise is to allow each of the women to learn what their partner's complaints are and to learn more about empathizing with them. In listening, B is not to correct or respond. She is simply to listen to what it is like to hear those complaints. The second part of this step is for B to read A's list as if it were her own. A does not respond or correct.

Step 4: After each woman has explained the other's list, they can tell where the other completely understood the problem. A might say: "I never really thought you understood how not paying your bills really frightens me, but now I see that you do." Each can also identify where the other was not responding correctly. B might say, "When you were talking about how nagging is upsetting, you left out that every time I tell you this you deny that you do it."

Step 5: Keep the list that your partner wrote. Read the list as if you wrote it about yourself. You may even want to begin each statement with "My life would be better if *I* would only..." Partner A reads about the nagging as if she herself was complaining. "My nagging you drives me crazy. I hate it in myself, that is why I deny that I do it. It is so awful." A finishes B's list reading each as if it were a complaint she had herself. B does the same with the list that A wrote.

This part of the exercise allows each to admit the shortcomings that she knows she has, but perhaps her partner is more willing to point out. If we nag or are not responsible with our housework, we know it. We are usually ashamed of it, and therefore become defensive when someone points it out to us. This is a chance for us to state it as fact and own what that means to us.

When you are hearing your partner read your list as if it is her own complaints about herself, it is important to simply listen. Do not comment, do not make it even more difficult by saying unnecessary things like "I told you so." You are going to have your chance at admitting shortcomings, and you will be glad for some mercy too.

Step 6: Take back your own list and see if anything on there applies to you, too. For instance, B might look at the list and realize that she nags A also. Read the list including the ones that do apply to you. This way you will see that what you complain about is often within yourself.

Step 7: Talk to each other about what you do appreciate in one another. Thank one another for doing the exercise. It is a difficult one to do under the best of circumstances and is very hard when communication has already broken down.

C-4: Trading Places

One of the ways we can detach ourselves from our own view of the world and try to understand what is going on for our partner is to take her place in an argument. This exercise is designed to do that. Each of you takes a chair and states your side of the argument that seems to be impeding your relationship. The chair that A sits in first will be the one that always represents her point of view.

That is, when either one of you sits in that chair, you assume the role of A whether you are her or not. The same applies for the chair that B sat in first.

The first step then is for each woman to state her case. The second step is to trade places. That means to literally take the other woman's chair. After this change, you are to continue the "argument" as if you are the person whose chair you occupy. Continue to play act as if you are your partner until you find that you are slipping back into your own character. When this happens, each of you can trade places again. State the major points of your argument at this stage, and then trade places once more.

You can continue trading places as long as you need to, until you come to an understanding of what your partner's pain is about. You may not agree with it, but being able to see the world from her eyes just for a moment will help to change your perspective.

C-5: "My Client Feels..."

This exercise is set up in a similar manner to C-4. Please read that one first. In this one, you set up four chairs. Each of you will move between two of the chairs. Woman A sits in chair "1"; she states her case. Woman B sits in chair "2" and states her case. Woman A moves then to chair "3." In this chair, she becomes her own lawyer. That is, she begins to interpret for herself as if she is representing her case. From chair "3", A may say, "You must understand that, when told that she is nagging, my client A becomes so upset that she cannot talk with you rationally. Her mother nagged and this makes her feel like her mother. She then must fight to win or else she won't be able to live with herself."

The procedure is to be continued with B moving to chair "4" and becoming her own lawyer to interpret the argument for A's lawyer. From chair "4", B might say, "When my client hears what she feels is nagging, she feels that she's like a child with her father yelling at her. She feels she has an obligation to herself to point out that your client is nagging."

The purpose of becoming your own representative is to learn to detach some from your own position. A lawyer is not emotionally attached to their client's position. The lawyer just wants to make the client's position understood. This takes rewording sometimes. Sometimes it takes making an analysis of the client's motives. Whatever the need, the lawyer figures something out. This is the job of A when she is in chair "3," and the role of B when she is in chair "4."

Continuing the discussion in these chairs can often clean up the communication considerably. Whenever either A or B moves back to saying "me" or "I" when explaining something, she should move back to her original chair so that it is clear that she is being the client at this point, not the lawyer. This moving between chairs is often helpful as each has an opportunity to see how much is communicated from which chair and how that is done. Often we just need to explain something in another language, or way, to give our partner the opportunity to understand us.

Relaxation Exercises: Exercises R-1 to R-10

These can be used in any situation that feels appropriate.

R-1: Simple Letting Go
Lie down where you are comfortable. Breathe slowly and deeply. Imagine the tension in your body being drawn out of you. Allow your muscles to relax. Start with your feet and work up gradually to your head. Spend time last on your genitals if you are trying to relax for sex. Let your genitals have special time. See them close, then open, close then open. Allow the tension and heat that is in them to leave your body. Let the air have all your anxiety and tightness from the day.

R-2: Filling with Air
Turn on some music that is soothing to you. It may be best to have music with no words to distract you. Lie down on a flat surface that is comfortable for you. Start breathing very deeply. With every breath you take in, allow there to be warm soothing air coming into you. For every breath you let out, imagine all your tension and anxiety being released.

Imagine your whole body filling up with air like a balloon and slowly deflating again. Start with your left foot. Let it be filled up with air. Imagine air filling up every vein with warm soothing air. Move up your leg gradually filling up every inch with warm soothing air. Now, go down to your right foot and fill it up with air. Make sure every toe is included. Move up your right leg slowly soothing it with warm, loving air. Start next with your left hand, moving up your arm. Next is your right hand and arm. Then come back down

225

to your vagina and pelvis. Fill each up with warm soothing air, allowing the tension and anxiety to flow outside you. Move up to your stomach and rib cage. Fill them up with warm, loving air. Now your breasts. Move to your shoulders and neck. Finally to your face and head. Concentrate on relaxing your mouth, tongue, nose, eyes, forehead, cheeks and chin. Then move to your head and ears filling all with loving air and releasing tension and anxiety.

R-3: Cradled in Your Vagina

Make sure you have read the physiology chapter so that we are both using the same vocabulary for the parts of your genitals.

Close your eyes and imagine yourself somewhere that is a beautiful place to you. Be in a peaceful, calm setting. Imagine that there is lots of sunshine and it is very safe to be naked there. Allow an image of your genitals to come into your mind. See your clitoris, lips, vagina, urinary opening, anus, pubic hair and surrounding skin.

Imagine yourself very small, and go inside your vagina and explore it. Touch the walls, feel their texture. See if they are moist or dry, smooth or bumpy. Feel how strong the tissue is. Push against the skin inside and see how much it can stretch. Imagine how large it can get if a baby can move through it. Crawl slowly up your vaginal canal. Feel how safe it is inside. Touch your cervix. (If you have had a hysterectomy, feel the dome of your vagina, love it with its changes.) Breathe slowly and deeply and allow yourself to be cradled in your vagina for as long as you like.

R-4: Snuggling with Your Lips

Lie down somewhere that you enjoy. Put on low music, make sure the room is warm. Take off your clothes. Touch your genitals slowly. Look with a mirror if you want to. Breathe very deeply. Allow the air you breathe in to go all the way through your body out through your vagina. Imagine getting very small, and moving down to your genitals. Part the lips you encounter. Touch them and feel their texture. Let the pubic hair touch your face. Allow in the pleasure of touching your clitoris, vagina, anus. Take your lips and curl them around your body. Snuggle into them like a comforter and relax into their nurturing safety.

R-5: Breathing to a Count of Seven

The following is a simple version of meditation practice. Many of the books on meditation have elaborate explanations of breathing and how to use it for concentration. You may want to read further. This exercise is meant to be used as a simple way to relax.

Sit or lie in a comfortable position. Allow your mind to be clear. When thoughts come in, allow them to go through. Try not to get stuck in them. Start concentrating on your breath. As you breathe in, count to seven, hold your breath for a count of seven, then exhale to a count of seven again. Continue to repeat this as long as needed to bring calm into your body.

R-6: Counting Exhaled Breath

Sit or lie down in a way that will not cut off your circulation. Breathe very deeply. Imagine the air going all through your body. Count each exhaled breath. Starting with one and going through until ten. If you loose track of where you began, start again at one. If you find you are counting the breath you take in as well, begin again at one. When you get to ten, start again with one. Do this as long as you like.

R-7: Breathing With a Partner

Lie together on your sides with your partner's back against your chest. You can do this with clothes on or off. Bend your knees where it is comfortable with your partner snuggled up against you. Some women call this lying like "spoons." Both of you start to breathe. Continue to cut the speed of your breathing until you are both breathing very slowly. The woman who is wrapped against the back of her partner begins to time her breathing with her partner's, eventually surrendering totally to the rhythm of her partner. Allow yourselves to spend a long time in this position. At least a half hour to experience the soothing effects.

R-8: The "Ah" Breath with a Partner

[This is taken directly from Stephen and Ondrea Levine's "Concious Living" workshops. There are many other wonderful meditations they suggest in *Who Dies.*]

This can be done for as long as both women want, but should continue for at least twenty minutes for each partner, in order for both to feel the effect. Partner A is lying down first, partner B kneeling or sitting beside her. A closes her eyes and begins to beathe slowly. B watches A's torso to see the rhythm she is breathing. When B feels she can, she begins to breathe at the same pace as A, inhaling and exhaling together. She does this for a while and when it is comfortable begins to emit a soft 'ahhhhhhh'' sound when exhaling. This sound will settle comfortably at it's own pitch and intensity. After a while it may seem at times that A is not even breathing or is taking too long between breaths. This is a good sign, as it means that the two of you are slowing down. Sometimes A may even feel as though B is breathing for her. Just allow the experience to carry each of you. When you have done this for at least twenty minutes, you may want to trade positions. Or you may continue for a long time, and agree to trade positions only at some future time. This is a wonderful exercise for communicating on a profound and non-verbal level.

R-9: Massaging Yourself

You may have done massage with a partner numerous times, and yet never have taken that kind of loving, relaxing time with yourself. Decide to unplug your phone, lock the door and spend an hour with yourself to relax and enjoy your body.

This can be done by using some sort of lubrication (massage oil, vegetable oil), pouring it on your feet, hands, face, legs, arms, genitals, body, or breasts. Probably the only place you cannot touch effectively is your own back. Take your time in loving all the parts of your body that you can reach. Just spending time quietly and alone can give you calm and peace.

R-10: Massage with a Partner

See P-5 for a suggestion of a series of massages. Any adaptation can work for physically relaxing one another.

Homophobia: Exercises H-1 to H-3

This has been written about at great length in this book. Take your time to read the chapter dedicated to this topic. These exercises are meant to help with the pain of homophobia with some attempts to actually work on the feelings.

H-1: The Reasons I Am Afraid of Being a Lesbian

You may not have chosen the word "afraid" when you thought of your homophobic self. You may think more of words like, "dislike," "hate," "am bothered." The reason I chose this word was because I think it really more accurately describes homophobia. It really is a fear. A fear that is often felt as hatred.

Make a list of all these reasons. They can be any reasons. I'll get caught at work, my family will reject me, my friends are anti-male, the community is so conservative, sex with women seems wrong, I can't hold hands with my lover on the street, and on and on. Make this list at least 25 items long. Make sure this list is thorough. No one is going to read this except you. There are no grades, you don't have to tell anyone. This is for you to learn the ways you are concerned about your sexual orientation.

Answer honestly which ones of this list are because of others, either other lesbians or the culture at large. See which ones are directly generated from within. Let yourself see how many are left. Most of us have great fears that have little to do with what is inside. Of course, there are bound to be some. Take that portion of the list and honor them. Let in that you indeed have these homophobic parts of you. Let them be comfortable within you. The struggle often happens when we are trying to fight with these parts and get them out of us. They just get bigger.

Make a list of all the reasons you love being a lesbian: I like being around women, I don't have to explain myself, oral sex with women is wonderful, we are part of a secret society, and on and on. See if those parts can be visible in light of the homophobia you have been exploring.

Work on SL-1 and see what sub-personalities the homophobic and lesbian-positive selves represent. Create a dialogue between these two parts. See if the two can think of something fun to do together that each would like. Work at creating a friendship within yourself of all the contradictions.

H-2: Open Your Heart to the Lesbian Within

This is to be a repeat of SL-2 and with your lesbian in your heart. All the parts of her you love, hate, are afraid of. Make your heart as big as you can and make her feel your security; not always security with her lesbianism, but always with your connection to her.

H-3: Homophobia Meditation

Repeat the breathing and relaxing exercises in SL-2. Let your body relax and close your eyes. Allow yourself to see the last situation you were in that caused you to have homophobic reactions. That could be a confrontation with your lover, a friend, your family, work, on the street with a stranger, or simply inside yourself. Let the details of that situation come into your consciousness. Imagine that you are there again. You are beginning to feel more and more uncomfortable. You are becoming anxious or sad. Make sure the scene is very clear and succinct. Let the two sides of you, or the people involved, begin to argue. Let them carry it to even greater extremes than they have in the past. Make it very exaggerated so that there are clear sides, with the idea being that one is right and the other is wrong.

Let yourself come into the picture as a third party. (This can be done even if the argument is purely within yourself—let a centered self come in as the third party, a part of you that has no investment in the outcome.) Let this third party view the whole situation. Get the two who are arguing to start to plead their case with this part. Imagine this part taking each of the other parts by the hand. As this is done, imagine that the two warring parts are turning into little children. The two parts may even be becoming babies. The details of the arguments begin to fade, and the essence of these two little beings are beginning to come into consciousness. All these two want is recognition. They just want someone to see they exist and that they are filled with love and affection. Imagine that this third party is taking them into her arms and rocking these two children. They are being held with great love and affection. The homophobia becomes an essence of love. Imagine that the energy of the pain is being turned into energy for connection.

Self-Loving: Exercises SL-1 to SL-5

We have all been taught that we aren't supposed to spend much time loving ourselves. We are supposed to concentrate on loving others, our work, or our possessions. We do not learn how to re-center ourselves when we have had something occur in our lives that overwhelms us. We are not taught how to help create some self-esteem. We are encouraged to believe that spending time and energy learning how we can support and encourage ourselves more is something that is a waste of time. I feel that to have a full sex life we often need some extra help with loving ourselves. Like it or not, we sometimes have sex tied in with our self-esteem; we don't always know how to continue to get what we want out of our sex life when we are feeling uncomfortable with ourselves. This can be especially true if we feel we have been rejected by someone sexually. These exercises are designed to help us learn ways to work on loving ourselves.

SL-1: *Making a List of Our Sub-Personalities*

Within each of us lurks numerous players. We are not just one simple person who always reacts to emotional or physical stimulus the same way each time. We have many "sub-personalities" within us. This is a phrase coined by Roberto Assagoli in *Active Will*. These extra personalities have been formed throughout our lives. They have been established in response to the environments we have moved through. For instance, we might have a feminist sub-personality that hates cooking and cleaning and in fact puts it down. In addition, we may have a Future Homemaker of America within us that has to have the dinner taste just right when guests come. Often our sub-personalities have conflicts with one another. These two may be stumped when it comes to how to ask someone on a date. The feminist within may feel you should be assertive, ask her out and live with the consequences. The homemaker may feel you should wait until the other woman makes the first move.

The helpful part about knowing our sub-personalites is that when one of them takes over and runs the show, and you are caught standing there reaping the consequences, at least you'll know how you got there. Knowing you have a homemaker within lets you know that she will struggle and maybe even sabotage when asking someone else out. The feminist may dial the phone number of the potential date, but the homemaker will chatter on about her day without getting down to business. If you know that your homemaker is talking now, that she's afraid of appearing too bold, you can help her by allowing another part of you to ask the potential date.

Another valuable part of making this list is to get to see that there are many parts of you. That you are not really always an asshole. You can see that you are more than the shy self. You can see that you have numerous children inside who are afraid of this grown-up world and need some assistance.

Take a sheet of paper and write down something about each personality. You may want to give them each a name, age and approximate time of arrival in your life. Write what you know about this part of you in the greatest detail. See how you feel abut each part. If you like this one or not. If you see any use for this other one. Would you introduce this one to the neighbors? Family? Friends? A lover? Do you feel this one should be hidden from everyone? See if you can bring up reasons why the personalities you don't like are inside you. They all have a gift and all have been a protector for you in the past. They may no longer be effective, but they indeed helped you in some way along your path.

Allow yourself to write about the core of you. The self that is surrounded by all these sub-personalities. See what that core is about. Learn as much as you can about the essence of you. Look at how these sub-personalities pull you off that core and get you to look at life from their eyes. See if you are willing to love each of these beings even if you don't like the way they try to run your life.

SL-2: Open Heart Meditation

Allow someone to read this to you, or read it into a tape recorder then play it back to yourself in a room that is quiet.

Close your eyes. Breathe slowly and deeply. Imagine that your body is filling with warm soothing air every time you breathe in. As you exhale, imagine that you are breathing out tension and anxiety. Continue to breathe slowly giving yourself all the time you need to gradually relax. Imagine that as you exhale, you are letting go of self-hatred. Imagine that you are breathing out all your doubts about self worth. Breathing in brings the love and caring of the universe.

Begin to focus on your heart. Imagine that it is beating with love, warmth and healing energy. As you move closer to it, you can feel its acceptance and openness. Imagine that you are getting very small and being able to move inside your heart. Let yourself sit quietly inside watching the walls of our heart moving in and out bringing you healing love. Allow yourself to feel the warmth and the encompassing feeling of safety. As you hear your self-hatred inside your mind, allow your heart to get bigger. Allow your heart to get big enough to take in all your self-hatred, your feelings of lack of worth, your anxiety and doubt about your life. Imagine that your heart can get big enough to allow in all these feelings you have.

If you have worked on SL-1, learning about your sub-personalities, now is the time to allow in all your sub-personalities. Take in even the ones that you feel you hate. Your heart can handle them. It can get big enough to allow in all parts of you. Imagine that your heart is getting as big as a huge stadium. Let its boundaries move wider and wider to allow in all of you.

Let your mind move to your sexual self. Let the fear, anger, regret and sorrow of your sex life come into your heart. See that even the hurt there can be healed. That you can accept the past and present when it comes to your sexual self. You are a loving being that only wants to gain love and give love. Allow your heart to encompass all of you.

Keep breathing with this image of your heart loving and holding you as long as you like. When you do want to make contact back with the rest of the world, breathe slowly and make it a conscious transition back. Let your body slowly readjust to the prospect of letting go of your image and coming back to the world. Open your eyes when you are ready.

SL-3: List of Positives

This can be used for whatever the issue is in your life. Whether you are feeling pain about sex, oppression, homophobia, abandonment, work, children, a lover, or yourself, you can use this.

Make a list of all the positive parts of you that work in your life. If you feel you cannot think of any, you are not thinking. The very fact that your are reading this and willing to try to do something which makes you feel better is something positive. You may even choose something very minor, like "I got out of bed this morning." You can move right along to such things as, "I went to the bus stop to catch a bus for work." Whether you went to work then or not, at least you have two positives on your list. Make the list as specific as possible. Not just items like "I've been nice." Remind yourself to whom, under what circumstances, and what other positives that led to.

Keep a copy of this list with you. It can be by your telephone, in your book bag, your purse, your desk at work, or your car. When you are starting to turn to self-hatred, look at the list and be willing to at least read each entry. Add to them when you are willing. This is meant to encourage you to see that even during hard times, you have charactertistics that are postitive.

SL-4: Suspended Judgment

When we are dealing with nearly anything in our lives we usually have judgments involved. We can come up with them instantly and hold onto them forever. ("I can't get over that I couldn't think of the name I was choosing for my confirmation in 1955.") The idea in this exercise is to suspend our judgments. You don't have to worry, they will always be there. They will not be lost to antiquity never being able to be reported to the generations that follow.

Close your eyes and allow all the judgments you have over a certain specific situation (not wanting to have sex last night for the seventh month in a row) or in general (I'm sure I'll never want to be sexual again). Let these judgments flood in. Just see them there in all their ugliness. Let the judgments of your lover, family and friends flood in too as long as you are at it. Feel what it is like to have these judgments inside you, how painful it is.

Take all the judgments, and put them into a helium balloon. Imagine stuffing each last one of them inside. Let the helium float the balloon away. Watch as it drifts above your head. You can always reach out for the string and pull the balloon back down. But right now, let yourself feel the relief of not having any judgments stuffed inside your head right now. Feel what it is like to have so much room in your mind to move around. Let your judgments stay suspended until you need them again. They are there, just suspended from making any demands on you at the moment.

SL-5: Seeing Yourself As Sexual

Many of us do not even believe we are sexual beings. This is something reserved for others. This exercise is meant to allow you to look at yourself as a sexual being.

1. Make a list on a piece of paper as to why you are not a sexual being. Put all the evidence you have, like not being sexual with another woman for a while, not having a desire for sex, not masturbating, not having a body that looks sexual. There may be hundreds of reasons that you have that "prove" you are not sexual. Get all those reasons out so that you can really build a case.

2. Make a list of factors that would prove someone is a sexual being. Let the list grow as much as you need it to. There could be things on it like the amount of times one is sexual in a month, the size that breasts need to be, the personality one needs to possess. Try and make this list at least ten items long.

3. Write down all other reasons why you could never be or live up to the list in step two. Take everything into account—your allergies, your religious training, how your parents acted towards you, anything you can find that supports the premise that you could never have the characteristics of a sexual woman.

4. Close your eyes and begin to imagine that you are this mythical woman that possesses all the characteristics that make some able to achieve step two. See yourself in her form. Imagine what she does with her day, her nights. Imagine what kind of job she

would have, what kind of clothes she would wear. Imagine what kind of car she would drive. Give her a name if you find one that fits. Allow yourself to imagine being her and engaging in a sexual encounter with another woman. See how this mythical woman asks the other woman out. See what she chooses to do for the evening. Allow yourself to go through the whole sequence. She and the other woman go to dinner, a concert, go dancing, or just stay home and watch T.V. or play cards. Let yourself move into her realm and see her engage the other woman in some extremely overt flirting. Let yourself watch her techniques in sitting closer and closer to the woman and finally touching her hand, leg or thigh. Imagine asking this woman if it would be all right to kiss her. Let your imagination take you to kissing this woman, holding her tight. Then move to the next stage of fondling the woman; watch how she is more and more willing to be sexual with this mythical sexual woman. Imagine taking off the other woman's clothes, piece by piece. Go slowly and allow yourself all the pleasure this kind of teasing brings. Then let the other woman take off the clothes of your mythical sexual woman. Move slowly into a more graphically sexual situtation. Allow in whatever activity you have decided is very sexual. Oral sex, fingers in vaginas, anal sex, fondling and kissing breasts—anything that makes you feel full. Carry the sex to whatever conclusion your imagination takes you. Lying peacefully in one another's arms watch your mythical woman and her partner float off to blissful sleep. Do not move onto reading the next step until you have completed these four.

5. Once the visualization is completed, read this. If you are tempted to read it before, try to follow these directions and the exercise will work better. The point of this exercise is that *you* are the one that imagined all this, your mythical sexual woman. This sexual woman is inside you, not somewhere else on earth. You have a sexual woman within and she only needs an avenue of expression. If you feel your visualization was not that sexual, try again. Work on this until you have exercised your imagination as far as you think you can. Come back and try it again another day.

6. Finally, you may want to put some of your imagination into practice. Start by masturbating with yourself and your imagination. When you are ready begin to use some of the techniques that sexual woman inside you has taught you.

Loving Your Partner: Exercises PL-1 to PL-5

PL-1: *Open Your Heart to Your Lover*

Read the meditation in SL-2. In this exercise, we are changing the focus into accepting our lover. Allow all her little people inside your heart. Let yourself take in all the parts of her that you do not like. Let those parts into this loving huge heart that has only love and compassion to give. Even if you have resistance. Even if your mind says to you—don't accept that part, it hurts you all the time. Usually what is true about ourselves and others is that the parts that are hardest to love are the parts that need it the most. Try a short form of this meditation every day; being open to your lover and accepting her into your heart often softens a relationship that is painful. It also allows relationships that are full and happy to become even more so. It is a great relief to accept our lovers exactly as they are.

PL-2: *Why Did We Get Together Anyway?*

This is an exercise for both women in a relationship. The "relationship" can be defined in any way that feels appropriate to you.

Each of you take out a piece of paper and write down all of your reasons for getting together. You can create this list together, or each write down your own reasons. You may be surprised as to all the reasons that can emerge. Make sure the list has at least fifteen reasons why you got together. After the writing, discuss the list and make additions and elaborations on the writings.

Now, take this list and display it somewhere. On the refrigerator, on the wall somewhere. If you live separately, make sure to have two copies to display in each dwelling. This list visibly displayed will help to affirm that you are together and for good reasons. When you are fighting, this is an excellent reference to remind each of you that you are not always fighting. This is an affirmation of your connection that is important.

PL-3: *Suspended Judgment*

This is again a repeat of SL-4. Please read this; use only very specific judgments about your lover, the ones that you put in that helium balloon and let go.

PL-4: *No Shame and No Blame*

This is a phrase that is to indicate that whoever you are, there is no shame for that person. There is no reason for you to be ashamed of who you are. You may have some shame for an act you committed, something you said, but you have no reason to be ashamed of yourself the human being. The woman who works so hard everyday to be on this planet. Both women in the couple should talk together about what shame you are carrying around, and try to let it go. If you are doing this after a very specific argument, talk about what shame you are trying to make up for. Say how you feel you were wrong; see what it is like to own that and not carry it anymore. You are not someone who should be ashamed, you are a woman who is full of contradictions and humanness.

Equally, there is to be no blame. Your love is not a woman that is "out to get you." She is suffering on this planet too. You may have some anger at her, you may feel she did something that is "wrong." this still is no reason for blame. Imagine what it would be like to discuss the argument you are having, or your lives in general, without any stigma of blame attached. It would be quite a new way of seeing one another.

PL-5: What Sub-Personality Is That?

Look at exercise SL-1 to understand what this is about. The use of it here is to learn more about your partner and how to love different parts of her even if you are sick of the way those parts rule some parts of the relationship.

When you are trying to negotiate with your partner, it may help to have a list that each of you has made of your sub-personalities. You may want to look and find out which sub-personality of yours is talking to what sub-personality of hers. I see this often in working with couples on communication. Usually each of them is operating from a two year old place in which they each feel scared and abandoned. They are not going to let the other woman scare them even more, and will become stubborn and angry. If each one is able to move out of the two year old position, she may be able to get more accomplished. Especially if each is able to connect to their adult self that has compassion and understanding for themselves and their partner.

Once you see what sub-personality is speaking for your lover, you may be able to detach from the personalized feeling you have about the way she is treating you. If you know that it's her abandoned child that is not listening to you (rather than her adult that you have told so many times how you need to be listened to), you may be able to try and not make more demands on that child.

237

Children are not always capable of doing what we want. Wait until you know her adult is available and start over. You may not like how you feel when her abandoned child takes over, but you will know that that isn't all of her, just one part.

Desire: Exercises D-1 to D-7

Many women do not have the desire to be sexual. This section is written with the assumption that you have read the chapters on desire issues and homophobia. Also it is important to at least start with the assumption that you do not have to feel desire to actually engage in sex. Often, once a woman begins to have sex, she begins to have a good time with the experience, although left to her own devices, she may have never initiated the sexual connection. Many women find that once they start to set a specific time for sex it is more acceptable. Once a woman has chosen to have sex and has set boundaries about what is all right to do in a sexual situation, she often finds that sex becomes an activity that is enjoyable.

The rules for the other exercises apply here also. Make specific times to have sex with yourself or with your partner. This should be pre-arranged and agreed on by both women. The exercises should be carried out unless there are specific reasons why either woman feels unwilling to do so. It is not that you have to have sex against your will. The point is to push yourself through a resistant barrier that may be ruling your sex life.

Please look at the other homework sections that may also pertain to your issues. Make sure that the ones that apply to genitals and sexual behavior are used along with this work. Don't go through the steps for sex with yourself and sex with a partner until after working on the desire section.

D-1: *Writing*
Step 1: Write all the reasons you do not want to have sex. Make sure you include pertinent information like what your family, church and community has taught you about sex between women.

Step 2: Write about why you are willing to work on your sex life. This needs to be divided into two sections. One that addresses why you want to change your sex life for yourself and one that addresses why you want to change your sex life for a relationship (which you may be in now). If you find that there are no reasons for yourself that encourage you to work on your sexuality, and that you are doing it because you think you have to for a relationship, then there are problems. If you find that you have given your partner all the responsibility for your sexual life, and you feel that she is the one motivating this change, then look more closely. You may find that, indeed, you do want to change things also.

If you find that you really have no desire to change your sex life, then you must wait until that reality is different. There is no point in forcing yourself to go through a process you do not want.

D-2: Getting Honest

This is the time for you to tell the truth to yourself and your partner if there is truth to tell that you haven't already said. Is there something about her that is turning you off? Have you fallen in love with another woman? Are you having an affair with someone? Do you want out of the relationship with your parnter and just do not know how to tell her? Do you have a serious alcohol or drug problem that may be inhibiting your sexual desire? Are there sexual activities you want to engage in and do not know how to tell her? Do you think your partner is having an affair or is not in love with you anymore? Are you angry at your lover? It is important to tell her if any of this is going on. It will never become any easier to tell her. Telling the truth does not necessarily mean you want to break up your relationship with her. It may only mean that you both have some negotiating to do that will enhance your relationship in the end.

D-3: Willingness Or: Expanding Your View of Desire

Step 1: If you are willing to change your sex life even if you do not have desire, that is the most important element. This can become your definition of desire. That is, you have the desire to change your sex life. You may not have "desire" that you see in the movies. Few people do, and if they do, it usually ends relatively early in a relationship.

Step 2. Make a date to have a sexual time with yourself or a lover once a week. Look at the introduction to this chapter and the exercises on sex. If you want to have this sexual experience with yourself, spend a certain amount of time each week being sensual and sexual with yourself. Do not slight yourself. Keep a commitment to work on your sexual self. If you want to have these sexual experiences with a partner, decide what would be acceptable sex behavior to you and let your partner know that. Remember that you do not have to be sexually excited about this activity to engage in it.

D-4: *Expanding Your Definition of Sex*

This is important. Sex can mean anything that has to do with exchanging special energy with another woman. That can happen just by holding someone. It can come while snuggling with your pajamas on. It does not have to be genital sex. You may want to go through each of the exercises in the sex section. If you have not had desire to have sex, it may be that you feel you have no choice in sex. Work at looking at sex in many ways.

D-5: *Masturbate*

This is intended to help you learn what about touching your body feels good to you. See exercise S-6. Some women find that with more sexual stimulation of their bodies, they want to be more sexual. This may not be true for you, but it will help you learn about your body and will be helpful in future sexual situations.

D-6: *Erotica*

Look into the lesbian erotica that is available in your town. If there is none, you may try the lesbian publication *On Our Backs*. It is a magazine specifically meant for lesbians. It has many types of erotica, stories, poems, photographs, drawings. All meant to help women learn about their sexual selves. Whatever type of erotica may seem like a turn-on to you, explore it. See if you become aware of any sexual feelings. If you have some do not worry that you have to tell anyone or do anything about it. Simply revel in your sexual side and give her continued support.

D-7: *Sexual Abuse and Its Effect on Desire*

There is a section of this chapter devoted to this, and there is also a chapter in the book on "Barriers to Sexuality." Please refer to these. It is important to know that sexual abuse can affect your sexual desire for many years.

Partner Dynamics in Lack of Sexual Desire: Excercises DP-1 to DP-4

DP-1: *What Are Your Roles*

Step 1: Read the chapter on "Desire Issues" in this book which deals with this directly. Talk about how your relationship looks to both of you. Discuss the dynamics and see if you fit into one of the categories mentioned in the chapter by Marny Hall, "Lesbians,

Limerance and Long-Term Relationships." See if each of you can discuss what you think is your own and the other's part in not having sex.

Step 2: Sometimes it takes an outside facilitator to figure out what each of your roles are in the relationship. If this is necessary, it is more important to seek professional help in the form of couple's counseling than to have your relationship break up.

DP-2: Only One of Us Has a Problem

Step 1: It is important that one of the women does not get labeled as the "identified patient." That is, if the two of you have decided that A has the problem because she lacks sexual desire, the two of you have not been clear about what is going on in the relationship. Or conversely, you may blame B for being "too sexual." It always takes two to make difficulty in a relationship. B has just as much a part in the problem as A. This is true even if it is so that A never wants to have sex and B always does. That in fact may be the problem. If B is pressuring A to define sex as she does (i.e. you have to have sex twice a month to be real lovers), A may never want to have sex. Saying "no" is the only power she has.

Step 2: See what B does that is irritating to A. Look at where else either B or A is seen as the identified patient. Does B spend money in a way that A feels is irresponsible? Do each of you think that B needs to learn more about money? Does B resent A for this attitude? Has this resentment contributed to your not wanting to be more responsible with money? This may also be happening in sex. Most of us resent being told what is "right" and "wrong." Sex is no different.

Step 3: Each of you go for one day without telling the other about their irritating behavior. Try that once a week for a month. Then move to two days a week. See if that helps you each learn how much you nag each other. See if it will give you relief that you are not being nagged by your partner.

DP-3: Communication

See the section in this chapter on communication between partners. Try any of the exercises C-1 through C-5.

DP-4: Stop Demanding Sex

If you are the partner who feels deprived by your partner who has no sexual desire, see what happens if you stop demanding sex. Make an agreement with yourself that you will not ask for sex (verbally or non-verbally) for a period of a week. Discuss with your partner what that was like for you at the end of the week. See what she says about the experience. Try it again for a month. You may discover that your partner is so relieved to not have to refuse you for a month that you become more appealing to her. Whatever happens in terms of her desire, you may find that actually choosing not to ask for sex for a month starts to change your attitude about sex. It may not seem like an affront to you if you are the one choosing not to have sex.

Learning Comfort With Genitals

Your Own Genitals: Exercises G-1 to G-9

G-1: Daily Contact

Look at your genitals every day in a mirror. Do not spend a long time. Just do this as a matter of course like you look at your face every day. Begin to assume your genitals are part of your body and that they deserve some attention every day.

G-2: Drawing

Draw a picture of your genitals. Color them in and make the coloring elaborate. There is a great book that will give you ideas about this, *Labia Flowers* by Tee A. Corinne. Use her book to become familiar with coloring genitals and with what they look like.

G-3: Corresponding

Write a letter to your genitals telling them how much you hate them. Now write a letter telling them how much you love them. Make sure that you include incidents that give examples for your reasoning. A great book that will help you with this is *The Women's Playbook About Sex,* by Joani Blank. Writing often helps us learn information that we don't readily think of. Just let yourself write anything. Do not agree to show it to anyone. This way, you will write what you need to, not what you think someone else wants to read.

G-4: Picturing

Take a picture of your genitals if you can. Find a friend that you trust that will do it for you. (When the companies develop pictures, they are done on a conveyer belt and no one looks at individual pictures. Don't worry, the camera store will never know you did it.) Look at this picture as often as you can. Get to know your genitals by sight. Look at the book *I Am My Lover* by Joani Blank which features Tee A. Corinne's photographs of women's genitals. It is a beautiful book on masturbation. The photographs are wonderful.

G-5: Looking

Take an hour and look at your genitals. A lighted make-up mirror is an excellent tool. Let in how foolish you feel. Take note of the feelings that come up when you start to hear the tapes of your family or religious leaders come in that say "what are you doing this disgusting activity for?" The voices you hear are going to be those that come in during any sexual activity, but they may not be this loud under normal circumstances. There is nothing like being alone to amplify the noises in our heads that keep us from functioning as we would like.

Looking at your clitoris, lips, vaginal opening, anus and surrounding tissue can be very moving. Read the physiology chapter first to learn what the names are that you're looking at. Say the words out loud to yourself. Touch each part of your genitals and see what they feel like.

G-6: Vagina

Touch yourself inside your vagina. See how that feels. Smell your finger once you take it out of your vagina. See what it's like to taste. Do this when you have your period so you know what your own blood smells and tastes like. You will be surprised that it is nothing like the smell that comes off a tampax or menstrual pad. The blood you smell and taste that has been taken from your vagina is usually quite sweet.

If you have are having trouble smelling your vaginal smell, put something that you like in your vagina—whipping cream, part of a fruit that you like—and see what this tastes likes mixed with your vaginal fluid. Don't worry, no one will know you are doing this unless you tell them. Your mother really cannot see what you are doing—I promise.

Spend a day with the smell of your vagina on your finger. If that is disgusting to you, explore what feelings come up that prompt this. Do you believe your vagina is unsanitary? Do you feel that you smell terrible? Do you think someone else will smell you and think you are perverted? We have been taught in our culture to believe that bodily fluids are a necessary evil. Fluids can be exciting. Many women like the smell of their underarms. Others really have fun with the fluid in their vaginas. You may be able to learn to love the smell of your vaginal secretions.

G-7: Anus

Do not forget that your anus is a part of your genitals. It has been associated with waste for too long. It also has much pleasure to offer. You can wash yourself thoroughly and touch the outside of your anus. Watch what the sensations are. You may be surprised at the sensitivity of the nerves in that area of your body. If you want to experiment, put your finger inside your anus a little way. Do this slowly and with lubrication. Spit may be enough. You will usually not find any excrement inside until you have gone at least an inch up into your rectum. There is a good book that can help you to learn about your anus and ways to have fun with it, *Anal Pleasure and Health* by Jack Morin.

G-8: Clitoris

Most of us do not have trouble making friends with our clitoris. After all, it can bring us a lot of pleasure for very little trouble. Spend time looking at your clitoris. Read about it in the physiology chapter. Learn what feels good about your clitoris. Pull the hood back and look at the tip of the glans. See what kind of pressure feels good. Notice what about the clitoris looks beautiful to you, what part looks awful.

Close your eyes and imagine what your whole clitoris looks like—the part that goes back through your body. Look again at the physiology chapter to see a picture of it. Imagine it wrapping its "legs" around your vagina and anus. See if you can imagine it wanting to give you pleasure in any way you ask. Feel the sensations it offers throughout your genital area. Remember it is the only organ in the animal world that is for pleasure only. There is no other use for it on this earth.

G-9: Lips

Loving our genital lips is sometimes difficut as we have been taught to hate them. Look at your lips in a mirror so that you really know what they look like. Touch your outer lips so that you begin to know what they respond to. Touch their wrinkles, pubic hair. Feel how slippery they are on the inside. Touch your inner lips. Feel your fingers on the skin. Revel in the slippery, wet surface. Watch how you react to the look and touch of your lips. See if the length and shape is hard to accept. If it is, imagine looking at them as an art object. Something that you have never seen before. Allow in their unique shape, color, texture and size. Do exercise R-4 to allow you a loving experience with your lips. Remember that your lips are unique, warm and a beautiful protection for your clitoris and vagina.

Your Partners' Genitals: Exercises PG-1 and PG-2

You may want to do these exercises because you are having problems or just to increase your sensitivity to your lover.

Please go through the section on your own genitals first. This may not seem like an area where you have problems. But if you do have problems with your partner's genitals, you probably still have some issue with your own. Go through those exercises and see what surfaces before you go on to these.

PG-1: Looking Together At One Another's Genitals

Read G-5 to see how to look at your own. Now do that with your partner present. Let her see what you like and do not like about your genitals. Explain what kind of touch you like where. Explore each of your genitals visually. Do not turn this into a sex session. This is to begin to introduce you in a more formal way to one another's genitals. If you have been partners for a long time, do this exercise even if you feel you have nothing to learn. You probably have never dealt with each other's genitals in quite this way.

Look at your partner's genitals with an exploring eye. Make sure you look at all parts, the vagina, the anus, the clitoris, the lips. Talk about her pubic hair, the skin around her genitals, make sure you explore every part that is there.

PG-2: Touching Another Woman's Genitals

Set aside an hour to do this and make sure you follow the directions for couples (given at the beginning of the Sex Exercises)— choose a giver and receiver, set a pre-arranged time to trade positions, making sure each has a chance on different days.

Spend some of your time just getting to know one another's body as a whole. Holding, being in a hot tub, can be one way to get comfortable. You may want to do some massage beforehand to help you begin to feel more relaxed. See exercise P-5 for suggestions.

245

Some women have a problem with the smell of another woman's genitals. Before you begin this exercise have both of you wash your genitals. This can be done together as part of the sexual experience. If you eliminate the natural smell of the genitals, you both may be more comfortable. If this does not matter to you, say so. Although, if you are having problems touching genitals, you may not know this is a part of the discomfort. The washing eliminates one factor that may be inhibiting you. This does not always have to be the way you touch each other, but it can be a start in learning to be comfortable with sex. If both of you do wash before you touch one another, you may even eliminate hurt feelings. It may be hard for someone who has a difficult time with sex to say "I don't like the smell of your genitals." This will eliminate that problem.

The giver begins to stroke the genitals of the receiver. This is done at the pace of the receiver. She should be verbally giving directions as clearly as possible. You may each want to start at the clitoris and move methodically down to the anus. You may each want to wander all over the area. Whichever method works, try it. Just make sure you include all the parts of the genitals.

The receiver's job is to communicate what she feels like. Trying to manuever your body and make moans at appropriate times does not necessarily allow your partner enough information to please you. Be as specific as possible: "I love to have strong sensation in my clitoris, be as quick as possible also." Or, "No don't touch my anus, I don't like it." Show her with your hands and fingers if you need to communicate what you like. The receiver may put her hand on top of the giver's to show exactly what feels good.

If you are the giver, ask your partner what she is experiencing. This is a time of feeling and talking. We all would like sex to just magically happen, but it is not possible. As a giver, you need to ask to find out what your partner really wants from a physical experience. Tell the receiver what is exciting or fun for you. "I really do like touching your clitoris, and the juice in your vagina is a turn on." The reciever can finish by masturbating if she wants, but this is not to turn into a sexual exchange between you.

At the end of the time, spend a few moments discussing the exercise. Be as honest as possible. Tell one another what you liked and what you didn't like. Now is the time to start telling the truth.

Make sure you do this exercise again on another day with the giver/receiver positions exchanged.

Sex Exercises

The following exercises are only suggestions, and should be altered according to how you want to use them. You may want to try them in the order they are listed. You and your partner(s) need to decide together which ones to do together. Decide on an exercise ahead of time and agree to it. Do not do another exercise until you re-negotiate. This will allow each of you to absorb the impact of the exercise. It will also allow the partner who is having the most trouble with sex to learn how to set limits and boundaries without necessarily having to say "no" to sex altogether.

While each partner must be invested in doing the work, this does not necessarily mean that each has to have "desire" to have sex. It simply means that each has an intention to make their sexual life more complete.

Make a date to have time each week to do any of these exercises, exercises from any of the sections. The time set aside should be agreed upon ahead of time. Mark it on your calendar so that you each do not have to rely on your memory. The time should be at least an hour of uninterrupted time.

If it is an exercise that takes two people, that means schedule two different one hour times together. Do not have each person do the exercise one right after the other. This puts too much pressure on both of you. Set two different times on two different days. The point of making the exercise happen on two different days is so there will be no anticipation during one person's time about what the other person's time is going to be like. In addition, neither partner has to be anxious about stopping this exercise, so that the other has equal time.

Sex with Yourself: Exercises S-1 to S-6

S-1: Sensual Time
Spend an hour of uninterrupted sensual time with yourself. This can be defined any way you want to. Soak in a hot tub, jog, take yourself on a walk in the woods, or sit quietly with yourself. The time is to be spent focusing on how your body feels and how sensuous it is.

S-2: Looking at Your Body
Look at yourself in the mirror for an hour. Talk with all parts of your body. Let each part know what you think of it. Let each part

reply to you. Take in all the feelings you have about your body. Allow in the uncomfortable feeling you get about spending time doing this activity.

S-3: Looking at Your Genitals

Spend some time with your genitals. See G-1 for details on this.

S-4: Touching Your Body

Spend an hour stroking yourself all over your nude body. Allow yourself to vary the speed, intensity and pressure. Pay attention to what feels good to you. Make a commitment to do this every week until you start to let in how good it feels to notice your own body and take this kind of loving care in regards to it.

S-5: Touching Genitals

Spend an hour touching your genitals without the purpose of having an orgasm. Just explore to experience what feels good and what feels bad. Change pressure. Put one finger on your clitoris and press different ways, now put two fingers on and see how that feels. Lie on your back at first, then your side, then your stomach. See what different sensations you get in each position. Put something else on your clitoris. A feather, a piece of cloth, something cold, something hot, anything that seems like it may feel good. You have many nerve endings in that organ, and see what it takes to stimulate them.

Try all types of activity with your vagina. Put your finger(s) inside and around. Try other objects to put inside your vagina if you wish to: a vegetable that is warmed by water, a rubber tube that slides easily in and out of your vagina. Be creative. This is your vagina, nobody else is going to see you, nobody else is going to have any say-so in this activity. Let your imagination go and have fun. Even if this does not feel like fun, keep at it for an hour and see what you feel afterwards.

Do not forget your anus. It is part of your genital area. You may only want to touch it on the outside. You may want to touch inside but are afraid. The main rule to remember is to make sure you do not put anything inside your vagina that has been in your anus. You can get infections from bacteria that live happily in your colon but can cause great damage in your vagina. Also remember to have as much lubrication as you need if you are going to put something inside your anus. Do not force anything. You can use saliva, vegetable oil, K-Y jelly, anything that is not a vaseline base, as this does not allow your tissues to breathe.

S-6: *Masturbate*

Masturbate for an hour. If your immediate response is "how can I spend an hour on that in my schedule" rethink this whole process of improving your sex life. If you are unwilling to give yourself an hour of your own time, you are going to have problems creating more full sex.

If you do not have orgasms easily and feel you will get too frustrated masturbating for an hour, remember that this is for the purpose of loving your body and spending time with it, not to have an orgasm. If you are a woman that has orgasms easily, spend an hour not having an orgasm until the very end. Try all kinds of touching and loving of your body and do not bring yourself to climax.

However you masturbate is fine. If you never have masturbated before, you may want to explore other books on masturbation. (See the bibliography.) It is simply giving yourself sexual pleasure. You do not have to do anything special.

You may want to touch it lightly or very hard. The important issue is to stimulate your clitoris. This is the focus of our nerves in the genital area. If you look in the physiology chapter, you will see the shape of your whole clitoris. However you want to stimulate this organ, do so. This may mean putting something inside your vagina to create pressure on your clitoris. The anus has access to the clitoris also.

The clearest access is on the head of the clitoral gland itself. This will usually bring the most intense type of response. Keeping this stimulation even and at the same intensity is usually necessary to create an orgasmic response, if that is what you are looking for.

Many women like to use vibrators when they masturbate. You can get them at most department stores, and in the larger cities there are now appearing stores that are dedicated to vibrators and other sex toys. If you cannot find them, look in the bibliography for mail order houses where you can get them. They can greatly enhance your masturbating. The machine may seem cold at first, but many women learn to love vibrators after receiving lots of pleasure from them. There are many types, some go inside the vagina, some rest on the outside of the genitals. Some women lie on their backs to massage their genitals, some lie on their stomachs. Give yourself plenty of time to explore how you like the vibrator.

Do not forget to touch and stimulate your breasts while you masturbate. They are as much as part of your sex life as you allow them to be. They often send great sensations to the rest of your body. Make sure that you do not give up without trying all types of activity with your breasts. Some women like to have their breasts touched lightly, some like a good deal of pressure. Some women only like to have their nipple touched, others like to have their whole breast felt with a hand all at the same time. See what is right for you. This is an opportunity to decide when and how any sort of physical activity is going to happen.

Sex with a Partner: Exercises P-1 to P-8

Each of these exercises is meant to have a time period on one day for partner A to be the receiver and partner B to be the giver. Then they are to reverse roles on another day, with partner B being the receiver and partner A being the giver. Please read the information at the beginning of sex exercises for more information.

Do not move on to another exercise without feeling accepting about the one you have just done. You may repeat these exercises from one time to one million times or anywhere in between. The goal is to become comfortable with the physical part of your relationship. It is not a race. You will not be graded. No one is watching over your shoulder. Take your time.

P-1: Sensual Time With a Partner

Repeat S-1 with a partner, making sure that the time is spent without physical contact. This is meant to encourage the expansion of your definition of "sex." The two of you can spend sexual time together that has nothing to do with you physically touching one another.

P-2: Talk About Sex

Talk about sex together every day. Read about this exercise in C-2.

P-3: Holding

Spend half an hour holding one another with your clothes on. This can be done anywhere, but with just the two of you in attendance. It is supposed to be intimate time alone. The temptation is to talk during the time. I strongly encourage you to spend this time communicating with your bodies only. No talking, t.v., or music. The holding is to be simply that, not touching of genitals, breasts. It is to be a non-threatening time for both women.

P-4: Holding Naked
Hold one another for half an hour with your clothes off. This again is not to include touching with breasts or genitals. Read P-3 for specific instructions.

P-5: Massage
Begin a series of massages. They are to begin with the most non-threatening areas and continue only as each partner feels comfortable. Follow the instructions to have each partner be a giver and receiver on different days. You may want to have classical music on (something you will not follow with your mind, nothing you can sing the words to), but no t.v., no kids, no other people in the room.

As the giver, allow your loving energy to flow through your arms and hands into your partner's body. Do not use pressure that creates spasm or tension in your body. If this begins to happen, stop and shake your arms. Rest if you need to. This is a place to begin to learn your limits and do not ask yourself to go beyond them.

As the receiver, allow yourself to take the loving energy that is coming into your body. Watch how you resist any sort of show of love. Watch how uncomfortable you are with the focus being on you. Let this go through your mind. When you get anxious about your partner giving you that much time, ask her if she is tired. Find out if she wants to stop. If she says "no" believe her, let her continue for the time which the two of you agreed upon If she says "yes" she is tired, the two of you can negotiate. Does this mean you both will continue later? Does it mean she will keep going even if she is tired? It is fine to talk about the process. This is not a magic spell that will stop if you talk about it. Let yourselves become more honest with one another.

Suggested below are a number of massage exercises. You can go through these exercise in order or you may want to see which ones make you most uncomfortable. "Uncomfortable" includes not feeling comfortable spending that much time with one of the steps. Pick a discomforting exercise, then start practicing with the next to last exercise before that. Work your way along gradually, paying attention to feelings.

If you and your partner find yourselves "forgetting" to make appointments or breaking ones you have made, try backing up to earlier, less threatening exercises. Breaking appointments is often a sign of resistance.

None of these massage exercises are to lead to actual genital contact in a sexual, love-making way. The best way to pursue this series of exercises is to not have sex at all afterwards. It allows each of you to be experiencing the actual activity that is going on rather than anticipating what may happen afterwards.

A. Massage hands with clothes on. Take your time getting to know your partner's hands. Allow this exercise to last at least half and hour and work towards an hour.

B. Massage feet with clothes on. Once again take your time. When we go quickly through an exercise like this, we lose the essence, which is communication.

C. Massage your partner's face while both of you have your clothes on. Slowly, slowly.

D. Massage hands, feet, and face with clothes off. No other part of the body is to be touched. This is to learn gradually how to be together with your bodies. Have the room warm so that each may be comfortable.

E. Massage the body without including breasts and genitals. Again do this slowly. Get re-acquainted with parts of your partner's body that perhaps you do not remember with your hands. Feast on all the sexual energy that's available without having genital contact.

F. Massage the body including the breasts. This is to be done under clear permission from the woman who is the receiver. It will also be important to find out how she likes her breasts massaged. Does she like a light touch or a heavy one? Does she like long strokes or short ones? The giver must watch her intention and make sure she is not touching her partner's breasts in a way that is sexually stimulating. This massage is meant to acknowledge the breasts in a loving way, not to insist they are sexual instruments.

G. Massage the body including breasts and genitals. Once again, it is important to have information about how the receiver likes to be touched. Even if you think you know, ask her and see what she says. If it is not clear how the touching should be done, the two of you may spend time during the massage communicating clearly about that. Does that kind of touch feel good? Does this type feel too intrusive? This is not to be a sexually stimulating massage.

P-6: Oral Sex

If you do want to have oral sex but are having problems with it, this exercise may be helpful. Talk about your concerns on oral sex when you are not in the sexual setting. This will help to keep you from sabotaging the actual experience. If one or both of you continues to talk negatively when you are in a sexual situation, eventually that situation becomes loaded with unpleasant memories. Hopefully through reprogramming, this can be changed.

Make sure each agrees to do this exercise before you begin. You may feel funny setting aside time to have oral sex, but unless you do, your discomfort with it may only increase.

You may want to wash off one another's genitals. I say this not because I feel that genitals smell bad, but only because I feel that many women have a difficult time with the smell of something as unfamiliar as women's genitals. Therefore, to help those women have access to oral sex, I have suggested this measure here. You must of course do what is the most comfortable for each of you.

Some women prefer to have oral sex with their eyes closed. Others like to watch what is happening. Still others insist that it be done in the dark with bed covers over each woman. Whatever works for you, do it. Make sure your partner has agreed to your suggestions and then create the atmosphere you like.

Making your partner's genitals familiar to you is the important part of getting comfortable with oral sex. This can be done with sight, touch, smell and taste. Doing exercises PG-1 and PG-2 may help to facilitate becoming familiar with sight and touch. Smell can be helped by washing. It can also be helped simply by becoming familiar with the smell of your partner's genitals . Smell them whenever you get a chance. Do it every day as part of your exercise.

Tasting genitals is often one of the most favorable parts of lesbian sex. However, many women find it difficult to do. Put your tongue on her belly, her arm, her breast, now move to her genitals. Watch the difference in the sensation for you. Genital skin is just skin. In fact, the skin that covers our whole body is considered one organ. Even though there are different kinds of skin cells, the skin "bag" we live in is one organ. See if reframing how you think of the skin of the genitals helps with your ability to taste it.

To start the tasting process, cover the genital area with your own spit. That will help make the taste familiar. When there is not enough spit, stop, and apply some more. If the spit is not enough, try something which tastes good to you. Whipping cream, jelly, avocado, bananna, strawberries—anything that will stick to the skin and that tastes good. Put this on the genitals and lick it off. If you come to skin, and are still not ready to lick it, put some more of the food on. Do this process over and over if you need or want to. Keep checking with your partner as you go. Spend a little time actually putting your tongue onto the skin of your partner's genitals. Do this even if you do not want to.

Start by doing this exercise for short periods of time. Make a date once a week to practice oral sex and do it for five minutes. Then move to some other sexual activity that is unambiguously enjoyable for you. Many women feel they have to have oral sex with their partner until she has an orgasm. This is not the case. It can only be one small part of your sexual activity. If you do not want to have it, sex can still be fantastic. The point of this exercise is to make oral sex a positive experience rather than a traumatic one.

P-7: *Having Another Woman Enter Your Vagina*

If you are a woman who would like to include in your sex practices having your vagina entered, but have found it difficult emotionally or physically, this may help.

Step 1: Begin by telling your partner in a non-sexual setting why having something in your vagina has been difficult for you. You may have been a survivor of incest or rape. You may have a spastic vagina. You may have been abused by another woman during sex. You may never have done this before and are afraid. It is important for your partner to know what in your past has contributed to the present.

Step 2: If you have been a survivor of sexual abuse which resulted in an emotionally negative response to something in your vagina, you will have to work at de-sensitizing yourself. Read some of the excellent books that have been published on rape and incest. (See the bibliography.) They will help you begin to learn about these crimes. Read the chapter entitled "Barriers to Sexuality" in this book. You may also want to look over the other exercises in this homework chapter and figure out if you need to do them before you get to this one. A-1 through A-7 may be especially helpful.

Step 3: To begin the process of de-sensitizing yourself, make sure that you take your time with this. Only practice for five minutes at a time. That may even be too long. Stop whenever flashbacks of old incidents happen. Talk to your partner about them. Let her know what is happening in your head even if you think it is stupid or silly or that she will be bored hearing it again and again. Educate yourself about the fact that incest and rape are acts of violence, not acts of sex. They were perpetrated from a need of power, not from positive sexual desire. This is different from your current situation. Let your partner remind you of this when you stop the action to reground yourself.

Step 4: The receiver is always directing the action. Begin with having the giver put a finger at the entry to the vagina. The receiver takes a hold of the finger and when she wants to, she moves the finger into the vagina. This is done slowly and with a great deal of awareness.

Step 5: The receiver allows the finger to lie quietly in the vagina for as long as she feels comfortable. This may only be seconds. This may last up to twenty minutes. There is only a change when the receiver wants to change.

Step 6: Once the receiver wants to move further into the exercise, she moves the hand of the giver so that the finger is moving in and out of the vagina. This is done slowly and with much love. If the giver becomes tired, she needs to let the receiver know this so they can stop when it feels appropriate. Continuing when you do not want to will result in the giver having a great deal of resentment.

Step 7: Only when you feel comfortable, allow the giver to put one finger in the vagina without the receiver holding her hand. Increase the number of fingers only as it is comfortable.

P-8: Vaginismus—Spastic Vagina

Some women have spastic vaginas. This can be the result of nerve damage, pressure on nerves, or vaginismus. Vaginismus is a condition that results in spasm of the lower portion of the vagina when anything is introduced into it. With this spastic condition, there usually is a great deal of discomfort with even one finger put into the vagina. Spastic conditions that are the result of nerve damage are not possible to change, but can be made more a part of love making rather than something to avoid. Vaginismus is a condition that can be changed. The woman who, for any reason, has a spastic vagina should carefully consider whether she indeed wants or needs to deal with it. It may be fine to have sex without someone entering your vagina. If you indeed want to include your your vagina as a part of your love making and find the spasms inhibit you, the following exercises may help. Make sure you are doing these exercises for you and not because you think you should.

The intention of the following exercises is to gradually introduce something into the vagina. This should start with something very thin and graduate to larger sizes as you continue. You may want to try your partner's little finger at first. That could be increased gradually to two, three or more fingers. If that is difficult, there are other options. If you have access to any medical or laboratory supplies, obtain a set of graduated syringe covers. A doctor who wants to be helpful could also get these for you. They start very small and come in increasingly larger sizes. They are plastic and have one end that is narrow. These can be helpful as they can be used by the woman with the spasms herself. They also are not a part of another person's anatomy and thus may not have the psychological implications of a finger.

You may also try any safe narrow object, as small around as possible. Do not use anything that can break or that is rough or cold. Be creative. Tampax inserters work well, and come in different sizes. Vegetables can be used—warm them with water first, and start with something as thin as a small asparagus spear. Make sure that whatever you use is well lubricated with vegetable oil or K-Y jelly.

These exercises are certainly something you can do yourself. You simply need something that is long enough for you to hold comfortably that you are able to move in and out of your vagina. If you are working with a partner, the woman with the spasms needs to be the one directing action at all times. She determines how large an object to start with, how it should be introduced into her vagina, and what should be done with the object once it is inside her.

Step 1: Set this up like any exercise that has been mentioned here. Set aside a time and make this separate from the love making you do with yourself or your partner. This is a problem area and your love making can certainly continue without involving your vagina if you want it to.

Step 2: Start any work on your vagina with some physical exercises for relaxation; you may try exercises R-1 through R-8, depending on your circumstances. When you are in an actual sexual situation, use these exercises beforehand. Let your partner know what your concerns are and ask her to do the relaxation with you.

Step 3: Take the narrowest object in the series that you have chosen. Take it in your hand, and holding it, close your eyes. Picture it being put at the opening of your vagina. In your visualization, see it going into your vagina. See it going in smoothly, slowly and with your permission. Imagine that your vagina is relaxed and open to the experience. If your vagina starts to spasm in your visualization, stop the action and start it only when you are relaxed and fully open to the exercise. Do this visualization any time you are working on these spasms, especially when you are introducing something new to your body.

Step 4: Put the narrowest object at the opening of your vagina. Making sure it is well lubricated, put it in the opening of the vagina very slowly. If your vagina starts to spasm at the introduction, stop, breathe and use the relaxation exercise again.

Only go in as far as is comfortable. This may only be 1/16th of an inch. Accept your vagina for what it has to offer you. Your vagina may only be able to accept this object 1/64th of an inch. Hurrying through this will not change your experience. That will only make it more difficult. Let the object sit in this position for a few minutes. If that is too much, take it out when necessary. You be the judge of your own experience. Trust your instincts.

Step 5: Gradually move the object you have started with into your vagina farther. Do this very slowly and if your vagina starts to spasm, stop the process. Let the object stay in the position it is in, if you are able. Do the relaxation exercises; breathe. Allow yourself to visualize the object inside your vagina. See the object as something you choose to have inside you.

If you are doing this with a partner, make sure you touch the object when your vagina starts to spasm. This way you will have some contact with the process other than just feeling it in your vagina.

Step 6: When you are ready (it may be hours, weeks, months, it may be never) move the object in and out of your vagina very slowly. If you are doing this with a partner, take a hold of the object also so that you know you can control the speed and the deepness. If your vagina starts to spasm, stop the action and begin to breathe deeply again slowly and work on relaxation.

Step 7: Repeat the series of exercises as often as you need to. You may want to use the narrowest object for months. It may be all you really want to have inside your vagina. You may not want to have a finger in your vagina ever. You may want to learn only how to have one finger inside you. Whatever your goal, you should be the one who chooses, not your partner, not your idea of what you think you should do.

Step 8: If you want to, move to a slightly larger object. Repeat the exercises above until you are comfortable. Again, this may be a long time.

Step 9: After getting comfortable with objects that you have chosen as safe for your vagina, move now to fingers if you would like to have them in your vagina. These fingers can be your own or those of a partner. Go through the steps in this exercise again beginning with one finger and gradually move to as many fingers as you feel are desirable. Whenever your vagina starts to spasm, make sure you slow down, go back a step and begin again. The key to this is patience, relaxation, visualization and self-love.

Step 10: There may be physiological reasons that your vagina is unable to completely stop spasms. If you continue to have involuntary spasms no matter how much you try and relax, do a visualization of your vagina. Imagine the spasms and trace them to the nerve that causes them. Imagine stroking that nerve so that it can relax. Allow yourself to forgive that nerve for its condition. See if there is a way for you to accept your nerve and the resultant effect on your vagina. There may be compromises you and your nerve can make. Perhaps you'll be willing to settle for one finger in your vagina occasionally, rather than as part of your love making every time. Have a conversation with your nerve and vagina and see what the three of you can figure out.

You may have to give up the idea of having something in your vagina. This may be a sad thought for you, and you may need to mourn this loss. Perhaps this is a good time to re-read the chapter "What We Do in Bed." See what other possibilities are open to you. Staying attached to what you cannot do stops considerations of what you can do. Read the chapter on disabilities; this may give you some insight.

Exercises for Orgasmic Response

This is intended to go along with the chapters on "Tyranny of Orgasm," "Orgasmic Problems and Concerns," and "Physiology." Please read those and thoroughly examine what your intentions are. Do you want to have orgasms? Do you feel that you are missing something if you haven't had orgasms? Do you get frustrated on a physical level because you don't orgasm? Do you wonder if you do have orgasms? Do you have resentment that your partner has them so easily? Do you think you are not vulnerable and open because you don't have orgasms?

The book *For Yourself* by Lonnie Barbach is an excellent book for you to read. Even though she aims it at heterosexual women, there is much good information for any lesbian.

The following exercises may not result in your having an orgasm. Even if you do one time, the exercises may not be effective for you another time. Please be gentle with yourself and honor whatever your body is doing.

Orgasmic Response With Yourself: Exercises O-1 to O-7

O-1: Writing
Step 1: Write a letter to your sexual response. Tell it how dissatisfied you are. Let it know how you cannot trust it and how it therefore makes you not like to have sex. Really let your body know how it has let you down. When you feel a response from the opposite side of yourself, ignore it. This is to bring up all your disappointments and angers at your problems with orgasm. This is to bring up any issues that you may not have dealt with. It is geared to allow that anger to come out in an appropriate way and not when you are actually in a sexual situation.

Step 2: Write a letter filled with the appreciation you have for your sexual response and body. Even if you feel you don't have any, think until something comes into your mind. You may only appreciate that your body is not dead and thus it is alive to respond. Whatever you can find, make sure you write it down. This is to allow you to see that there is opportunity for reconciliation with your sexual response cycle. It cannot expand and heal without your support.

O-2: Relaxation

Look through the exercises in the relaxation section and choose which feel appropriate for you.

O-3: Masturbation

This is the next step. You must learn to be able to give yourself some pleasure. Whether or not this results in orgasm, the pleasure your body receives is important. Look at exercises S-5 to S-6. You may also want to look at all the exercises on Learning Comfort with Genitals (G-1 to G-8) and Sex Exercises (S-1 to S-6). They may give you some good insights.

O-4: My Body Feels Dead

Step 1: If you are reading or being read this book, you are not dead. It is important to reassure yourself. Even if you currently have a life-threatening illness, you are not dead. When you are masturbating and you feel your body has stopped any sort of feeling, you are not tuning in to the subtle messages. Stop your activity when this occurs. Lie very still and feel your body. Tune into the itching that occurs while you lie there. Feel where you are constricted. Pay attention to your breathing. Experience how hard it is to lie in one place for any time. All of these messages will begin to prove to you that you are not dead.

Step 2: Focus on your genitals while you are lying still. Feel what they are experiencing. Your clitoris may be numb—that tingly feeling means you are alive. You may not have sensation in your vagina. Reach down and touch it very lightly. You will find a nerve responds to that touch. Push down on your muscles from within, as if you are peeing. This will give you sensations in your genitals. You are alive.

Step 3: Start masturbating again slowly. Take your time and make the pressure very light. Increase this only when you are sure your body is going at the same pace as your mind. Sometimes our heads try to hurry our bodies. They will not be hurried and may "play dead" to get your attention off your mind and its expectations and back to your body's ability.

O-5: Working with the "Edge"

Many women describe that they get to an "edge" when they are having sexual contact with themselves or a partner. They are stimulated to a point where they feel they are just about to go over "the edge" and then their body stops feeling. It's as if the electricity is shut off and all forward momentum is stopped. Very like a sneeze that your body prepares for and then never happens. This is very common.

Step 1: Stimulate yourself in masturbation using whatever method pleases you. Stop before that edge comes. Wait a few moments before you stimulate yourself again. Begin the process again and stop before the edge appears. Do this several times. Part of what you can learn from this is that you are in fact able to stimulate your body in a way that you have some control over.

If you become numb from the stimulation, stop altogether and come back to this at another time. There is no sense in forcing your body. It will not continue to respond. The nerves can only take so much.

Step 2: When you masturbate again, allow your body to come to the edge. Increase your stimulation at that time and do not stop it. If you lose your momentum and the energy subsides, start the stimulation again. You may need the strength of a vibrator to push your body through this edge. If you are already using a vibrator, you may need to switch to a hand at this point to ease the stimulation and then switch back to a vibrator in a few moments.

Step 3: Experiment with the stimulation. You may take a long time to find the formula. Allow yourself to see this practice as something that is exciting. Not something that is frustrating. Try to frame it in a way that you can see the whole process as positive.

O-6: Expanding Your View of Orgasm

Step 1: Read the chapters suggested above. Allow yourself to tune into other body responses you have. Think about when you sneeze. How about when you laugh. There are times when those responses to stimulation are intense and some times when they are almost nonexistent. When you stimulate yourself to a certain point and you cannot go any further, when your body just will not tolerate any more stimulation, this can be your orgasm. It is not a spastic response that is pronounced. It is a diffusing of the tension around your genitals. It may take a long time. Just because partners you have been with have jerking, obvious, responses to stimulation does not mean they have an orgasm and you do not.

Step 2: Masturbate and afterwards talk to yourself about how wonderful your orgasmic response was. Act as if you had an orgasm. See what it is like to have had one, whether you feel you actually did or not. Tell yourself how lucky you are to have a fulfilling sex life. See how your body responds when you actually have something kind to say about it. You may be surprised. Orgasm may only be a state of mind.

Step 3: See what your physical concept of orgasm is about. Practice having an orgasm. Lie in bed and writhe around in a way that you would expect an orgasm would feel like. Make your face grimace. Let your legs wave wildly. Let your pelvis gyrate. You may be afraid of what you think a physical expression of orgasm would be. You may think it's rather ugly and base. You may be surprised at what you feel in response to your body's performance.

O-7: *Using a Vibrator*
Many women who do not have orgasms with their hands have wonderful orgasms with a vibrator. If you have not tried this yet, think of doing it. You can find one through the mail order house listed in the bibliography, at major department stores and erotica stores. There are many different types that work for different women. Some women use them while on their backs, others while on their stomachs or sides. It may just be the type of stimulation you need. It is not a substitution for another person, just an enhancement to your sex life.

Orgasmic Response With a Partner:
Exercises OP-1 to OP-7

Before you begin, review the exercises in the above section and the chapter on couple dynamics. You may also want to review the exercises on communication (C-1 to C-5) to help you both learn how to talk with one another about sex.

If you are the partner of a woman who does not have orgasms, you may be tired of dealing with her sexual problems and wish you could just be having to sex the way "everybody else does." Well, everybody else is doing it this way also, as usually women who do not easily have orgasms get involved with women who do have orgasms easily. The process can be frustrating. If you are a partner who has orgasms easily, be willing to tell the truth about your feelings. Your partner feels your energy even if you do not say anything. Make sure you read the chapters suggested to expand your ideas about orgasm. Make a clear choice about working on these exercises. If you do not want to, make sure you do not. If you are interested in a more fulfilling sex life, there are many alternatives. These exercises may help.

OP-1: *Make a Pact to Not Have Orgasm*

The purpose of this is talked about in the "Tyranny of Orgasm" chapter. Start these exercises with your partner by making this contract. This will take the pressure off having an orgasm and may allow each of you to work with the situation. Make this pact to last for one month. In the meantime, do the following exercises and see what happens.

OP-2: *Relaxation*

See Relaxation section.

OP-3: *Show Each Other How You Masturbate*

Partner A puts her hand on partner B's hand. Partner B shows exactly how she stimulates herself, how hard the pressure is and where. She shows A when and if she puts a finger or other object in her vagina. If B moves around on her clitoris or inside her vagina she shows A how she does it. Be very specific. Do not leave out any details. The more information you exchange in the process, the better. Trade positions when all the information about B's masturbation is gathered.

OP-4: *One Body Feels Dead and the Other Woman is Upset*

Read O-4 about how one of you can't be dead.

If you are the partner of the woman whose body is "playing dead," you may need to work through some of your resentment. You may feel that your partner is doing this on purpose to get out of love making. She is probably as upset as you are, though she may not be showing it since she is "dead"—usually feelings go when the body "dies". You can participate in O-4 with her. Lie together and, when she is willing, touch her in places where she feels "dead." Do this with much love, and not in order to create what you hope will be sexual feelings. The purpose is just for reacquainting each of you with her body that feels.

If you are the partner and feel so angry you cannot participate in this exercise, you may try to remember the last time you visited your parents. Remember the time when you were called in by your boss. Think of when you last "went dead" in a situation that was difficult for you. This may be a similar phenomenon. It does not have to continue to be negative if both of you are willing to work through the pain.

OP-5: Working with the Edge Together

Read O-5 together. This can easily be adapted to working with both partners together. If A is working on her "edge" she can either be stimulated by B, or can lay in B's arms while she masturbates. The same technique applies. Each woman is urged to give the other feedback afterwards about how she felt during the exercise.

OP-6: Expanding Both of Your Views of Orgasm

This again parallels O-6. You may both want to try this exercise together. Act as if A had an orgasm when she did not in actuality. Talk about how each of you think that would change your sex life. It may feel like a lot would change; it may seem like nothing would change. Talk about what each of you has invested in the orgasmic response changing to what you thought it "should" be.

If you are a partner of a woman who does not have orgasm as you do, stop and consider why you think your way of having orgasms is "right." It may be something you have never thought about before. It is important to question the arrogance of assuming the way you have a physical response to stimulation is the only way that is truly orgasm.

OP-7: Using A Vibrator Together

The truth is no person's fingers or tongue has anything on a vibrator. Some women need that level of intensity to have orgasms. Read O-7 for more information on this. If you are a partner of a woman who needs the stimulation of a vibrator to have an orgasm, do not feel this is an insult to your character or abilities as a lover. It simply means she needs the stimulation of intense constant movement to experience orgasm. If orgasm is a goal both of you have for your love making, then you may have to consider vibrators as a way of making that real for each of you.

There are many types of vibrators that have a head shaped like a sphere that allows both women to be stimulated by it at the same time. This can make using the vibrator not second best, but another way of love making.

There is an opportunity for women to share quite an intimate connection if one woman wants to masturbate with the vibrator while the other woman holds her. This can be love making at its best—giving support where it is really needed.

Exercises for Sexual Abuse Survivors and Their Partners

Please read the chapter on "Barriers to Sexuality." This will give you a good basis on which to start these exercises. You need to know you are not alone. These exercises are simply meant to help you begin the process of being sexual with yourself or a partner. They do not always heal the pain of your experience.

Incest and rape have to be self-defined. You may have lived in a household where you had to withstand daily bodily assaults. You may have been molested when you were five by a stranger. You may have had vague boundaries in your family where sexual innuendo was made, but nothing physical happened that you remember. If you read through these exercises and they feel "right" for you, that is the most important part. When sexual abuse is a part of your past it can affect your present sex life. Do whichever of these exercises feels appropriate. Only move to another when you feel safe in doing so.

Self-Healing of Sexual Abuse: Exercises A-1 to A-7

A-1: Separating Your Experience From Sex
Step 1: One of the most important factors in this process is learning that the sexual abuse you suffered had nothing to do with sex. It was a power play perpetrated on you by someone else.

Step 2: Write a letter to the perpetrator of your incest. Tell him or her what you feel about their act. This does not have to be a letter that you share with anyone. This is simply for yourself. Explain what it was like to be the age you were and have this happen to you. Let the person know how it has affected your current sex life. Tell her or him that you need to get them out of your bedroom and in their proper place. Keep the letter so you can refer to it when you forget why you don't want to have sex, or when you feel sad or angry and don't have a "good" reason.

A-2: Protecting The Little Girl Within

Step 1: As a survivor of abuse, you had a little girl that was unprotected. This may even have been the case if you were an adult rape victim. Each woman has a little girl within and if she is not cared for (by her mother, father, institution, peers, culture) she can be exposed to sexual abuse. In this exercise the point is to teach the little girl that you intend to do all you can to protect her from this behavior.

Step 2: You need to explain what boundaries you are setting with your body. This is important for a little girl whose boundaries were violated. Writing a letter about this can be very effective. You again may not choose to show this letter to anyone. This letter is for the safety of your little girl within. If the sexual abuse was done by a parent, let him or her know that you cannot accept their inappropriate parenting. Explain to them that a parent has no right to use such power over their children. Tell the parent that there is no excuse that allows them the opportunity to abuse a child in that way. Alcohol and drugs are not an excuse. Loneliness is not an excuse. Attraction is not an excuse. Their own feelings of abandonment are not an excuse. That they could not get sex from an adult is not an excuse. That they were "over-sexed" is not an excuse. That you were their favorite daughter is not an excuse. That you were assumed to be "seductive" is not an excuse. There is no excuse that could allow sexual abuse to be acceptable.

Step 3: If the perpetrator was a stranger or another family member, you can write the same type of letter that is in step 2. The important aspect is letting your little girl know there are limits and that you are going to set them for her.

A-3: Setting You Sexual Limits Today

Step 1: Whether you have a partner or not, write down what you see as your sexual limits. If you would feel more comfortable, record them on a tape recorder. The goal here is to come up with a list of what is acceptable sexual behavior for you today. You may just make a list of what you are willing to do sexually and what you are unwilling to do. The "don't" list may include oral sex or penetration of the vagina. It may even include kissing. The "do" list may only have holding on it right now. What is important is being honest with yourself. Again you do not have to show this to anyone. It is for yourself. You may be surprised as to what limits you commonly do not uphold for yourself. You may not have known that kissing really bothers you—it seems so ordinary. Any activity may have many connotations for you that do not make it ordinary. Respect yourself.

Step 2: You may want to give this list to your long-term partner or casual sexual partners. You may want to get an agreement from them that they will respect your limits and support you in doing so. This will at least give you some ability to be in a sexual situation with an ally rather than someone you fear is a potential attacker.

A-4: Learning to Say "No"

Step 1: This is something which every incest and rape survivor must learn. Practice with little things. Make an agreement that you will say "no" to three things this week that you normally would have said "yes" to but did not really want to do. For instance, if your best friend wants you to go to the laundromat with her and you really don't want to, say "no." This may seem silly, but once you begin to see how often you say "yes" when you would like to say "no," you will see how valuable this experiment can be.

Step 2: This is especially important in sex. If you do not want to have sex, you must learn to say "no." This is true even if you have said "no" for the last two years. It may take a long time before you really want to say "yes." Wait for that time.

Step 3: If you want to have sex but have specific activities that you do not want to do, say "no" to those activities. You must listen to your inner self and respect her. She has had experiences in the past that taught her no one would listen. Help her turn this concept around by learning to believe her discomfort.

A-5: Masturbating with Consciousness

This is an experiment in being sexual with yourself and learning what makes you uncomfortable. Go through a regular session of masturbation. Do it slowly, taking great care of yourself. Whenever you have an uncomfortable feeling or a flashback of a negative scene, stop. Comfort yourself at that moment. If you can contact your little girl within, let her know that you and she are alone, that you will take care of her and that you will not let anyone

267

hurt her. Do this hundreds of times during a masturbation if you need to. If discomfort does not arise, don't push it. Let it happen naturally. Let your masturbation be a caring, loving investigation for you.

A-6: *Forgiving Yourself*
Many of us hold ourselves responsible for something that was perpetrated on us. It's important to go beyond these feelings and forgive ourselves for what's happened in the past.

You may not know that you are holding yourself responsible for your rape or incest. As a child, some part of you may have enjoyed the attention and thus you feel that you must have invited it. It is a statement of the general deprivation in your family that incest was welcome attention. You may feel you should not have been out on the streets after dark or you wouldn't have been raped. No one has the right to overpower a girl or woman. There is no excuse. You may be ashamed that this is in your past and feel that only terrible women have this history. One in three women is a sexual abuse survivor. It crosses all race, class and cultural boundaries. There is no such things as a woman who is bad because she is a survivor of sexual abuse.

Begin today by spending some small time each day forgiving yourself for your sexual abuse. You didn't cause it. You are a survivor of it. You are a heroine. Treat yourself with respect. You have lived to see the day when you would no longer be a victim to someone else's lack of control.

A-7: *Ritual for Cleansing*
There are many women who feel "dirty" because of their sexual abuse. You may want to try a ritual to cleanse and heal yourself. There are many books on the subject of ritual; *The Spiral Dance* is one you may try. A simple exercise is as follows. Do this alone or with loving supportive friends. Light white candles around the room. Take a long hot bath (or sit in a hot tub), take that opportunity to imagine soaking the impurities out of your skin. See them flowing out of your genitals, breasts, lips, mouth. Come into a warm room and anoint yourself with oil. If you feel willing, allow your friends to rub some of the oil into you. Ask the universe to remove the vestiges of the sexual abuse from your body, and give yourself loving energy to replace the negative energy. Imagine yourself birthing again into a pure body that will keep its purity throughout life.

Imagine yourself coming into the protection you deserve that will protect you. Allow yourself to dance or rest curled into a blanket—whichever feels a proper resolution for this scene.

Becoming Sexual with a Partner
As a Survivor of Sexual Abuse:
Exercises AP-1 to AP-5

AP-1: Talking About the Sexual Abuse

Step 1: Many women do not know how to explain their abuse to someone else. Even if you have had a partner for a long time you may not have told her about the incest or rape in your life. This is not uncommon. We are taught not to talk about these things. Some have said the culture teaches that incest is not the crime—talking about it is the crime. It is important to talk about it. If nothing more than to let your partner (or friends) know about your past. It is important that you not keep yourself silent. You committed no crime (even if part of you enjoyed the attention, as is common).

Step 2: Make a decision to tell your partner some part or all of your sexual abuse story. Make a deadline for yourself today or next month. The important aspect is to make a date that you are willing to keep. Ask her in advance for support on that day and that you would like her time. Tell the incidents leading up to and during the incident(s). Include also what happened afterward. Let her know that this is important to you and that you expect her to respect the magnitude of your disclosure. Ask her in advance to give you only positive feedback and support. After your telling, see if you are willing to be held. This has been an important undertaking.

AP-2: Giving Your "Limits" to Your Partner

Look at exercise A-3. This may be something that is helpful for you and your partner. Discuss the list if you are willing. See if she understands your limits and why you have set them.

AP-3: Becoming Actively Sexual

Step 1: You may want to start with only having contact with a partner with all your clothes on. This stage may last six months or more. You may want to go through all the exercises on genitals and sex in the other homework sections. You may need a lot of time to gradually open up your sexuality.

Step 2: Give yourself as much time as you need. This may be two or three years after you have been raped. It may be a long time (years even) after you have started dealing with your incest before you have interest in sex with a partner again. Be gentle with yourself. Forcing yourself is only ignoring that little girl within. It will not help your sex life.

Step 3: When you are actually in a sexual situation, stop and start as often as you need to. You may have flashbacks of the sexual abuse scene. It may only be a smell or a feeling that comes through your brain as something that is uncomfortable. Whatever it is, stop the action between you and your partner. Discuss this with her ahead of time so she understands what is happening. Do not push yourself; pamper yourself. You may need to stop and start every minute. How often does not matter. You have to heal. If your partner does not have the patience, you must give yourself a gift and not be sexual with her. Take care of yourself first.

AP-4: Discusing Sex Outside of Bed

Spend time after you are sexual with your lover discussing what was good about your sexual time together and what was difficult. Each of you has an opportunity to let the other one in on what you need, like, or are afraid of. Doing this out of the usual sexual setting is helpful. Do it the next day, in the kitchen. Hearing difficult material during the love making or right after is often damaging to future sexual times.

AP-5: Support the Courage Both of You Display

Whatever side you are on in this relationship, make sure you give one another and yourself lots of loving support for being willing to go through such difficulty with one another. Creating a loving, sexual relationship in the midst of dealing with incest and rape is a tremendous feat indeed. Both of you need to be supported and applauded. Spend some time every week telling each other why you are there and how important the other is to you. Let your partner know she is special. Allow her to tell you how special you are.

Partners of Incest or Rape Survivors: Exercises PA-1 to PA-4

PA-1: Nothing That Happened to Me Was That Bad

This is often a reason that many partners become resentful and angry. While the statement looked at objectively may be true, it is also true that the hard things that happened to you in your life are important. If you continue to discount your experiences because your partner's were so bad, you will never get the healing you need. We have all had hard times.

PA-2: I'm Getting Sick of Dealing with This

Step 1: It is difficult to deal with someone else's problems on an on-going basis. But if you got into the relationship because you only wanted to share her joy, you have made a false commitment. The true gift is being willing to share her pain. If you feel you are willing to share her pain, but are just sick of doing it in the moment, let your partner know. Tell her that you want to be available to her, and you will be back with renewed energy next week (month, whatever feels right), but that this week you must take a rest.

Step 2: Spend some time with your friends that have extra to give you. You need attention and love, and if your partner is depleted from dealing with her incest or rape, you must find that loving energy someplace else.

PA-3: I Want to Have Sex

Step 1: If you need sexual connection and she is unavailable, you may need to masturbate. This may be your second choice of sexual expression, but in a relationship with a sexual abuse survivor it may be all you have access to.

Step 2: Discuss with your partner if she is willing to have any type of sexual relationship with you right now. She may be willing for you to hold one another, or massage each other, or kiss. Try to look at how you can expand your definition of sex and have some of your needs taken care of.

Step 3: It can be manipulative and unfair to both of you for you to go have sex with someone else, unless you have both agreed to that ahead of time. Often partners of sexual abuse survivors have sex with others from a place of resentment. If you are that resentful, try exercise PA-1 and PA-2. You may also need to get out of the relationship now for your own sake. It may be the only way for you to feel good about yourself.

PA-4: Why Are You With a Sexual Abuse Survivor?

This is a question to explore. Is it because you are attracted to her vulnerability? Does it give you a chance to look at how you had abuse in your own life? Is this an opportunity to help someone feel good about herself? Are you attracted to her strength in exploring this in her life?

When you get frustrated, start asking yourself why you are with some woman who needs a lot of extra time and consideration. It may be a way for you to slow down and take care of yourself. It may be a way for you to feel superior. Whatever the thoughts that come up, let yourself have them. We are all basically selfish and want to do things that enhance ouselves. Choosing partners is no different. Be willing to explore your selfishness and ego in this relationship.

Appendix

APPENDIX A:
Specific Issues on Sex and Disability

There is almost nothing written on the topic of lesbian sex and disability. Disabled lesbians find that the culture provides no support for having sex lives. When disabled women ask questions about sex, from our medical workers, we are discouraged from having sex at all. Sometimes we are told that women in wheelchairs shouldn't get pregnant (as if all sex is heterosexual) although there are no reproductive or physical reasons that totally rule out pregnancy. Sometimes we are told that there will be no positions available to us in which sex is comfortable. That's not true. Or it may be assumed that we ought to forget sex because our disabilities will make us unattractive to possible partners. That is certainly not the case.

> "I was actually told to 'forget sex' because of my polio that would keep me wheelchair bound. Doctors only dealt with sex because I insisted and then usually discouraged it. 'Get involved in other things' one doctor advised."

> "People in the able-bodied community do not realize how much some disabled people rely on their doctors and other medical workers. When they tell you, either by silence or in actual words, that your sex life will be non-existent, you believe them."

This culture encourages disabled people to concentrate on our disabilities, not figure out our abilities. Women are seen as people who can easily get along without sex. So, all in all, we are neither encouraged to be sexual nor to figure out how to meet our sexual needs.

"How am I supposed to know what I want in a sexual relationship? Women have not been allowed to talk. Lesbians have not been heard, and disabled people have not been seen. Once again in sex I have to be the one to explain myself. I have to be the one to say what I need. Why doesn't someone teach able-bodied women so the disabled don't have to?"

Sex is just as important for us as it is for any woman. As with all women, we have sexual issues to explore, techniques to teach and learn, and support to find. We have the right to experience sex in any way we choose. The primary source for sexual information will be our bodies.

Listen and feel very carefully to what is happening inside of you, both physically and emotionally. Read the chapter on tyranny of orgasm. Try questioning yourself on the assumptions you make about sex. Have you accepted the dictates of the culture? (Who hasn't?) Does it have to be spontaneous to count? Are orgasms essential? Is good sex only when you can reciprocate with a partner?

"If I paid attention to what I read in books, I would never be able to have sex that was great. I am paralyzed from the neck down. I need a lot of preparation to get my body in the right position. I mean it's a little weird asking my attendant to help me get in a position so that I can masturbate. But I have learned to do it."

Some of us with physical differences can never have "spontaneous sex." We must arrange our bodies in a way that enables us to have sex comfortably. Others of us are constrained by the schedules of our attendants. When we are having sex with another woman for the first time, we must explain what is painful and what is not. Some of us may not be able to get in certain positions. Others may not have what Masters and Johnson would refer to as "orgasms," although we have an orgasmic release. You may have to re-define the meaning of orgasm. You will have to learn your own unique sexual response pattern. Forget what the books say; listen to your own body. If you feel that your sex life is positive, then it is. You are the one who is right about you.

276

Exercise for Any Disability

Practice is the most valuable activity you can engage in around sex. Start by practicing with yourself. Take some uninterrupted time and relax with yourself. Stroke yourself all over. Try different positions on the bed or floor. If you need help with your body positioning ask your attendant or a friend to help. See what positions bring you pain and which bring you pleasure. See what touch and what positions are in between pleasure and pain. Be very specific with yourself. For example, note: "Intense touching in my genitals brings me pain, but stroking gently with a piece of cloth brings me pleasure. Touching my breasts is out of the question. Lying on my side feels better than lying on my back or stomach. Having one finger in my vagina is just fine, more than that and I begin to hurt."

Put together all the information you gather. This is all you need if your sex life does not include partners. If you want to include a partner, you must then relay all this information to her.

Saying all this to a partner may seem overwhelming but there are ways to make it less difficult. Arrange an occasion to talk together when you are not in a sexual situation. Talk at a time that is not your customary time for being sexual. Remind your sexual partner that neither of you is in a position to have to act on anything you say. Give both of you time to digest the information.

If you have had this partner for a while, she may be upset that you didn't share this information with her before. You may need to share with her your reasons for not having been explicit. You may have been worried that she would leave you. You may have felt self-conscious about having to specify your needs again. You may have hoped she would figure them out without your having to tell her. There may have been a denial on your part that you had to more specifically deal with sex.

You may want to explain that you need to do this exercise because you want to ensure that you have a wonderful sex life together. Let her know that your being able to do this with her is a mark of your trust. You may both want to talk about how the whole process makes you feel. Acknowledge that most women do not deal with sex this explicitly and that both of you are brave to do so. Keep in mind that you are having this discussion in order to have a more exciting sex life and remind your partner, too.

Paralysis

Nerve impairment can alter sex. It can be the result of birth traumas, spinal cord injuries, and a number of acute and chronic diseases. Impairment may be intermittent or constant, may be increasing or decreasing in severity. If you have nerve impairment, the functioning of your nervous system will affect your sexual responding.

Read the chapter on physiology for a basic understanding of the sexual response cycle. Remember that there are two sexual response arcs. One describes a circle from the brain through the body to the genitals and back to the brain. The second arc is in the pelvic region. Even if your particular disability has impaired the arc in the pelvic region, your sexual response may not be gone. The first arc is still operative. There is still nerve activity in the rest of your body and the brain. Sexual response is still available to you. Some of us experience orgasms in our genitals even if we do not have feeling in that region.

> "I have been in a wheelchair since I was 14. I have no feeling from my waist down. There is feeling on the inside somehow, because I do have orgasms when my lover caresses my nipples in a specific way."

If you have a reaction in your pelvic region that you think you could not be having because of your particular nerve impairment, trust yourself. Make sure you embark on your own exploration of this response. Ask your partner(s) if the two of you can practice very specific sexual stimulation. Ask her to simulate you in different parts of your body. Have her vary the pressure and speed of the stimulation. While she is touching you, close your eyes and allow the sensation to move through your body. Experience how different types of touch feel. See where the feeling starts and where it ends within your body. Have your partner stimulate you in parts of your body that "do not have feeling." See if you do in fact feel sensations in parts that you thought were unfeeling. All parts of your body need touch. All parts respond even if you cannot feel the sensation in a way that the able-bodied community says you should be able to.

Make sure you let your partner know when different types of stimulation feel good. Tell her specifically what does not feel good. Do not make her figure this out by herself. Do not expect her to know by the movements of your body or the sounds that you make. Tell her.

"Even though my lover and I had been together for two years, we decided to learn very specifically what my body liked and what it didn't. I was so surprised to learn that she had not known most of the information I gave her. She had been my attendant for a year before we became lovers. I guess I just always thought she knew everything about me."

Spasms

Pressure on nerves can cause a variety of symptoms, including spasms. Those of us who have cerebral palsy or other types of spasmodic responses may have little or no interference with our sexual response cycle. Others of us may have periodic breaks in the sexual response arcs due to the spasms (see the section on paralysis for a discussion of sexual arcs). Spasms may create problems in continuity; you may need continuous stimulation to experience your sexual response fully. You will have to communicate very specifically with your partner. Doing this effectively and with a minimum of distress will come after practicing. You do not have to forego positive sexual experiences because you have spasms. You will just have to prolong sex so that you receive all the pleasure you are entitled to.

"My spasms are frustrating sometimes. They seem to increase when I get excited. So when I get into sex with another woman I often start to shake more than normal. Telling someone that I want her to follow my body with her hand or mouth even if my body is jumping has been hard. Saying just that has gotten easier the more I do it."

"I start feeling guilty because not only does it take me longer than it does my lover to walk someplace, but it takes me longer to feel satisfied with sex. She has never complained, and finally I asked her if she got tired of having to caress me over and over. She says no, so I guess I'll have to believe her."

If you ask your lover to do certain things to your body to make you feel good, please believe her when she says she is willing. In sex, it is particularly difficult for anyone to accept what another gives. If you have difficulty receiving, you are not alone. But the greatest satisfaction in giving is having your gift accepted. If you ask and she says she is willing and then you sense resentment later, do not make guesses about her feelings. Ask. She may not have the feelings you're attributing to her. If she is resenting the kinds of sex you need, it is better to hear that directly from her rather than making up what you think she feels.

Pain

Pain can be a result of any kind of physical disability. Pain can be intermittent or chronic, increasing or decreasing. Whatever the cause of pain, it affects our sex lives.

Talking to your partner(s) about your pain and how it changes your sexual behavior is crucial. Although pain may not inhibit the actual functioning of your body's sexual response, you may have to go through quite a process to get to pleasure. Your pain may effect what positions you can assume, your willingness to be touched, the level of stimulation your body is able to tolerate, even your ability to be present for sex. Spontaneity may be out of the question for you. You may have the urge, but may not have any physical ability to act on it. You may feel you have to avoid sex because it seems too frightening to lose control of a body that is already in pain. You may fear attempting some activity because it may bring more pain.

> "I finally had to admit that having oral sex was painful for me. I was unable to have my legs spread far enough apart without being in terrible pain. I was also unable to get in the right position. I finally had to tell my partner. I found myself avoiding sex instead of not wanting oral sex. She and I have been trying to come up with different positions that may help, some work sometimes. The best part is that we are working on this together; I am not suffering in silence."

Give yourself permission to start and stop when it comes to sex. If an activity begins to hurt, stop. Let your partner know ahead of time that you will stop if you feel pain. Do not push yourself beyond your limits because you're afraid of your partner's anger. Pushing yourself beyond your pain threshold will negatively reinforce sex for you. Sex does not need to equal more pain.

Sight Disabilities

Sight impairment may present some difficulties in regard to sex, although the culture encourages us to have sex with our eyes closed. If you have special needs in regard to your sight, you will have to learn to express them to your partner(s). If you are able to see images in strong light, you may want to turn the lights up during sex. Since the culture seems to think that sex is better in the dark, you will need to let your partner know ahead of time about your desire for light. Don't be afraid to state your need for light during sex. Experiment with having the lights on. You may want to try a bulb with a lesser wattage. Gradually increase the light until your needs are met.

Hearing Impairments

One of the signals (we learn through reading, movies and advertisements) of our partner's sexual pleasure is the sounds she makes during lovemaking. Those of us who are hearing impaired can feel the "sounds" a lover is making in other ways.

> "I used to think I was crazy because I could 'hear' my lover's body moaning when she was sexually excited. I decided to respond as if I were right and I found I was. Even though I am totally deaf, I can respond to sound."

If your impairment is partial, let your partner know the extent to which your hearing is impaired. She may not have been aware of the extent of your hearing impairment. If you hear in one ear better than the other, let her know that. Demand accessability during sex. Tell her to talk loudly if need be. If you would enjoy sex more with your partner making louder sounds, let her know that. Each of you may practice making loud sounds when you are out of bed to learn unself-consciousness. It may be painful if sounds are too loud. Experiment until you find the pitch that is just right.

Invisible Disabilities

Invisible disabilities include diseases that affect our bones, gastrointestinal tracts, blood, organs, or brain. Chronic illness may become disabilities.

Hidden disabilities may be the hardest to teach partners about. If disabilities cannot be seen, they are often forgotten. You may collude in that denial, desiring to ignore your physical and emotional limitations.

Many of us with hidden disabilties often push ourselves beyond our threshold of pain or discomfort. If this happens with sex, it can begin a pattern of uncomfortable sexual situations. Talk to your partner(s) about your limitations in order to create freedom for yourself. Then your limits will be up front. You will not have to draw the line in the middle of a sexual situation. Allowing your partner in on the issue gives her a part of the responsibility in curtailing uncomfortable activity.

Allow yourself to figure out what special treatment you need in regard to sex. If you have hidden disabilities, you have the same rights as all of us. Treat yourself to getting exactly what you need from a sexual encounter.

Emotional Disorders

Disabling emotional disorders include emotional problems that severely intrude on our functioning. Disabling emotional disorders includes severe depression, suicidal concerns, schizophrenia, manic-depressive illness, and borderline personality problems.

People assume that everyone has emotional problems or that no one has them. Most people treat those of us with emotional illness in the same way they treat those of us with physical disabilities—with ignorance and fear. You can have a good sex life even if you have severe emotional disabilities. It may take time to accomplish a satisfying sex life, but it is possible. You need encouragement from people who care about your life. It may be especially difficult for you to find a support group; you may have to create a support structure of your own.

"Sometimes people don't believe that I have
emotional problems. Some people are afraid of my

problems. I feel pushed away by most people. Then I get scared and think I'll never find a woman who will want to have sex with me. Finding other women who feel that way has helped me. I don't always trust them, but it does feel better than being alone."

If you have disabling emotional problems, you probably have had little if any information given to you about your sexuality. You may have been in therapy for years and learned nothing about how to actually deal with, and survive, a sexual relationship. Or you may have been given a lot of information about how to have relationships, but little on sex itself.

"I think my therapist would just as soon I didn't have sex at all. She keeps telling me that I have to take good care of myself but that I don't have good judgment when it comes to choosing sex partners. I figure I have to learn somehow, and practice is the best way."

As a lesbian with severe emotional problems, you may have been told that your lesbianism is causing your emotional illness. Do not believe this for an instant. Just because your counselor said it, doesn't make it so. Read the chapter on homophobia. Have your therapist read it also. There are more heterosexuals with emotional illnesses than lesbians. Does your counselor tell heterosexual women that they are ill because they have sex with men? Probably not. It is too pat an answer to say that someone is emotionally unstable because they emotionally and sexually identify with their own sex.

"When I found a lesbian psychiatrist I was relieved. She told me that I was a lesbian who had severe emotional problems. I had always heard that I had emotional problems because I was a lesbian. Now that I think back, I wonder if those doctors expected me to stop being attracted to women and then I would not have anymore problems. That would be really strange."

Emotional disorders can severely affect our sex lives. For example, depression can slow down the central nervous system until the sexual response cycle temporarily stops working. Anxiety may render you unable to tolerate any more stimulation. Paranoia may render you incapable of the intimacy required of a sexual encounter. You must learn to go slowly during your sexual activity. Remember that you are the expert on yourself. Give yourself as much time as you need. You have the right to create a satisfying sex life for yourself. Find out what works for you in your sex life. If the pressure is too much this week, try next month. Try in six months. You do not have to give up on sex. Take all the time you need.

Joint and Bone Problems

Joint and bone problems include arthritis, bursitis, and post-polio difficulties. The problems may be traced to diseases, injuries, operations or hereditary issues. Whatever their origin, living with them can be painful and will affect your sex life.

Let your partners know under what circumstances you experience pain. Let your partners know what sexual positions give you pain. Relay information about how you can be more comfortable in sexual situations; for example, you may need pillows under a leg or your hips.

Experiment with a partner you trust when you are not in a sexual situation. Fully clothed, practice taking different positions. Each contributes ideas that may make sex more comfortable for you. Try sex standing, sitting, laying on one side or the other. Try things that you do not normally think of. If both of you are willing to be creative, you may find out more about sex than you thought you could know. Doing this fully clothed, during a time when you are alert and not ready for bed, may make your communication easier. Experiment and use the information later if it helps.

When you are having a flare-up of pain, get in a comfortable position and allow your partner to caress you without the expectation that you will reciprocate. This may help you to relax. Your partner may masturbate with you holding her if she wants to. Spend some time together doing things that help relieve your pain. Soak in hot water or stroke the affected area with ice. Make this a sensual event. Redefine what may have been a source of resentment into something that enhances your sex life. Ask your partner about her feelings; she may experience joining in your recovery from pain as a gift rather than a burden.

Diabetes Mellitus

Varying in intensity and disabling effects, diabetes can cause energy fluctuations and mood swings which create havoc with sex. If you have diabetes, treat yourself with great care. Stay very aware of your body. Do not push yourself beyond your stamina threshold. Put yourself and your needs first, and those of your partner second. Your sex life may suffer from time to time, but remember that you are the most important element in your joint sex life.

Diabetes does not seem to inhibit sexual desire or excitement, although some of us experience problems with the nervous system that prevents us from experiencing orgasm. Read the tyranny of orgasm chapter and find types of sexual activity that are fulfilling and exciting for you.

Life-Threatening Illness

Dealing with dying will undoubtedly affect your sex life. A diagnosis that causes one to face death plunges you into depression. Depression can prevent you from feeling any sort of sexual desire; your sexual desire may not vanish, it may simply decrease. You might desperately want to feel "normal" sexually in order to be close to your partner(s) during this time.

Women with life-threatening illnesses are forced to conserve their energy. You will find yourself unable to be as active as you have been in the past. The energy you do have will fluctuate with medication, operations, rest, your emotional state, and the severity of your illness. If you are unwilling to accept the information your body gives you, you will find yourself exhausted and unable to continue.

The stages of dying carry with them different possibilities of sexual experience. You may find yourself wanting to have sex but be physically unable to do so. You will have to find sexual activities that satisfy you. Your partner may feel a tremendous need for sexual activity to satisfy her needs for intimacy. You may be unable to comply. Talking about why you cannot fulfill her needs may take the pressure off of both of you. Or your partner(s) may have difficulty facing the finiteness of life and may emotionally or physically abandon you. Being intimate with someone who is dying may be more than they can bear. There is a particular pain about this if you are wanting sex. You may deeply miss your ability to have sexual connection up to the very end of your life.

Whatever your experience during your life-threatening illness, you must put yourself at the center of your life. You must constantly validate the reality that you are experiencing. Do not allow anyone to make you feel inadequate around your sexual feelings or lack of them. Self-respect is the key to your having the sex life you want during this period.

Medication

Most people with disabilities are on medication either constantly or periodically. Many of these medications have side effects that affect sexual functioning. One of the simplest ways to find out if the medicine you are on affects sex is to look it up in the *Physicians Desk Reference*, referred to as the "PDR" in the medical community. Your doctor has at least one copy of it. Your local library should have one. It is published by the pharmaceutical companies and has every medication listed by brand and generic name with long lists of side effects caused.

When checking for the drug's impact on sex look for: depression, lethargy, anxiety, agitation, loss or decrease in libido (which means sex drive), any mind alterations (ie. paranoia, psychosis, auditory or visual hallucinations), and loss of appetite.

Drugs that are known to decrease sex drive and sex functioning in people are listed below (from *Disorders of Sexual Desire*, pp. 203-211). The amount that will affect you depends on your size and tolerance. If you are taking drugs that you feel are inhibiting your sexual desire or functioning, see what alternatives you and your health care worker can find.

The following list is given by classification and includes both "street' drugs and prescription drugs:

Sedatives: alcohol, barbiturates.

Anti-anxiety drugs: diazopines, valium, librium, tranzene, meprobamate.

Narcotics: morphine, codeine, paragoric, methadone.

Antipsychotics: stelazine, mellaril, thorazine, haldol.

Antidepressants: lithium carbonate.

Stimulants: cocaine, amphetamine.

Hormones: adrenal steroids (includes cortisone), spironolactone.

Antihypertensives: alpha-methyl dopa, quaternary ammonium compounds, guanethidine, bretylium, propranalol.

Miscellaneous: tryptophan.

Neuro-toxic agents: halgenated aromatic hydrocarbons (agricultural fungicide), carbon disulfide and mangan intoxification (industrial exposure).

If you take any of these drugs regularly, and you seem to have a lowered sex drive, ask your physician to work with you on lowering the dosage. If that is not possible, you may have to wait until you no longer need such a high dosage to experience a return of your usual sex drive.

Below is a list of diseases and illnesses that are associated with decreased sexual desire and functioning. If you have one of these diseases/illnesses, you may experience a disruption in your sexual life: Multiple sclerosis; alcohol neuropathy; diabetes mellitus; removal of adrenals, ovaries, or pituitary for treatment of estrogen-sensitive breast cancer; thyroid deficiency; muscular distrophy; fibrosis, degeneration; weakness of the pubococcygeal muscles; pituitary tumor; psychomotor epilepsy; herniated lumbar disc; radical pelvic surgery (sacral resections, rectal and bladder operations); leukemia; sickle cell disease; cardiac disease; coronary artery disease; hypertension; endocrine disorders; carcinoid syndrome; kidney problems; liver problems; debilitating diseases (advanced malignancies, degenerative diseases, pulmonary diseases).

Partners Who Are Able-Bodied

You are in a unique position. You have a partner who is physically different, from whom you can learn a great deal. You do not get to make the same assumptions about what she is experiencing. To really know what is happening to your partner inside her body, you must ask. Do not expect your partner to always be the one who has to bring up her special needs. Even though she probably has been dealing with her physical differences longer than you have, that does not make it easier for her to talk about them. It certainly does not make it simpler for her to bring up issues that affect your sex life together. She, in fact, may not be able to bring up the changes she needs in your life together. She may feel that once again she is requiring time, energy and attention. She may be tired of always having to be the one that asks for concessions. Let her know that you are willing to make those concessions, and that you want to know what they are.

"I was always taught that whatever problems other people had was no concern of mine. Now that I am lovers with a woman who is disabled, I see that I am just as responsible for making overtures that will make our life together more comfortable. In sex I take a lot of time asking her what she needs. I receive so much in return. I am so lucky."

You must also be willing to explain your own concerns around sexuality. Just because you call yourself able-bodied does not mean that you do not have your own issues with sex. Certain positions may be painful for you. Some sexual activities may be emotionally difficult for you. Make sure that you own these. Do not assume that because your partner has the "real" disability that you cannot have problems of a physical or emotional nature. Your needs are important also. Voice them, giving your partner some relief from always being the one with the sexual concerns.

If you have resentments about your partner's disability, make sure you let her know. Let her know in a way that will encourage a dialogue. Do not let your resentments pile up until you can no longer contain them and then find yourself letting loose in a destructive manner. We able-bodied women sometimes do not say what we need to to disabled women because we do not want to "hurt" them. If you think your partner does not know that your are holding resentment, you are fooling yourself. She may not be able to voice it, but on some level she realizes it. Resentments will always get in the way of sexual functioning. It is not up to your disabled partner to pull your resentments out of you. She has enough to deal with in terms of her own disability. She should not have to be responsible for voicing your resentments too.

Appendix B:

Sexually Transmitted Diseases And Problems

Lesbians have less venereal disease than the rest of the population. "Veneral" means that the malady is transmitted through actual sexual contact. We as women loving women are lucky in this regard that our sexual lovemaking creates fewer problems than that of the heterosexual, bi-sexual, or gay male communities. However, this does not mean that we are not vulnerable to sexually transmitted problems. In fact many women mistakenly believe that because lesbian love is "so pure" there is no way to have problems because of it.

The diseases and problems we *do* get are covered here so that you will know they exist. For a more complete study consult other books which cover this subject more fully. *Lesbian Health Matters!*, *Sapphistry,* and *A New View of a Woman's Body* are good sources on this material. (See the bibliography for author and publisher.)

Above all, remember that sexually transmitted diseases do not make us or our lovemaking "bad" or "wrong". Bacteria and viruses are transmitted from one human to another all the time. That's how we get colds. These germs can be transmitted through all kinds of touch, or even through the air. Some particular ones are passed from one woman to another through kissing, putting fingers in vaginas, anuses, or mouths, or through touching genitals together. We seem to view the bugs and viruses that can be caught through genital contact as ones that are "dirty". This is just a carry-over from the puritanical attitudes about genitals that we inherited from our ancestors. Do not worry about your morals if you contract one of these. And, do not let a fear of being judged prevent you from seeking help if you suspect you've contracted something.

Vaginitis

"Vaginitis" simply means that there is an "itis" or infecion in the vagina. This is women's most common complaint by far. Vaginas get numerous types of infections and for a good reason. The vagina is dark, moist, warm and virtually closed off from air—a perfect place for bugs to thrive. They love it. In fact, under normal circumstances, we have millions maybe trillions of bugs living in our vaginas at one time. This is a delicately balanced world and once it is disrupted, lots of difficult symptoms can follow.

Many things besides making love can disrupt the world of the vagina. The use of some types of medicines kill off the helpful bugs and allow others to take over. Particularly notable are antibiotics which, while given regularly by physicians to cure one part of your body, are very likely to wreck havoc in your vagina.

Transmitting vaginitis from one woman to another is easily done through the mixing of vaginal discharges. Fingers transport the juices, touching genitals together mixes things up, and sharing toys (vibrators, dildos) can introduce new germs from one vagina to the other. Stress can also make your vagina more susceptible to these disorders.

The three most common forms of vaginitis are: yeast, trichomonas or bacteria. All of these are found in your vagina all the time. The problem is when they take over.

Yeast (Monilia)

This is exactly what grows bread. It is a friendly fungus that is normal in our vaginas, but too much is uncomfortable. It itches and causes a discharge that may smell like bread yeast. The itching often feels unbearable. The most common home remedy for this is to douche (wash out the vagina) with a solution of vinegar and warm water (¼ cup to 1 quart). This is to be done each day (sometimes twice) until the symptoms go away. Also spoon in some plain, unsweetened, yogurt every day in your vagina. Or coat a tampax with yogurt and put it in your vagina. Both these remedies can help to restore the balance in your vagina. If these do not work, there are other methods which can be recommended by a health care worker including suppositories or creams that are anti-fungicides.

Trichomonas

Lovingly called "trich" by many women, this is a protozoan (one celled animal) that multiplies to the point it causes any one of the following: redness of the genitals; itching; pain on peeing; yellow-green vaginal discharge. Its one-celled seige on your vagina is usually hard to stop. Many women end up taking flagyl, a prescription drug that can cause side effects of nausea and headaches. Be sure not to use alcohol for a few days either before or after taking flagyl. Also, this is not a safe drug for pregnant women or nursing mothers. There are some women who suffer from chronic trichomonas. Be sure your health care worker knows that some chronic trichomonas has been linked to pre-cancer cells in the cervix. This does not always happen, but should be watched closely.

Bacterial Infection

These bugs exist normally in the vagina, but in smaller numbers. The most common one to get out of hand is the hemophilus. Once again the symptoms are uncomfortable: itching, burning while peeing, red genitals, discharge that smells very different from normal odors A common treatment is to douche with betadine and water. Betadine (which is basically iodine) can be bought at any drug store. Mix it with water and put it in your vagina (a douche bag and tube makes this easy) and on your genitals. You may also want to put plain, unsweetened yogurt in your vagina to prevent the betadine from setting off a yeast infection.

Cervixitis

This is an infection of the cervix (the bottom end of the uterus up inside the vagina). It has the same symptoms as vaginitis. Some women suffer from chronic trichomonas infections which can be linked to pre-cancer cells in the cervix and looks like cervixitis. Make sure that you care for your vagina and cervix and get regular checkups to know what is happening inside your vagina.

Herpes Simplex Type I and II

Herpes has probably gotten more press in the last four years than any political candidate. Fear of herpes swept the nation in 1982 and was once labeled the modern day "scarlet letter." Again, there have been moral judgments made about a virus because it is transmitted through sexual contact. Most commonly, it is passed from a person who has active herpes to someone else via contact with the mucous membranes. However, this virus is also suspected of being passed on in many other ways as well. There is some belief that herpes can be contracted by sitting in a hot tub where someone with active herpes has been—not necessarily at the same time.

The herpes virus appears most commonly in two types. One is termed herpes type I, the other herpes type II. The first is found 95% of the time on the lips, 5% on the genitals. The second type is found 95% of the time on the genitals, 5% of the time on the lips. The duration of either is ten days, the normal span for viruses. There can also be a series of outbreaks, one helping to encourage the formation of another. Outbreaks usually occur at the same site over and over again. The theory is that the virus stays in the cells and is always present, only manifesting outside the tissue from time to time. The outbreak of sores can be aggravated by stress, ill health, heat, wind, the menstrual cycle and friction.

Many of us are immune to this virus. We do not "catch" it from contact. However, often the immunity diminishes as the person ages. Caution is wise under any circumstances.

Herpes I, on the lips, is the most obvious. It appears on the lip as a small, raised red dot which often itches when it first begins to form. Usually within 24 hours, it swells with fluid and becomes a painful sore. From the moment it first appears, it is communicable—that is, someone could catch it. (Some believe there could be some contagion even a day or two before the sore appears. Since there is no sign of the virus, this is difficult to determine.) Do not make contact between your lips and any part of anyone's body at this time. Kissing, having oral sex, kissing your partner before she has oral sex with you, all can spread the virus. It is not safe during any of the ten days of its cycle. Remember too, that kissing children, though not sexual, will still cause transmission of the virus.

The type of herpes (II) that appears on the genitals is more elusive. It takes many shapes and forms. Some women have herpes on their genitals that look exactly like that which appears on their lips. Other women have herpes that look like tears in the skin, not raised bumps. The outcome is usually the same however: shooting pains inside the body; swollen lymph nodes; fatigue; sometimes cold symptoms; sores draining with puss; itching; burning sensation from urination or touch. All women do not have every symptom but if you have any, they probably will last ten days. Consider the duration and pattern of appearance carefully when trying to determine whether the sore on your genitals is herpes.

Today's medical knowledge has not found a way to "cure" a virus once it appears in the body. Viruses go through a cycle whose visible symptoms usually last ten days (an arbitrary number chosen by the medical community). Many treatments are surfacing in trying to *con-*

trol the herpes symptoms once they appear. Probably the most common is L-lysine therapy. This is an amino acid that one can find in pill form usually wherever vitamins are sold. It is taken in large quantities and in conjuction with other healing vitamins, minerals and amino acids (L-cysteine, vitamins A, B complex, C, D, E, calcium, and zinc). Some dietary suggestions include increasing the intake of dark, leafy vegetables. One helpful measure is to wear all cotton underwear so the area gets as much air as possible. A good pamphlet that explains herpes and help for it is *Herpes! Something Can Be Done About It.* See the bibliography for other books that may help.

Venereal Warts

Just like warts on your hands, these are caused by a virus that can be exchanged between two women, but also can get into our bodies in ways that no one can explain. They can appear inside the vagina and anus, but usually appear outside the vagina. Health care workers burn them off with an acid solution. Sometimes if there are a lot of them, they have to be surgically removed.

Scabies and Crabs

These creatures deserve to live on the earth, but on our bodies they are really a drag. They cause intolerable itching.

Scabies attach on the skin of the genitals, nipples, ankles, in between fingers and toes, and anywhere else the skin is thin enough for them to penetrate. They burrow under and lay eggs. A small blister forms inside where they have their little families. They can spread to bedding and clothes, and to fully eliminate them, any cloth that has had contact with your skin has to be washed or dry cleaned at once. In addition, Kwell or a similar shampoo obtained by prescription should be used to poison them. The directions are very clear and should be followed.

Crabs are a form of lice that live exclusively on the pubic hair. They burrow into the skin between two pubic hairs and lay their eggs. They usually do not move from their treasured home, but to be sure, wash clothes after a treatment with Kwell (the poison shampoo).

In both cases, if you may possibly have had sexual partners after you became infested, it is important to tell those people. To prevent reinfection, all involved parties must use the shampoo even if some do not have symptoms. It is possible to have the bugs and not have the itching for a few days. Usually just telling someone that they have been exposed to scabies or crabs gets them itching, so there probably won't be much resistance.

Urinary Tract Infections

This problem shows up in your urethra (see the physiology chapter) and may also be present in your bladder or kidneys. It often is caused by too much movement in the area of the urethra from fingers, dildos, vibrators or anything else put in the vagina. The urethra is very tender so too much or too hard pressure in the vagina can cause problems. The activity need not be avoided; just be careful. Symptoms may include: pain and frequent peeing, pain in the abdomen and lower back, blood or pus in the urine. It is very important to treat this problem to prevent serious infections in the bladder and kidneys.

Women usually depend on prescription drugs to cure these infections, but Chinese herbs and acupuncture are effective. If you have symptoms of a urinary infection, go to a clinic, nurse practitioner, or doctor and have a culture (they grow the bugs to see what kind they are). They will prescribe sulfa drugs or antibiotics depending on the kind of bugs causing the infection. It is important that they know exactly what the problem is before you take the drug. You may jump at the chance to take something that day, but wait the 24 hours it takes for a culture just to be sure.

On your own, it can help to increase your liquids (one gallon a day at least), put wet heat on your pelvis and belly (soaking in the tub or using a hot water bottle), and drinking some acidic juice (orange, grapefruit, cranberry, etc). You may also want to wear cotton underwear, and after going to the bathroom, wipe your genitals from the front towards the back. This prevents bugs from entering the urethra from the anus which can really upset the balance.

Gonorrhea and Syphillis

These are rarely found in the lesbian community, but since they are not totally unheard of, they should occasionally be tested for. This is especially true if you are genitally sexual with men or bi-sexual women. Because of the fact that these diseases can often go undiscovered because of the lack of symptoms in women, they can cause a good deal of damage in your body.

Gonorrhea is a bacteria that may be found in the vagina, anus, or mouth. They can travel also to the cervix, rectum and throat. There can be a variety of symptoms, though you may not experience any, or only after you have had the disease for a while: unusual discharge from the vagina or anus; pain in the lower abdomen; sore throat; or burning with peeing. Diagnosed by a culture (growing the bug by taking a smear from the infected area), the treatment is antibiotics. You must tell every person you have had sexual contact with.

Syphillis is another bacteria and can be found through a blood test (VDRL) after the bug has been in the body for a few weeks. The only symptoms in the early stages are raised bumps that are not painful. They may multiply in later stages, and become open draining sores in latter stages. This bacteria can cause severe damage to organs, so it is important for it to be treated. Once again, the cure is antibiotics. You must tell every sexual partner so they may be treated and refrain from sexual activity until you are no longer infectious.

Sex During Genital Problems

Even though these problems may have cures or ways to avoid them, waiting for them to go away can be difficult. In addition, women who have chronic cases of any of these may find them debilitating to their on-going sex life. If this is true for you, refer back to the sex and disability chapter. The very important advice there can help you create a sex life that is positive. You may not feel disabled, but if these problems interrupt your bodily functions, they are disabling.

Learn to re-educate and love yourself during a time that is emotionally and physically draining. See the homework section for exercises that apply to you. You may need to re-learn how to touch your genitals. You may need to have your partner practice with you on some of the sex exercises. You may want to do some of the communication exercises to allow you and your partner to verbalize the difficulty you experience. The relaxation and self-esteem exercises may help you to learn to accept and love yourself again. Do not put this emotional work off because "you'll get over it" or because you feel it's unimportant. Allow yourself the pleasure of taking care of yourself today.

Remember, never equate venereal disease with punishment for immorality. Just as you accept a cold or a sore throat without guilt, accept infection of your genitals as one of life's little inconveniences. They may be unpleasant, or in the case of herpes even incurable, but if treated they are tolerable and they won't kill you. Ignored for reasons of embarassment or guilt, however, some of these bugs can become life threatening! Take care of yourself emotionally and physically.

Appendix C:

Checklists for Alcohol and Drug Abuse

I. Self-Check For Alcohol Or Drugs

1. Do you lose time from work due to drinking?

2. Is drinking making your home life unhappy?

3. Do you drink because you are shy with other people?

4. Is drinking affecting your reputation?

5. Have you ever felt remorse after drinking?

6. Have you gotten into financial difficulties as a result of drinking?

7. Do you turn to lower companions and an inferior environment when drinking?

8. Does your drinking make you careless of your family's welfare?

9. Has your ambition decreased since drinking?

10. Do you crave a drink at a definite time each day?

11. Do you want a drink the next morning?

12. Does drinking cause you to have difficulty in sleeping?

13. Has your efficiency decreased since drinking?

14. Is drinking jeopardizing your job or business?

15. Do you drink to escape from worries or trouble?

16. Do you drink alone?

17. Have you ever had a complete loss of memory as a result of drinking?

18. Has your physician ever treated you for drinking?

19. Do you drink to build up your self-confidence?

20. Have you every been to a hospital or institution on account of drinking?

If you have answered YES to any one of the questions, there is a definite warning that you may be alcoholic.

If you have answered YES to any two the chances are that you are an alcoholic.

If you have answered YES to three or more, you are definitely an alcoholic.

(The above test questions are used by Johns Hopkins University Hospital, Baltimore, Md., in deciding whether or not a patient is alcoholic.)

II. Another Test for Alcohol Abuse Problems

Once you have answered the self-check above, and you still do not know if you have a problem, do this test for one month.

Drink only two ounces of any alcoholic breverage within any 24 hour period (this includes beer or wine). Even if there is a wedding, a funeral, a break-up with a lover, drink no more than two ounces. Any excuse you find yourself making in order to drink is cause for concern. If you do drink more than two ounces within 24 hours— yes, this means even three ounces—you must start the month over again.

If you cannot do this for thirty days straight, you are an alcoholic.

III. Family Alcoholism Quiz

Do you think that someone in your family drinks too much? This quiz may help you to determine whether someone's drinking is directly affecting your life. Alcoholism hurts everyone: how much is it hurting you? Please try to answer the following questions honestly.

1. Does someone in your family undergo personality changes when he/she drinks to excess?

2. Do you find yourself bewildered by what's happening in your life?

3. Do you feel that drink is more important to this person than you are?

4. Do you feel sorry for yourself and frequently indulge in self-pity?

5. Has excessive drinking ruined special occasions?

6. Do you find yourself covering up for the consequences of someone else's drinking?

7. Do you often feel guilty or apologetic?

8. Is drinking involved in many of your family's activities?

9. Do you feel that you're different from other people?

10. Have you ever tried to fight the drinker by joining in the drinking?

11. Do you often feel depressed?

12. Is your family having financial difficulties because of drinking?

13. Do you have an unhappy homelife?

14. Have you ever tried to control the drinker's behavior by hiding the car keys, pouring the liquor down the drain, etc.?

15. Do you find yourself doing things out of character?

16. Do you find yourself distracted from your responsibilities because of this person's drinking?

17. Do you find yourself responding inconsistently to other members of your family?

18. Have you ever been embarrassed or felt the need to apologize for the drinker's actions?

19. Do you no longer feel good about yourself?

20. Have you ever feared for your own safety or the safety of other members of your family?

Bibliography

Alyson, Sasha, ed., 1980, *Young, Gay and Proud.* Alyson: Boston.

Anonymous, 1981, *Al-Anon's Twelve Steps and Twelve Traditions.* Al-Anon Family Groups: NY.

Anonymous, 1976. *Alcholics Anonymous.* Alcoholics Anonymous World Services, Inc.: NY.

Anonymous, 1982, *Each Day a New Beginning.* Hazeldon: Box 176, Center City, MN.

Anonymous, 1976. *One Day at a Time in Al-Anon.* Al-Anon Family Groups: NY.

Apter-Marsh, Mickey, 1982. *The Sexual Behavior of Alcoholic Women While Drinking and During Sobriety. Unpublished Ph.D. dissertation.*

Armstrong, Louise, 1978, *Kiss Daddy Goodnight: A Speak-Out on Incest.* Simon & Schuster: NY.

Bach, George and Goldberg, Herb, 1974, *Creative Aggression.* Doubleday: NY.

Bar bach, Lonnie Garfield, 1975, *For Yourself: Fulfillment of Female Sexuality.* Doubleday: NY.

Barbach, Lonnie; and Levine, Linda, 1980, *Shared Intimacies: Women's Sexual Experiences.* Doubleday: NY.

Becker, Elle Friedman, 1978, *Female Sexuality Following Spinal Cord Injury.* Cheever Publishing: Bloomington.

Bennett, Gerald; Vourakis, Christine; Woolf, Donna, eds., 1983, *Substance Abuse.* John Wiley: NY.

Biren, Joan, 1979, *Eye to Eye: Portraits of Lesbians.* Glad Hag Books: Washington, D.C.

Black, Claudia, 1981, *It Will Never Happen To Me.* M.A.C.: Denver, CO.

Blank, Joani, 1982, *Good Vibrations: The Complete Guide to Vibrators.* Down There Press: Box 2086, Burlingame, C, 94010.

Blank, Joani, 1980, *I Am My Lover.* Down There Press: Burlingame, CA.

Blank, Joani, 1977, *The Women's Play Book about Sex.* Down There Press: Burlingame, CA.

Blank, Joani, 1980, *The Playbook for Kids about Sex.* Down There Press: Burlingame, CA.

Blumstein, Phillip and Schwartz, Pepper, 1983, *American Couples.* Morrow and Co.: NY.

Brecher, R. and Brecher, E., 1966, *An Analysis of Human Sexual Response.* New American Libary: NY.

Brownmiller, Susan, 1975, *Against Our Will.* Simon & Schuster: NY.

Bregman, Sue, 1975, *Sexuality and the Spinal Cord Injured Woman.* Sister Kenny Institute, Chicago Ave., Minneapolis, MN, 55407.

Butler, Sandra, 1978, *Conspiracy of Silence: The Trauma of Incest.* New Glide Publications: San Francisco.

Bullard, David and Knight, Susan, *Sexuality and Physical Disability.* C.V. Mosby: St. Louis.

Califia, Pat, 1980, *Sapphistry: The Book of Lesbian Sexuality.* Naiad: Tallahassee.

Campling, J.O., 1981, *Better Lives for Disabled Women.* Virago: London.

Carnes, Patrick, 1983, *The Sexual Addict.* CompCare Pubs: Minneapolis, MN.

Cedar and Nelly, eds., 1979, *A Woman's Touch.* Womanshare Books: Grants Pass, OR.

Clark, Don, 1977, *Loving Someone Gay.* Celestial Arts: 231 Adrian Rd., Millbrae, CA, 94030.

Corbett, Katherine and Carrillo Cupolo, Ann, eds., 1982, *No More Stares.* Disability Rights Education and Defense Fund, Inc.: Berkeley.

Corinne, Tee, 1982, *Yantras of WomanLove.* Naiad Press: Tallahassee.

Corinne, Tee, 1978, *Labia Flowers,* Naiad Press: Tallahassee.

Cornelius, Debra; Makas, E., and Chipouras, S., 1981, *Getting Together,* RRRI-ALLB: 1828 L Street NW, Suite 704, Washington, D.C. 20036.

Cornwell, Morique, 1978, *Motherhood: How to Cope.* Disabled Living Foundation: London.

Daly, Mary, 1971, *The Church and The Second Sex.* Beacon Press: Boston.

Daly, Mary, 1973, *Beyond God The Father.* Beacon Press: Boston.

Daly, Mary, 1978, *Gyn/Ecology.* Beacon Press: Boston.

The Disability Rights Review, Disability Rights Education and Defense Fund, Inc., 2032 San Pablo Avenue, Berkeley Ca 94702. (This organization also keeps a list of names of disabled women's groups, caucuses and organizations and can provide a national list of Independent Living groups. Also, support and networking is available from the Disabled Lesbian Alliance: Room 229, 5 University Place, New York, NY, 10003.)

Duggy, Yvonne, 1981, *All Things Are Possible.* A.J. Garvin: Ann Arbor.

Elana, Myrna and Sundahl, Debi, eds., 1984, *On Our Backs: 1.* Box 421916, San Francisco 94142.

Evans, Arthur, 1978, *Witchcraft and the Gay Counterculture: A Radical View of Western Civilization and Some of the People It Has Tried to Destroy.* Fag Rag Books: Boston.

Fairchild, Betty and Hayward, Nancy, 1979, *Now that You Know: What Every Parent Should Know about Homosexuality.* Harcourt, Brace and Javonovich: NY.

Federation of Feminist Women's Health Centers, 1981, *A New View of a Woman's Body.* Simon & Schuster, NY.

Galana, Laurel and Covina, Gina, 1977, *The New Lesbians: Interviews with Women Across the U.S. and Canada.* Moon Books, Box 9223, Berkeley, 94709.

Gardner-Loulan, JoAnn; Lopez, Bonnie; and Quackenbush, Marcia, 1981, *Period.* Volcano Press: San Francisco.

Garden, Nancy, 1982, *Annie On My Mind.* Farrar, Straus and Giroux: NY.

Gearhart, Sally and Johnson, William, 1974, *Loving Women, Loving Men: Gay Liberation and the Church.* Glide Publications: San Francisco.

Gill, Eliana, 1984. *Outgrowing the Pain: A Book for and about Adults Abused as Children.* Launch Press: Box 40174, San Francisco, 94140.

Gail, Marilyn, *What Lesbians Do.* Godiva Publications: San Francisco.

Golombok, Susan; Spencer, Ann; and Rutter, Michael, 1983, "Children in lesbian and single-parent households: psychosexual and psychiatric appraisal" *Journal of Child Psychology and Psychiatry and Allied Disciplines, 24:* 551-572.

Goodman, Bernice, 1973, "The lesbian mother" *American Journal of Orthopsychiatry, 43:* 282-284.

Gordon, Sol, 1978, *Facts About Sex for Today's Youth.* John Day: NY.

Grahn, Judy, 1984, *Another Mother Tongue: Gay Words, Gay Worlds.* Beacon Press: Boston.

Green, Richard, 1978, "The best interests of the child with a lesbian mother" *Bulletin of the American Academy of Psychiatry and the Law, 10:* 7-15.

Greenwood, Sadja, .1984, *Menopause, Naturally.* Volcano Press: San Francisco.

Guy, Rosa, 1976, *Ruby*. Bantam: NY.

Hall, Marny, 1978, "Lesbian families: cultural and social issues," *Social Work, 23:* 380-385.

Hall, Marny, 1985, *The Lavender Couch: A Consumer's Guide to Psychotherapy for Lesbians and Gay Men*. Alyson: Boston.

Hamilton, Richard, 1980, *The Herpes Book*. J.P. Tarcher: Los Angeles.

Hanscombe, Gillian and Forster, Jackie, 1982, *Rocking the Cradle— Lesbian Mothers: A Challenge in Family Living*. Alyson: Boston.

Hautzig, Deborah, 1978, *Hey, Doll Face*. Bantam Books: NY.

Heiman, Julia; LoPiccolo, Leslie; and LoPiccolo, Joseph, 1976, *Becoming Orgasmic: A Sexual Growth Program for Women*.Prentice-Hall, Inc.; Englewood Cliffs, NJ.

Heron, Ann, ed, 1983, *One Teenager in Ten: Writings by Gay Youth*. Alyson: Boston.

Hite, Shere, 1976, *The Hite Report: A Nationwide Study of Female Sexuality*. Dell Publishing: NY.

Hoeffer, Beverly, 1981, "Children's acquistion of sex role behavior in lesbian mother families" *American Journal of Otheropsychiatry, 51:* 536-544.

Jay, Karla, and Young, Allen, eds., 1972, *Out of the Closets: Voices of Gay Liberation*. Douglas Book Corp.: 905 West End Ave., NY, 10025.

Kaplan, Helen Singer, 1981, *The New Sex Therapies*. Bruner-Mazel: NY.

Kaplan, Helen Singer, 1979, *Disorders of Sexual Desire*. Simon & Schuster: NY.

Karen, Jeanine and Skope Sue, eds., 1981, *Sapphic Touch*. Pamir Productions: San Francisco.

Kenoff, Dorothy, 1979, *Love and Limerance*. Stein and Day: NY.

Kinsey, Alfred; Pomeroy, Wardell; Martin, Clyde; and Gebhard, Paul, 1953, *Sexual Behavior in the Human Female*. W.B. Saunders, Co.: Philadelphia.

Kirkpatrick, Martha, 1982, "Lesbian mother families" *Psychiatric Annals, 12:* 842-848.

Kreiger, Susan, 1983, *The Mirror Dance: Identity in a Women's Community.* Temple University Press: Philadelphia.

Krestan, JoAnn and Bepko, Claudia, 1980. "Problems of Fusion in the Lesbian Relationship" *Family Process, 19:* 279.

Kushi, Michio, 1978, *Natural Healing through Macrobiotics.* Japan Publications, Inc.: Tokyo.

Lesbian Health Information Project, 1979. *Artificial Insemination: An Alternative Conception.* San Francisco Women's Centers, 3543 18th St., San Francisco 94110.

Levine, Stephen, 1982: *Who Dies: An Investigation of Conscious Living and Conscious Dying.* Anchor Books: NY.

Lewis, C.E.; Saghir, M.T.; and Robins, E., 1982, "Drinking Patterns in Homosexual and Heterosexual Women" *Journal of Clinical Psychiatry 43(7):* 277-279.

Lorde, Audre, 1980, *The Cancer Journals.* Spinsters Ink: San Francisco.

Macdonald, Barbara with Rich, Cynthia, 1983, *Look Me in the Eye: Old Women, Aging and Ageism.* Spinsters, Ink: San Francisco.

Mann, George A., 1979, *Recovering of Reality: Overcoming Physical Dependency.* Harper & Row: NY.

McNaron, Toni and Morgan, Yarrow, 1982, *Voices In The Night: Women Speaking About Incest.* Cleis: San Francisco.

Masters, William and Johnson, Virginia, 1979, *Homosexuality in Perspective.* Little, Brown and Co.: Boston.

Masters, William and Johnson, Virginia, 1966, *Human Sexual Response.* Little, Brown and Co.: Boston.

Meiselman, Karin C., 1976, *Incest.* Jossey-Bass: San Francisco.

Milam, James R.; and Ketcham, Katherine, 1981, *Under the Influence.* Madrona Publishers: Seattle.

Michael, John, 1976, *The Gay Drinking Problem: There is a Solution.* CompCare: Minneapolis.

Mitchell, Tom, 1980, *You're not Alone with Herpes.* Skylite Books: Novelty, Ohio.

Mooney, Thomas; Cole, Theodore; and Chilgren, Richard, 1980, *Sexual Options for Paraplegics and Quadriplegics.* Little, Brown and Co: Boston.

Morin, Jack, 1981, *Anal Pleasure and Health.* Down There Press: Burlingame, CA.

Neistadt, Maureen and Baker, Maureen Freda, 1979, *Choices: A Sexual Guide for the Physically Handicapped.* Massachusetts Rehabilitation Hospital: 125 Nashua Street, Boston, MA 02114.

Nomadic Sisters, 1974, *Loving Women.* The Nomadic Sisters: P.O. Box 793, Sonora, CA 95370.

Nowinski, Joseph, 1980, *Becoming Satisfied.* Prentice Hall: Inglewood Cliffs, NJ.

Osman, Shelomo, 1972, "My stepfather is a she" *Family Process, 11:* 209-218.

Pagelow, Mildred, 1980, "Heterosexual and lesbian single mothers: a comparison of problems, coping and solutions" *Journal of Homosexuality, 5:* 189-205.

Pelau, Letitia; Cochran, Susan; Pedesky, Christine and Rook, Karen, 1978, "Loving Women: Attachment and Autonomy in Lesbian Relationships" *Journal of Social Issues* 34:3.

Romano, Mary, 1978, "Sexuality and the Disabled Female" *Sexuality and Disability:* 27-23, Human Sciences Press: NY.

Rush, Florence, 1980, *The Best Kept Secret: Sexual Abuse of Children.* McGraw-Hill, NY.

Russell, Diana; Linden, Robin Ruth; Pagano, Darlene, eds., 1982, *Against SadoMasochism.* Frog in the Well: Palo Alto, Ca.

Samois members, eds., 1982, *Coming to Power.* Alyson Pubs: Boston.

Samois members, eds., 1979, *What Color is Your Handkerchief: A Lesbian S/M Reader*. Samois: Berkeley.

Sampsidis, Nicholas, 1980, *Herpes! Something Can Be Done about It.* Sunflower Publishing Co.: Glen Head, NY.

Sandmaier, Marian, 1980, *The Invisible Alcoholics: Women and Alcohol Abuse in America.* McGraw-Hill, Co.: NY.

Santa Cruz Women's Health Collective, 1979, *Lesbian Health Matters!* Santa Cruz Women's Health Center: Santa Cruz: CA 95060.

Scoppettone, Sandra, 1981, *Happy Endings Are All Alike.* Bantam, NY.

"Sex issue" 1983 *Heresies 12,* Heresies Collective: NY.

Further bibliographies developed upon request from SIECUS: Sex Information and Education Council in the U.S.: 80 Fifth Avenue, Suite 801, New York, NY 10011.

Smith, Barbara, ed., 1983, *Home Girls.* Kitchen Table Women of Color Press: NY.

Snitow, Ann; Stansell, Christine and Thompson, Sharon, 1983, *Powers of Desire: The Politics of Sexuality.* New Feminist Library, Monthly Review Press: NY.

Stanley, Julia; and Wolfe, Susan, 1980, *The Coming Out Stories.* Persephone Press, Watertown, MA.

Stern, Nancy; Browne, Susan; and Conners, Debbie, 1985, *With the Power of Each Breath: A Disabled Women's Anthology.* Cleis: San Francisco.

Stimpson, Kate, 1979, *Class Notes.* Avon: NY.

Sue; Nelly; Dian; Carol; and Billie, 1976, *Country Lesbians: The Story of the Womanshare Collective.* Womanshare Books: Box 1735, Grants Pass, Oregon. 97526.

Sumaje, 1984, *First Time: Sexual Fun on Cassette by Lesbians for Lesbians from the Light and Humorous to the Unspeakably Hot.* Sumaje: P.O. Box 30319, Philadelphia, PA 19103.

Swallow, Jean, ed., 1983, *Out From Under: Sober Dykes and Our Friends*. Spinsters, Ink: San Francisco.

Tanner, Donna, 1978, *The Lesbian Couple*. Lexington Books: Lexington MA.

Tripp, C.A., 1975, *Homosexual Matrix*. Signet: NY.

Vaeth, J.M.; R.C. Blombers; and L. Adler, eds., 1980, *Body Image, Self-Esteem and Sexuality in Cancer Patients*. Karger: NY.

Vida, Ginny, ed., 1978, *Our Right to Love*. Prentice-Hall: Englewood Cliffs, NJ.

Wegscheider, Sharon, 1982, *Another Chance: Hope and Health for the Alcoholic Family*. Science and Behavior Books: Palo Alto, CA.

Women's Braille Press, (newsletter & tapes) Box 8475, Minneapolis, MN. 55408.

"Women and Disabilities", May 1981, *Off Our Backs* XI: 5. 1724 20th Street, NW, Washington, D.C. 20009.

Mail Order Stores for Vibrators, Toys & Sex Information:

Good Vibrations: 3416 22nd Street, San Francisco, CA.

Eve's Garden: 115 West 57th Street, New York City, NY 10019.

Photo by Jay Linder

The tradition among the people in my family is one of great strength. My family came over on the Mayflower with all the other pioneers, rejects and escapees from England. I think it would be great to have a lesbian in the Daughters of the American Revolution. My maternal grandmother was a suffragist, my mother and her sister were feminists before there were words for that. My biological family has always loved and defended me even if they didn't agree with me.

I was raised in a small town in Ohio called Bath. We are everywhere. We come from everywhere, we live everywhere. Get used to it folks, lesbians are all around you.

My process of coming out as a lesbian ten years ago was prompted by Tee Corinne who was part of a class I took in graduate school. She said lots of wonderful things about lesbians out loud. Finally, what I had been feeling for so many years made sense.

Counseling lesbians has been my work for a long time with great success because I love it. I am very lucky to do the work I love with a community I love.

I have a chosen family in the lesbian community that makes me feel totally cared for and held, including two chosen sisters and their parents who have adopted me as their own.

My family is complete with the birth of my son and the entrance of a lover in my life who is dedicated to our relationship. Our family is precious and gives me the energy to continue through all of life's jokes.

I have come to believe that the universe works.

Spinsters, Ink is a women's independent publishing company that survives despite financial and cultural obstacles. Our commitment is to publishing works of literature and non-fiction that are beyond the scope of mainstream commercial publishers. We emphasize work by feminists and lesbians.

Your support through buying our books or making donations will enable us to continue to bring out new books — to publish between the cracks of what can be imagined and what will be accepted.

For a complete list of our titles, please write to us.

Spinsters Ink
803 DeHaro Street
San Francisco, CA 94107